Westfield Memorial Library
Westfield, New Jersey

W9-ACO-706

I Love New York

Westfield Memorial Library
Westfield, New Jersey

I ♥ NY®

Ingredients and Recipes

Daniel Humm
and
Will Guidara

Photography by Francesco Tonelli

641.5974

TEN SPEED PRESS
Berkeley

Contents

Introduction

A Moment in New York Cuisine

We were drinking Manhattans in a Paris hotel bar when Daniel first told me that he wanted to write a book about New York cuisine. It was a statement prompted by an ongoing conversation the two of us had been having, reflecting on trips we had taken over the past couple of years, to Lyon, Paris, Tokyo, Piedmont, discussing how in each of these places, there is a collective pride in place—each city's cuisine a celebration of its home.

Yet in New York City, one of the greatest dining cities in the world, it has never been this way. Here, for the most part, our cuisine has always had a sense of place somewhere else in the world. Our city, so often referred to as a melting pot, is brimming with virtually every culture and tradition. As a result, you can get almost everything here simply by going to an ethnic neighborhood—that microcosm of a foreign country—or to a local distributor. It's one of the coolest things about living in New York, but it can also be our downfall. Too often, because everything is available all the time, we forget to look at what's growing in our backyard. In spite of the fact that New York is one of the greatest agricultural regions in the world, we have never fully developed our own identity.

So we decided to write this book—to play our part in the conversation to define "What is New York Cuisine?" and to join the growing local movement that has begun to take shape around us.

We acknowledged early on that a local cuisine begins with its local ingredients. This book, then, we realized, had to be not only a collection of recipes but also a collection of the ingredients that comprise them and of the incredible men and women who work tirelessly to make their existence a reality. There was a lot we needed to learn.

So Daniel and his team spent weeks driving around New York, visiting countless farmers who cultivate amazing ingredients, learning about their land and their crops, tasting their products. What he found along the way was that New York is full of lush farmland and dedicated farmers who are producing some extraordinary things. We found that their stories are compelling, their products outstanding, and their commitment to preserving the New York agricultural tradition exemplary. He chose to highlight the farms and ingredients that he had come to respect the most on his travels throughout the state. The more he learned about these farms and their farmers, the more we became interested in New York's culinary trajectory throughout the ages.

This took us beyond the ingredients, to the historical narratives, and more research—and we quickly discovered that although our city's culinary identity is not quite intact, there are some wonderfully unique traditions that have existed over the years. We became obsessed with egg creams and soda fountains and Delmonico steak. We learned about their origins and their evolutions, about the legends that surrounded them and the people who invented them. An entire genre of food that was classically New York—smoked fish, potato chips, the oyster pan roast—all these dishes speak to this city's history not only as America's immigrant melting pot but also as a rich agricultural center. We decided to include these recipes and stories as well, because they had their cultural roots here in New York, but, perhaps even more so, because they had their agricultural roots here, too.

And so it was there in that Paris hotel bar sipping on that quintessential New York cocktail, reflecting on our relationship with New York and our budding fascination with it, that we decided to write this book. But it was through the process of writing it that we learned to fully understand the magnificence of our hometown—not only because of its lush farmland and the people that cultivate it, but also because its centuries-old culinary narrative has left an indelible imprint on American history. And we realized, in the humblest of terms, just as generations of immigrants and entrepreneurs had before us, that we love New York.

How to Use This Book

When we were writing our first book, *Eleven Madison Park: The Cookbook,* we asked ourselves whether or not people would cook from it. And as it turned out, there was no simple answer: plenty of people did cook from it with persistence and well-stocked kitchens. But plenty of others lovingly placed it on their coffee tables. With this book, though, we wanted the answer to be an emphatic yes. Our recipes, while designed in our restaurant kitchen, are meant to be cooked at home. While there are some that will require an abundance of time and tenacity, there are many that will yield almost instantaneous results. And while each recipe can be created with ingredients from anywhere in the world, the farm profiles should serve as a resource such that if you *are* cooking in New York, you'll know the best ingredients our state has to offer. It's worth noting, moreover, that all of the farms featured in the book are located within 150 miles of New York City, a characteristic that we found to be crucial to the essence of this book and its narrative.

As you read through the farm profiles, you'll come across the term *CSA*, which stands for "community supported agriculture" and is a way for consumers to buy local, seasonal food directly from farmers, usually through a membership or subscription program.

Unless otherwise noted:

Milk is whole	Butter is unsalted
Cream is heavy	Pepper is freshly ground
Eggs are large	Wine is dry
Flour is all-purpose	Foie gras is grade-A duck
Salt is kosher	Olive oil is extra-virgin
Gelatin is gold-strength sheet	Herbs are fresh

In some of the recipes, there are components that make more than what is necessary for the recipe itself. In those cases, we have suggested other uses, as well as storage methods, though we encourage you to use your creativity and your pantry to come up with alternatives of your own for using any leftovers.

Lastly, if at any point you get stuck or have any questions regarding a farm, an ingredient, or a recipe, please don't hesitate to e-mail us at iloveny@elevenmadisonpark.com. We're here for you.

Apples

Locust Grove Fruit Farm

The trees at Locust Grove Fruit Farm in Milton, New York, do not stand in the perfect lines that you would imagine in a successful commercial orchard. Surveying it, Chip Kent grins: "We aren't that symmetrical. Look around—there are trees going down, up, and across the hills. Every inch of this place is utilized." He proudly defends the haphazard planting scheme as the culmination of seven generations of work that his family has put into this land. Over half of the space is devoted to New York's state fruit and a Hudson Valley specialty: apples.

Chip moves about the place in a fully restored Ford Model T that his grandfather bought in 1926. He loads it with apples destined for the local market; this morning he's driven it down the steep hill to the Hudson River. As fog drifts along the terrain, escorting with it a wave of tree-ripened perfume, Chip discusses the orchard's proximity to water. "Ask my father, Jim, and he will tell you that the reflected moonlight off of the river adds more flavor to our fruit." Offering a more scientifically grounded explanation, he says, "Breezes come off the water and create a constant airflow around the property. Wind wards off potential fungus and creates an earlier harvest timetable, meaning a lower chance of late-season frost."

Most of the apple trees grow on the back hills of the property in well-draining soil, scattered among pear, quince, and plum trees in a patch-work. Locust Grove Fruit Farm expertly nurtures close to fifty varieties of apples and harvests them from late July to early December. Chip pulls out an elegant, hand-inscribed list, one that delineates every variety of produce he grows. He makes copies of it, distributing it to potential clients. Gazing at it, he confesses his greatest bias: "My favorite is the Golden Delicious." When this sweet-tart apple is crossed with the Cox's Orange Pippin, the result is another of Chip's favorites: the Suncrisp. Among all of these delights, there is one heirloom tree on the property that he is particularly fond of. Fifteen years ago, Chip's uncle threatened to cut it down. "To ward him off, I ate every last apple from the tree" just to prove it was worth keeping. From that time, the tree's apples became known as Chipper apples. This unique variety speaks to the heroic effort Chip made to save it, and, he says, "People ask specially for this apple at the market," loving it not only for its heirloom characteristics but also because of its unique association with Locust Grove.

Locust Grove Fruit Farm's commitment to growing extraordinary fruit honors the Hudson Valley apple farming tradition. It is because of the dedication of farmers like Chip that close to 120 varieties of apples abound at the Greenmarket today—a dramatic improvement over the selection of perhaps four varieties that were available a mere twenty years ago. Now, Chip is working on a plan that will enable him to invite more people to see his glorious orchards. A 250-year-old abandoned farmhouse on the property is begging for some restorative attention. Chip envisions its destiny: a brewpub. Playfully, he lets us know what his role will be in this venture: "I'll help cut wood for the fires, but the cooking . . . that's for somebody else."

Caramelized Apple Brioche

Brioche

3 cups bread flour
4 eggs
3 tablespoons milk
2 packed tablespoons fresh yeast
¼ cup plus 1 teaspoon sugar
2½ teaspoons salt
1 cup butter

Before beginning, refrigerate all of the ingredients plus the bowl and dough hook of a stand mixer until cold, at least 2 hours. Place all of the ingredients except the butter in the mixer bowl. Mix on the lowest speed with the dough hook until well incorporated, about 2 minutes. Increase to medium speed and mix until the dough begins to pull away from the sides of the bowl and is homogenous, about 5 minutes. While the dough is mixing, make the butter pliable by hitting it a few times with a rolling pin. Gradually add pieces of the butter and continue mixing at medium speed until the butter is incorporated and the dough is smooth and elastic; it may take up to 10 minutes. Transfer to a glass bowl that has been sprayed lightly with nonstick vegetable cooking spray. Cover with plastic wrap and proof for 45 minutes at room temperature. Lightly press any air out of the dough, cover the bowl tightly with plastic wrap, and refrigerate overnight.

Apple Honey

8 cups apple cider
2 cinnamon sticks
1 vanilla bean, split lengthwise and scraped
1 teaspoon green cardamom pods
1 teaspoon black peppercorns
Zest of half a navel orange

In a straight-sided sauté pan, combine all of the ingredients. Set over medium heat and reduce by half. Strain through a chinois, return the liquid to the pan, and continue reducing to ¾ cup. Strain through a chinois, cover, and refrigerate. **Note:** Any leftover honey can be stored in the refrigerator for 2 to 3 days and used in place of conventional honey in tea or over pancakes.

Apple Granité

¼ cup sugar
1 teaspoon citric acid
1¾ cups Granny Smith apple juice (from about 10 apples)

In a saucepan over medium heat, dissolve the sugar and citric acid in ¼ cup of water. Add the apple juice and stir to combine. Pour into a 9 by 9-inch ceramic or glass dish, cover with plastic wrap, and freeze overnight.

Apple Spread

½ cup butter, at room temperature
¾ cup sugar
1 teaspoon salt
⅓ cup Apple Honey
3 tablespoons cream
1 tablespoon Laird's apple brandy

In a stand mixer fitted with the paddle attachment, cream the butter with the sugar and salt until smooth. Add the honey, cream, and brandy. Mix until well incorporated, transfer to a bowl, cover, and refrigerate. **Note:** Any leftover apple spread can be stored in the refrigerator for 2 to 3 days and be eaten on toasted brioche.

Lemon Syrup

2 tablespoons lemon juice
1½ tablespoons sugar

In a small saucepan, combine the lemon juice with the sugar and 1½ tablespoons of water. Bring to just under a boil to dissolve the sugar. Transfer to a bowl and refrigerate.

To Finish

4 teaspoons turbinado sugar
2 Mutsu or Honeycrisp apples
½ cup Laird's apple brandy

Spread about 2 tablespoons of apple spread in the bottom of four pint-sized cast-iron cocottes. Cut the brioche dough into 24 pieces (approximately ⅓ ounce each) and form into balls. Place 6 balls in each cocotte, with 5 lining the outside and 1 in the center. Cover with plastic wrap and proof at room temperature until doubled in size, about 1½ hours.

Once the brioche has proofed, preheat the oven to 350°F. Sprinkle each brioche with 1 teaspoon of sugar and bake until golden brown, 15 to 20 minutes. While the brioche is baking, scrape the granité with a fork. Cut the apples into different shapes, such as slices, cubes, and Parisian scoops of different sizes. Toss with the lemon syrup and place in small serving dishes along with the granité. As soon as the brioche comes out of the oven, pour 2 tablespoons of brandy over each one. Serve warm with the granité and apples.

New York Sour

SERVES 4

Apple Shrub

6 Red Delicious apples
2 cups sugar
1½ cups white balsamic vinegar

Peel the apples with a paring knife, being sure to leave some of the flesh (about ¼ inch thick) attached to the peel. You should have about 2 cups of peels. Toss the peels with the sugar in a medium bowl. Transfer to an airtight container and refrigerate for 3 days.

After 3 days, combine the vinegar with ½ cup of water in a small saucepan and bring to a boil. Pour the hot liquid over the apple peels and sugar. Allow the mixture to cool to room temperature. Cover the container and allow to sit at room temperature for 2 days. Shake the mixture to ensure all of the sugar has dissolved and then strain through a chinois, reserving only the liquid. **Note:** Any leftover apple shrub can be served over ice and topped with sparkling water to make a refreshing nonalcoholic beverage.

Simple Syrup

½ cup sugar

In a small saucepan over medium heat, combine the sugar with ½ cup of water. Once the sugar is completely dissolved, remove from the heat and cool to room temperature. **Note:** Simple syrup can be stored in the refrigerator for up to 1 month and can be used to sweeten iced tea, lemonade, or cocktails.

Apple Sour

Jerry Thomas, affectionately called the Father of the Cocktail, described sours in his 1862 book, *Bartenders Guide: How to Mix Drinks*, the first recipe book for bartenders. After traveling the world in search of the latest in all things cocktails, Thomas opened his most celebrated bar on Broadway and 22nd Street. Our version of Thomas's sour is made with apple brandy from Laird's, America's first commercial distillery. Opened in Scobeyville, New Jersey, and in operation since 1780, Laird's has supplied everyone from George Washington's troops to visiting foreign dignitaries with its legendary apple-based spirits.

To Finish

8 ounces Laird's 12-year-old apple brandy
3 ounces lemon juice
4 egg whites

Combine 2 ounces of apple brandy, ¾ ounce of lemon juice, ¾ ounce of simple syrup, and 1 egg white in a cocktail shaker. Add ice and shake. Strain into a cocktail glass and slowly layer ½ ounce of apple shrub over the drink. Repeat with the remaining ingredients, to serve 4.

Apple Vinegar

MAKES 6 CUPS

2 Macintosh apples
2 Mutsu apples
1 Gala apple
5 cups white balsamic vinegar
1 cup maple syrup
1 tablespoon salt

Cut the apples in half and place in a clean jar. Combine the vinegar, syrup, and salt in a medium saucepan and bring to a boil over high heat. Pour the liquid over the apples, making sure the apples are completely submerged, and allow to cool to room temperature. Cover and store in the refrigerator for at least 1 month and up to 3 months before using in place of any light vinegar in vinaigrettes.

Asparagus

Wells Homestead Farm

In Long Island's Suffolk County, Lyle Wells, an eleventh-generation farmer, grows sensational asparagus. Although some of it makes it into some of Manhattan's most esteemed restaurants, most of it is sold locally, flying off the Wells Homestead shelves in Riverhead. "Two months out of the year I get to sell asparagus, and unlike some crops that I need to actively move, I've never had to pick up the phone once. Never once," Lyle says.

Opting out of rigid field organization and standard row arrangement, Lyle allows the asparagus to pop up wherever they please, and the effect is that of a miniature forest. Densely clustered stalks grow from the plant's base, called a crown. Once the crown is set, the plant takes two years to yield an edible crop. Only then does it begin to produce vegetables perennially. In very hot weather, asparagus stalks grow rapidly and become overly woody; this signals the end of the harvest season. However, they are purposely left in the field to flower while they fully mature to the fern stage. This induces more photosynthesis and prepares each plant for the next season's crop. Unless there is an asparagus beetle to combat (these feed on the spears and cripple the asparagus), Lyle has the luxury of being able to say, "I don't really have to do much."

Although part of Lyle's success with asparagus can be attributed to the ease of growing it, part of it also comes from the fact that farming is in his blood. His family history on this same land stretches back 350 years—the longest any Riverhead family has ever owned a piece of property. With deep family roots in Long Island, Lyle is wholeheartedly dedicated to the land and the work that he himself has been doing for over thirty years. On the whole, he says, "It's not easy, and if it was, everybody would be farming." His connection with the profession somewhat reflects the nature of his favorite crop—after the asparagus is set, it will continue to produce for nearly two decades. Lyle finds ease and comfort in this long-term commitment, as he ensures prosperity for the next generation of Wells family farmers one harvest at a time.

Asparagus Salad with Quinoa

Quinoa

1 cup red quinoa, rinsed
3 tablespoons Lemon Vinaigrette (page 500)
2 tablespoons sliced chives
1 tablespoon finely diced (⅛ inch) shallot
Salt

Bring a medium saucepan of salted water to a boil. Add the quinoa and boil until tender, 25 to 30 minutes. Drain and cool to room temperature, fold in the vinaigrette, chives, and shallot, and season with salt to taste.

Asparagus Vinaigrette

1 tablespoon butter
2 cups chopped asparagus
1 tablespoon tomato paste
¼ cup red wine vinegar
4 cups Chicken Stock (page 499)
Salt

In a medium sauté pan, melt the butter over medium-high heat until it begins to foam. Add the asparagus and cook until caramelized, 6 to 7 minutes. Add the tomato paste and continue cooking while stirring frequently, 1 to 2 minutes. Deglaze the pan with the vinegar, add the stock, and raise the heat to high. Reduce the liquid by two-thirds, to 1⅓ cups, skimming frequently. Strain the liquid through a chinois and return to the pan, discarding the asparagus. Continue reducing until there is only about ⅓ cup of liquid remaining. Remove from the heat and strain again through a chinois. Season with salt to taste.

To Finish

4 eggs
20 asparagus
Lemon Vinaigrette (see page 500)
Chervil sprigs
Chive tips and flowers
Tarragon sprigs
6 ounces lardo, at least 8 thinly sliced pieces

Place the eggs in a small saucepan, cover with cold water, and bring to a boil over high heat. Immediately remove from heat, cover, and let stand for 7 minutes. Quickly transfer the eggs to ice water to cool. Cut the asparagus down to 5-inch spears, discarding the woody bottoms. Peel the bottom half of each spear. Bring a saucepan of salted water to a boil. Add the asparagus and blanch until tender, 4 to 5 minutes. Transfer to a bowl of ice water. When the asparagus is cool, drain and dress in lemon vinaigrette. Arrange 5 asparagus on each plate so that the spears are pointing outward from the center in alternating directions. Spoon the quinoa at the ends of the asparagus. Peel the eggs, break up 1 egg for each plate, and arrange the pieces on top of the quinoa. Arrange the chervil sprigs, chive tips and flowers, and tarragon sprigs on top of the egg. Garnish with 2 slices of lardo and finish with the asparagus vinaigrette.

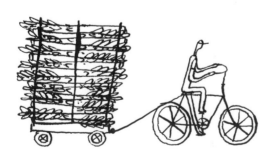

Oven-Baked Asparagus

SERVES 4

28 large asparagus
4 cloves garlic, crushed but kept whole
4 (⅛-inch-thick) slices lemon
4 sprigs thyme
4 tablespoons butter
Salt

Preheat the oven to 400°F. Remove the outer leaves from the asparagus tips, forming tight points. Trim away the woody ends of the asparagus and peel the stalks from the point down. Tie the asparagus with butcher's twine in 4 bundles of 7. Cut 4 pieces of parchment paper a little larger than twice the size of the asparagus bundles. Place 1 asparagus bundle on each piece of paper. Place 1 garlic clove, 1 lemon slice, and 1 thyme sprig on each bundle. Top with 1 tablespoon of butter and season with salt to taste. Fold the paper over the bundle to enclose, and fold the edges together to seal, creating a parchment paper pouch around the asparagus. Place the asparagus packages on a baking sheet and bake in the oven for 12 minutes. Remove from the oven and let rest in the pouches for 2 minutes before serving. Alternatively, you can grill the asparagus in their pouches over a grill.

Autumn Squash

Shaul Farms

To say that Dave Shaul is familiar with the lay of his land is an understatement. As the youngest of ten children, he has lived on the same property in Fulthonham, New York, since he was born. Dave, his wife, Becky, and their three boisterous children fill the house now, keeping alive the energy that's always permeated this home. Until recently, the couple had little time to raise a family, especially when Dave was growing vegetables for Beech-Nut, the baby food company. His father had established the farm's business plan such that its scale would allow them to provide squash for the large processing company. "One season, we harvested 120 tons of butternut squash," Dave recalls. This model was great for sales, but the farm lacked relationships with customers. It was an aspect of farming that Dave longed for, so to change that, he diversified their crops and "created an identity for Shaul Farms by starting a roadside stand."

Dave's comprehensive seed library, including almost 20,000 reserve selections of seeds, is catalogued in a notebook. This old-fashioned system speaks to Dave's personality, and it allows him to stay organized and keep his precious seeds safe. Paging through seed catalogs happens to be Dave's favorite winter activity, as he selects new varieties to plant in the spring. He devotes sixteen of his 1,500 acres to autumn squash; Becky takes the time to learn how to cook each of the farm's squash offerings. "I'm not a fancy cook but I want to teach customers how to prepare each one and to tell them what each different squash tastes like," she says.

Uniquely, the Shauls plant their squash in a greenhouse before transferring it to a plastic-covered field. This controls germination and prevents weeds from overcrowding the sprawling vines. Because of squash's long growing season, frost must constantly be monitored as harvest nears—exposure will make the squash unable to sustain storage in the cellar. Dave believes that this extra attention yields economically viable results, but his motivations are based on more than money. "I find high personal value in the product," he says.

On a normal year, Shaul Farms grows 10,000 butternut and 5,000 acorn squashes. On the parcel of his land where he grows less known specialties, his acorn squash varieties include the Gold Nugget, the Autumn Delight, and the Heart of Gold. Long Island Cheese Pumpkins are shaped like a wheel of cheddar, and Becky insists that they make the best pies. The Celebration is a festive looking, tri-colored squash; thick-skinned Hubbards are on the larger end of the squash spectrum; and the petite Turbans are popular for their ornamental appeal.

Dave farms with joyous enthusiasm and infinite wonder. His notion is that squashes are the cold season's equivalent to summer's heirloom tomatoes. Although his model includes farming tons of butternut squash, Dave explains that "growing so many varieties keeps things interesting in the field."

Acorn Squash Soup

SERVES 4

Roasted Acorn Squash

6 acorn squash
6 tablespoons dark brown sugar
12 sprigs thyme
12 tablespoons butter
Ground nutmeg
Salt

Preheat the oven to 350°F. Cut the top off of each squash and scoop out the seeds. Season the inside of each squash with 1 tablespoon of brown sugar, 2 sprigs of thyme, 2 tablespoons of butter, and nutmeg and salt. Pour enough salt into an ovenproof dish to hold the squash upright and place the squash in the dish. Roast the squash in the oven until tender, 1 to 1¼ hours. Remove the squash from the oven and pour out the excess liquid inside each squash into a bowl, reserving the liquid for the soup. Keep 4 of the squash whole to use as serving vessels and scoop out the flesh from the remaining 2. You should have about 3 cups of squash.

Acorn Squash Soup

2 tablespoons butter, plus 2 tablespoons cold butter
1 cup diced (½ inch) onion
½ cup diced (½ inch) celery
1 clove garlic, crushed but kept whole
3 cups Roasted Acorn Squash
Squash liquid, reserved from making
**   Roasted Acorn Squash**
Salt

In a medium stockpot over medium-low heat, heat the 2 tablespoons butter until foamy. Add the onion, celery, and garlic and sweat until tender, 6 to 7 minutes. Add the roasted acorn squash and continue to sweat for 2 minutes. Add the squash liquid and 5 cups of water and bring to a simmer. Continue simmering for 20 minutes and transfer to a blender. Add the 2 tablespoons cold butter and blend until smooth. Strain the soup through a chinois and season with salt to taste.

To Finish

6 tablespoons butter
1 cup torn bread
2 cloves garlic, crushed but kept whole
2 sprigs thyme, plus thyme leaves
1 cup baby chanterelle mushrooms, cleaned
Olive oil

Melt 4 tablespoons of the butter in a small sauté pan over medium-high heat. Add the torn bread, garlic, and thyme sprigs and sauté until the bread is golden brown, 2 to 3 minutes. Remove the croutons from the pan and set aside. Melt the remaining 2 tablespoons butter in the same pan over medium heat and sauté the chanterelle mushrooms until tender, 2 to 3 minutes. Add 1 tablespoon of water and reduce to glaze the mushrooms. Fill each squash bowl with soup and garnish with the croutons and mushrooms. Finish with olive oil and thyme leaves.

Butternut Squash Tortellini with Sage Brown Butter

Butternut Squash Filling

1 medium butternut squash
Olive oil
Salt
½ cup grated Sprout Creek Farm Ouray cheese
    (a raw cow's milk cheese similar to a dry cheddar)
¼ cup mascarpone
1½ tablespoons honey
Ground nutmeg

Preheat the oven to 350°F. Cut the squash in half lengthwise, scoop out the seeds, rub with olive oil, and season with salt to taste. Place flesh-side down on a baking sheet lined with parchment paper and roast until tender, 1 to 1¼ hours. Scoop out the flesh; you should have about 4 cups of loosely packed squash. Transfer to a straight-sided sauté pan and cook over medium heat until the squash is dry. The volume should reduce to about 2 packed cups. Place the squash in a medium mixing bowl and combine with the cheese, mascarpone, and honey. Season with nutmeg and salt to taste. **Note:** Reserve any leftover filling in the refrigerator for 2 to 3 days. Eat warm tossed with pasta or stirred into risotto.

Pasta Dough

1 teaspoon saffron threads
3 cups tipo 00 flour
1 teaspoon salt
9 egg yolks
1 egg

In a small saucepan, bring the saffron and 1 cup of water to a boil. Reduce the liquid to ¼ cup, strain, and reserve the saffron water. Combine the flour and salt and mound the dry mixture on a clean work surface. Create a well in the middle and add the yolks and whole egg. Use a fork to begin incorporating the egg into the flour. As the pasta dough begins to come together, add 2½ teaspoons of the saffron water. Start kneading the dough, incorporating the dry and wet ingredients, until the dough is firm and slightly dry but not crumbly. Note that depending on the size of the eggs and the humidity of the room, you may not need to incorporate all 3 cups of the flour into the dough to reach this consistency. Knead the dough for 10 minutes to develop the gluten. Wrap in plastic wrap and refrigerate for 30 minutes before rolling out.

Butternut Squash Tortellini

Pasta Dough
1 egg white
Butternut Squash Filling

Remove the pasta dough from the refrigerator and allow to come to room temperature. Set a pasta machine on the widest setting according to the manufacturer's instructions. Run the pasta dough through the machine, gradually decreasing the thickness until the thinnest setting is reached. Cut the rolled out pasta into 1-foot lengths, keeping the dough you are not currently working with covered to prevent it from drying out. Whisk the egg white with 1 teaspoon of water to create an egg wash. Lay out a sheet of pasta and drop ½-teaspoon mounds of the filling down the center of the sheet, spacing them 3½ inches apart. Brush around the filling mounds with the egg wash and fold the pasta down over the mounds so that they are at the folded edge. Press to seal around each mound, removing all air pockets by pressing the air bubbles to the edge of the pasta sheet. Punch out each section of filling in a half circle with a round 3-inch cutter. Using both thumbs and index fingers, pick up each tortellini, holding the straight edge away from you. Brush the left corner with a touch of egg wash, and push the middle of the pasta inward and up, creating a point. Then, fold the right corner over the top of the left and press together gently. Repeat with the remaining pasta and filling.

To Finish

7 to 8 tablespoons cold butter
8 to 12 sage leaves
1 teaspoon lemon juice
Salt
Amaretti cookies

In a small sauté pan, melt 3 tablespoons of the butter over medium heat. Add the sage leaves and continue cooking for 1 to 1½ minutes, until the butter is golden brown. Add the lemon juice and season with salt to taste. Reserve both the brown butter and the sage leaves. Bring a large stockpot of salted water to a boil. Drop the tortellini into the boiling water and cook until they float to the top, 1½ to 2 minutes. Remove the tortellini from the water and transfer to a medium sauté pan over medium heat. Add 2 tablespoons of pasta water and the remaining 4 to 5 tablespoons of butter to emulsify. Divide the tortellini evenly among 4 plates and drizzle with the sage brown butter. Crumble amaretti cookies on the plates and garnish with the sage leaves.

Butternut Steaks with Black Pepper

SERVES 4

Bacon

12 slices of bacon, ⅛ inch thick

Preheat the oven to 350°F. Place the bacon on a parchment paper–lined 13 by 18-inch rimmed baking sheet. Bake in the oven until the bacon is crispy and the fat has rendered, 9 to 10 minutes. Remove the bacon with a slotted spatula, reserving both the bacon and the rendered fat.

Butternut Steaks

3 large butternut squash
Bacon fat, reserved from making Bacon
4 tablespoons butter
4 sprigs thyme
2 cloves garlic, crushed but kept whole

Preheat the oven to 350°F. Halve the butternut squash crosswise, separating the neck from the bulbous bottom. Discard the bottom or reserve for another use. Slice the butternut squash neck into ½-inch-thick slices. Cut the slices into ovals measuring 2½ inches by 1¾ inches. Alternatively, use a round cutter to punch large circles from the slices. You should have at least 12 slices total. Discard the rest of the squash or reserve for another use. Heat the reserved bacon fat in a large oven-proof sauté pan over medium heat, add the squash, and sauté until lightly caramelized, 1 to 2 minutes. Turn the steaks and continue cooking for 1 more minute. Add the butter, thyme, and garlic and baste the steaks for 1 minute. Flip the steaks over and transfer the sauté pan to the oven. Roast until tender, 7 to 8 minutes. Transfer the steaks with a slotted spatula to a platter and reserve the browned butter.

To Finish

Sea salt
Cracked black pepper
Browned butter, reserved from making Butternut Steaks
8 sprigs thyme

Place 3 butternut steaks on a serving plate and top each with a slice of bacon. Season with salt and pepper. Spoon browned butter over the steaks and garnish with thyme. Repeat with the remaining ingredients, to serve 4.

Beans

BEANS

The Green Thumb Organic Farm

Driving down the picturesque Montauk Highway, it is hard to miss the sign depicting a green hand giving a "thumbs up." This insignia marks a produce stand that was founded by Peachie and Ray Halsey in the 1960s. Their family has been in Water Mill since 1644—the same year that Southampton's defining mill was founded. The Halseys' four children, Johanna, Patricia, Bill, and Larry, collectively refer to their niche in life as "vegelicious." Jo explains their close family bond, saying, "We get together on a weekly basis when possible. Having grown up as farm kids, we understand each other on a different level." The Halseys' work was praised early on by Long Island neighbor and original *New York Times* food critic, the late Craig Claiborne. He helped enrich the farm's portfolio by commissioning Green Thumb to grow arugula—a green the Halseys had not yet heard of at the time. But of the 350 organic vegetables that the farm currently grows, their bountiful beans are some of the most beloved.

This farming family has been experimenting with organic methods and biodynamic preparations since the 1970s. The fertile land stocks Green Thumb's stand with a cornucopia of vegetables while also sustaining their 500-member CSA. "The family works together and shares common goals," says Jo, the family's unofficial spokesperson. She and her sister, Patricia, co-authored their family cookbook, *The Green Thumb Harvest,* which features recipes written by local residents inspired by the farm's beans and other vegetable crops.

Starting in May, various beans are continually rotated through one hundred acres of sandy loam soil. This ensures that a single plant variety does not deplete the soil of too many nutrients. French, green, yellow, and purple beans grow to be tender and sweet. They are planted every two weeks, and thrive throughout the summer. Long, flat Romanos demand specific attention on account of the size and fleshiness of their pods. Favas, an enduring favorite, are in season for only a small window of time in July. Dragon Tongue beans are festively dressed in purple camouflage, while Chinese Red Noodles are long and slender. All of the beans come from nonhybrid seeds, distinguishing them from genetically altered and industrialized versions. This coincides with the Halseys' goal to grow "the best possible food for a healthier planet."

The Halseys' farm is thriving and popular, due primarily to their unwavering unity. The children are grateful to Claiborne for his contribution to their success; Bill recounts, "In the late 1970s, Craig wrote in the *Times* that the Green Thumb was his favorite farm stand. The next day was our busiest ever! How's that for the power of the *Times*, or maybe the power of Craig?" His sisters tell of when Claiborne volunteered—nearly insisted—that he not only write a recipe for their cookbook, but that he also pen the foreword. He wrote about the area, "The Hamptons is often called the most fashionable resort in America . . . to me, it is simply the place I call home."

Minestrone of Garden Beans with Oregano

SERVES 4

Minestrone Sauce

¼ cup olive oil
3 cups diced (⅛ inch) zucchini
1 cup diced (⅛ inch) carrot
½ cup diced (⅛ inch) celery root
4 tablespoons diced (⅛ inch) leek
2 tablespoons minced onion
2 cloves garlic, minced
2 teaspoons tomato paste
½ cup white wine
8 cups Chicken Stock (page 499)
3 cups diced (¼ inch) tomatoes
1 cup diced (⅛ inch) potatoes
2 cups basil leaves
½ cup mint leaves
2 tablespoons salt
½ teaspoon piment d'Espelette
4 tablespoons cold butter
4 teaspoons lime juice

Heat the olive oil in a large saucepan over low heat. Add the zucchini, carrot, celery root, leek, onion, and garlic. Sweat the vegetables until tender, stirring to prevent them from achieving any color, about 10 minutes. Add the tomato paste and continue sweating for 2 more minutes. Add the white wine, raise the heat to high, and reduce the liquid to ¼ cup. Add the stock, tomatoes, and potatoes, and simmer over low heat for 30 minutes. Remove the pan from the heat and add the basil and mint. Season with the salt and *piment d'Espelette* and allow to infuse for 20 minutes. Strain through a chinois, keeping only the liquid. Return the liquid to the pan and reduce to 5 cups over medium heat. Add the butter and mix with a hand blender until emulsified. Season the sauce with the lime juice.

Beans

½ cup dried gigante beans, soaked overnight in water
½ cup dried black-eyed peas, soaked overnight in water
½ cup dried coco beans, soaked overnight in water
½ cup fresh shelled cranberry beans
1 cup olive oil
Salt
¼ cup diced (⅛ inch) onion
4 teaspoons diced (⅛ inch) carrot
4 teaspoons diced (⅛ inch) celery
4 bay leaves
4 sprigs thyme
20 black peppercorns
10 haricots verts, ends trimmed
2 tablespoons butter

Drain all of the soaked beans. In separate saucepans, cover each type of bean with 3 cups of water and ¼ cup of the olive oil. Season with salt. Using cheesecloth and butcher's twine, make four sachets each containing 1 tablespoon of onion, 1 teaspoon of carrot, 1 teaspoon of celery, 1 bay leaf, 1 thyme sprig, and 5 peppercorns. Place 1 sachet in each saucepan. Bring to a simmer over medium heat and cook the beans until tender, about 45 minutes for both the cranberry beans and the black-eyed peas, and about 1¼ hours for the gigante and coco beans. Bring a pot of salted water to a boil and blanch the haricots verts for 5 to 6 minutes. Transfer to an ice bath and, once cold, drain. Cut into ½-inch pieces. Drain the cooked beans, discard the sachets, and transfer them to a medium sauté pan over medium heat. Add the haricots verts and the butter, tossing to glaze. Season with salt to taste. **Note:** Any leftover beans can be served family-style drizzled with olive oil and salt. They can also be refrigerated for 2 to 3 days and warmed up before serving.

To Finish

Confit Cherry Tomatoes (page 499)
Basil leaves
Flowering mint
Oregano sprigs
Olive oil

Divide the minestrone sauce among 4 bowls, reserving 2 cups. Arrange the cherry tomatoes in the sauce. Divide the beans among the bowls and garnish with basil, mint, and oregano. Spoon olive oil over the top. Aerate the remaining minestrone sauce with a hand blender to create a foam. Spoon over the dish to finish.

Salad of Summer Beans and Savory

SERVES 4

Savory Vinaigrette

¾ cup buttermilk
1 egg yolk
1 tablespoon lemon juice
1 tablespoon salt
½ cup olive oil
½ cup grapeseed oil
1½ tablespoons chopped chives
1½ tablespoons chopped savory

In a blender, combine the buttermilk, egg yolk, lemon juice, and salt. Blend on high speed and slowly stream in the olive oil and grapeseed oil. Blend until smooth, about 1 minute. Transfer to a bowl and stir in the chopped herbs. Marinate in the refrigerator for 1 hour before serving. **Note:** Any leftover vinaigrette can be stored in an airtight container in the refrigerator for up to 1 day. It is best as a dressing for a green salad or spooned over grilled chicken or fish.

Summer Beans

6 ounces (about 1 cup) green romano beans
6 ounces (about 1 cup) yellow romano beans
6 ounces (about 1 cup) haricots verts
6 ounces (about 1 cup) yellow wax beans
2 ounces (about ¼ cup) baby haricots verts

Cut the green and yellow romano beans at a 45-degree angle to create diamond shapes. Cut the haricots verts and yellow wax beans into ½-inch pieces. Bring a pot of salted water to a boil. Blanch the green and yellow romanos until tender, 4 to 5 minutes. Transfer to an ice bath and, when cooled, remove and reserve. Blanch separately the haricots verts and wax beans until tender, 5 to 6 minutes. Transfer to the ice bath, remove, and reserve. Finally, blanch the baby haricots verts until tender, about 1 minute, transfer to the ice bath, remove, and reserve.

To Finish

Red pearl onions
¼ cup Lemon Vinaigrette (page 500)
Salt
Savory sprigs

Slice the onions on a mandoline into ¹⁄₁₆-inch-thick rings. Dress the romano and wax beans in the lemon vinaigrette, season with salt to taste, and place in a small bowl. Dress the haricots verts and baby haricots verts with ¼ cup of the savory vinaigrette. Place the haricots verts on top of the other beans in the bowl. Garnish with a few pearl onion rings and savory sprigs.

Beef

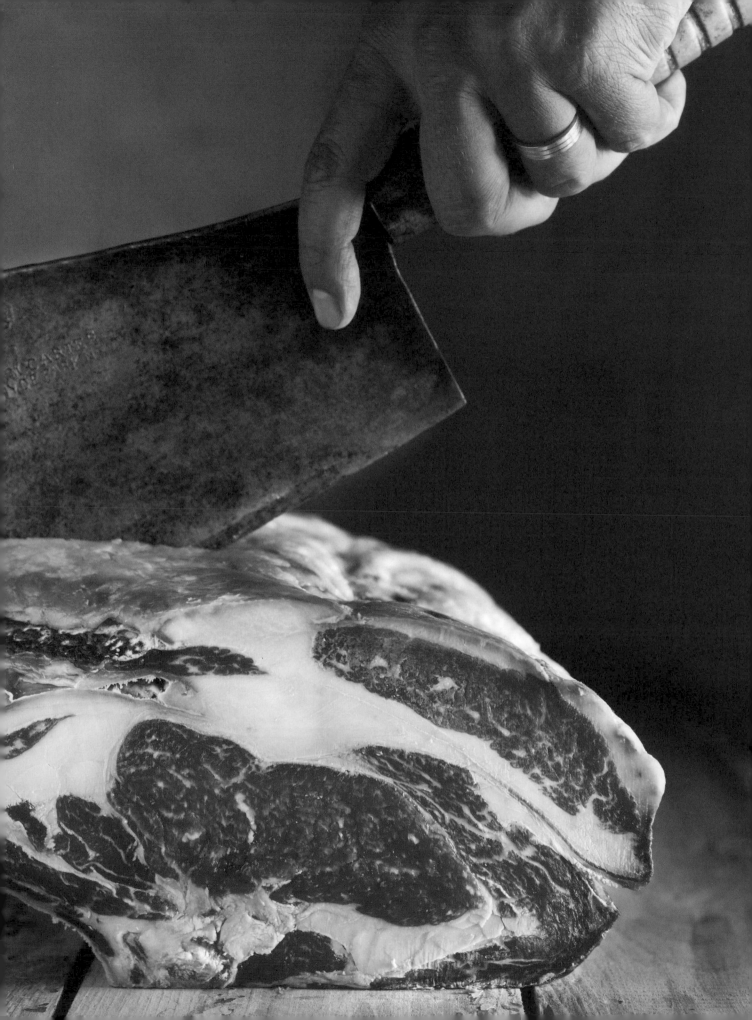

Rosenkrans Farms

Jeff Rosenkrans's story, and that of Rosenkrans Farms, is inextricably linked to those of his father, Bob, and their Seneca Falls farm. In 1980, with capital from his successful insurance company, Bob established his six-hundred-acre property, growing soybeans and other cash crops while also leisurely raising cows. It was in these cows that Jeff saw amazing potential. Recognizing that the local market had yet to encounter premium beef, he decided to raise the finest cattle in New York State. He took a very simple, intuitive approach to raising them, reasoning that, as he put it, "Grass feeding cows is common sense. If you give them what they naturally want to eat, they will feed for you." Starting in 2009, Jeff was able to share his grass-fed beef with New York City by way of a relationship he fostered with Manhattan's DeBragga and Spitler Meat.

The rainy Seneca Falls weather makes it nearly impossible to dry the hay Jeff needs to feed his cows. Instead of fighting the elements, he embraces them, cutting, baling, and wrapping the grass while it's still filled with moisture. It naturally ferments in an airtight environment, releases sugars, and transforms into something called balage. This product has greater health benefits than regular feed, as well as a superior flavor profile that is appealing to the animals. Jeff jokes that the addictive sweetness of the feed is like "cotton candy" for the cattle. The summer season, he says, yields "three hundred bales of forages to feed the cows during the winter." With this specialized feeding and foraging regimen, Rosenkrans's animals eat the same healthy food year-round.

Jeff can trace the lineage of his entire herd of cows—all 110 of them. This ensures a healthy gene pool for the eighty Black Baldy steers, which are crossbred from Hereford and Angus. When calves are born, they roam together with their mothers on fields planted with nutrient-packed timothy, alfalfa, and clover. When the calves are eight months old, gradual fence-line weaning begins. Although they are placed in separate pens from their mothers, both cow and calf are still in sight of the other, drastically reducing their stress levels and increasing the quality of the beef. After ten more months of feeding on Rosenkrans's balage, the young steers grow big and healthy and are ready to harvest.

Rosenkrans Farms yields well-marbled meat that starkly differs from typical lean grass-fed beef. Extra intramuscular fat allows it to hold up to dry aging and translates to rich, meaty flavor at the table. Fortunately, Jeff has no plans to abandon the fields any time soon. "So many guys are doing what I'm doing, but they spend the whole day on the phone as a meat distributor instead of as farmer." But Jeff's passion for farming, for his cattle, and for his extraordinary beef is sure to keep him on the fields and off the phones for many years to come.

Beef Tartare

SERVES 4

Consommé

8 egg whites
½ cup julienned carrot
½ cup thinly sliced onion
¼ cup julienned celery
½ cup sherry vinegar
2 tablespoons salt, plus more to taste
1 tablespoon tomato paste
2 sprigs thyme
1 bay leaf, julienned
2 cups Chicken Jus (page 498)
2 cups Chicken Stock (page 499)
6 gelatin sheets

Whisk the egg whites until soft peaks form. Fold in the carrot, onion, celery, vinegar, the 2 tablespoons of salt, the tomato paste, thyme, and bay leaf. Whisk in the chicken jus and chicken stock. Pour the mixture into a tall, narrow pot and set over medium-low heat. Bring the mixture to a simmer. The egg white mixture will float to the top and create a raft. Make a hole in the middle of the raft using the edge of a ladle, and baste the raft with the simmering liquid every 10 to 15 minutes for about 45 minutes. Dipping a ladle through the hole in the raft, spoon the liquid from the pot and pass through a chinois lined with cheesecloth. Discard the raft. Season the con-sommé with salt to taste. Bloom the gelatin in ice water until pliable, about 10 minutes. Remove the gelatin from the water and squeeze to remove excess moisture. Add the gelatin to the warm consommé and stir until melted. Pour into a container and refrigerate until set, about 4 hours. **Note:** Any leftover con-sommé can be refrigerated in an airtight container for up to 1 week or frozen for up to 1 month. It can be served alongside pâtés or terrines.

Pommery Mayonnaise

½ cup Mayonnaise (page 500)
1 tablespoon sherry vinegar
1 tablespoon whole-grain mustard
½ teaspoon salt

Whisk together all of the ingredients in a small bowl. Transfer to a squeeze bottle. **Note:** Pommery mayonnaise can be used as a condiment for cured or smoked meats, sausages, or sandwiches.

Pickled Radishes

8 baby radishes
1 cup white balsamic vinegar
1 tablespoon salt
1 tablespoon sugar

Trim the tops and bottoms of the radishes, leaving ½ inch of the green tops attached, then quarter each one. In a small saucepan over medium heat, bring the vinegar, salt, and sugar to a simmer. Place the radishes in a bowl and pour the hot vinegar mixture over them. Cover with plastic wrap and cool to room temperature. Refrigerate until ready to serve, up to 1 week.

Beef Tartare

12 ounces beef sirloin, diced (⅛ inch)
4 teaspoons minced rinsed salt-packed anchovies
4 teaspoons minced capers
4 teaspoons Cognac
2 teaspoons Pommery Mayonnaise
2 teaspoons sliced chives
2 shallots, minced

Mix all of the ingredients in a bowl. Finish and serve the dish immediately.

To Finish

4 quail egg yolks
Salsa Verde (page 89)
Fresh horseradish, peeled
Raw radishes, shaved
Radish leaves
Salad burnet

Place a 2½-inch ring mold in the center of a plate and spoon one-fourth of the beef tartare into the mold. Create a small indentation in the tartare with the back of a spoon and lay a quail egg yolk in it. Remove the ring mold. Spoon the salsa verde around the edge of the tartare. Grate horseradish on one side of the tartare. Arrange the pickled radishes around the plate and garnish with shaved radishes, radish leaves, and salad burnet. Squeeze dots of Pommery mayonnaise around the plate and spoon consommé onto the plate to finish. Repeat with the remaining ingredients, to serve 4.

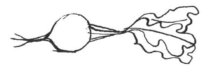

Bone Marrow, Shallots, and Anchovies

SERVES 4

Bone Marrow Panade

4 marrowbones
2 cups diced (⅛ inch) country bread
3 cups Chicken Stock (page 499)
6 tablespoons butter
½ cup minced shallot
2 cups white wine
3 tablespoons minced rinsed salt-packed anchovies
3 tablespoons chopped parsley
1 teaspoon thyme leaves
3 tablespoons olive oil
1 lemon
Salt

Ask your butcher to cut the marrowbones in half lengthwise. Remove the marrow to create a trough. Set the bones aside and dice the marrow into ¼-inch pieces. Preheat the oven to 200°F. Toast 1½ cups of the bread on a baking sheet in the oven until dry, 20 to 25 minutes. Cool to room temperature and then soak in the chicken stock. When the bread has completely absorbed the stock, place it in a quadruple layer of cheesecloth and gently press out any excess moisture. Combine the soaked bread and the diced marrow in a mixing bowl. In a medium sauté pan over medium-low heat, melt the butter with the shallot and sweat until tender, 3 to 4 minutes. Deglaze with the white wine and raise the heat to high. Reduce the liquid until almost dry. Remove from the heat and let cool. Combine the cooked shallot, anchovies, parsley, and thyme with the marrow mixture. To make croutons, heat the olive oil in a small sauté pan over medium-low heat. Add the remaining ½ cup of country bread and toast until golden brown. Using a Microplane grater, zest the lemon. Season the croutons with the lemon zest and salt to taste.

Shallot and Parsley Salad

1 shallot
½ cup roughly chopped parsley
2 teaspoons Lemon Vinaigrette (page 500)

Slice the shallot on a mandoline into ¹⁄₁₆-inch-thick rings. Place the sliced shallot in ice water to crisp, about 10 minutes, and then drain. Dress the parsley with the lemon vinaigrette and toss together with the shallot.

To Finish

4 marrowbones, halved lengthwise,
**   reserved from making Bone Marrow Panade**
Salt
Ground white pepper
Croutons, reserved from making Bone Marrow Panade

Preheat the oven to 400°F. Divide the bone marrow panade among the 8 marrowbone halves. Place on a baking sheet and season with salt and white pepper. Bake in the oven for 5 minutes.

Preheat the broiler. Top each bone with croutons and place under the broiler until golden brown, 30 to 45 seconds. Arrange 2 bones on each plate and garnish with the shallot and parsley salad. Season with salt and white pepper to taste.

Delmonico Steak

SERVES 4

Herb Butter

1 pound butter, at room temperature
1 tablespoon chopped chervil
1 tablespoon chopped chives
1 tablespoon chopped parsley
1 tablespoon chopped tarragon
Zest of 1 lemon
1½ tablespoons sea salt

Place all of the ingredients in a mixing bowl and combine with a spatula. Place on a sheet of plastic wrap and roll into a cylinder. Alternatively, use a piping bag and star tip to create small rosettes. Refrigerate until firm. **Note:** Any leftover butter can be tightly wrapped and frozen for up to 1 month. It is great with steak and roasted vegetables or potatoes.

Steak

2 tablespoons canola oil
4 (¾-pound) boneless rib-eye steaks, about 1-inch thick
Salt
Ground black pepper
1 tablespoon butter
5 sprigs thyme
1 clove garlic

Heat the oil in a 10-inch cast-iron skillet over high heat until it just begins to smoke. Season the steaks with salt and pepper and sear in the skillet until golden, 2 to 3 minutes. Flip the steaks and sear for an additional 2 to 3 minutes. Add the butter, thyme, and garlic. Lower the heat to medium-low and baste the steaks for 1 minute with the foamy brown butter. Flip and repeat. Repeat this process for 7 to 8 minutes, flipping the steaks every minute and basting until the internal temperature reaches 130° to 135°F. Allow the steaks to rest for 10 minutes before serving with herb butter.

The legendary Delmonico's, which opened in the financial district in 1837, revolutionized restaurants. It was the first in the U.S. to go by the French term *restaurant*, the first to allow women to dine without a male escort, the first to have printed menus, the first to have a wine list, the first to use tablecloths, and the first to have diners sit at private tables. It was there that American classics like lobster Newburg, eggs Benedict, and baked Alaska came into existence. Of all of the Delmonico's dishes, though, the most legendary is perhaps Delmonico steak, a dish whose exact preparation and exact cut of meat remain a mystery. In the years after the original Delmonico's closed its doors, a series of imitators opened restaurants called "Delmonico's" around the city, and in the process, the precise cut originally used for this fabled dish was lost along the way. The true identity of the Delmonico steak is thus one of the food world's enduring enigmas.

Brooklyn Brewery

Steve Hindy and Tom Potter transformed their home-brewing experiments into the Brooklyn Brewery in 1988, in a borough where over a hundred breweries thrived before the Prohibition Era. But their team would not be complete until six years later, when they were joined by Garrett Oliver—a match made in beer heaven.

After studying film at Boston University, Garrett lived in England, where the local beer and beer culture sparked his interest. When he returned to Manhattan to work in a law office, he continued his love affair with beer and began to home-brew every moment that he was away from his Park Avenue office. Gradually, Garrett came to realize that his corporate career was driven by a paycheck rather than a passion. One evening at a Homebrewers Guild meeting, he learned that the (now defunct) Manhattan Brewing Company needed an assistant brewer. Garrett seized the opportunity to trade his desk for a mash shovel and fermentation tanks—in fact, he literally took hold of the company's representative: "I grabbed the guy by the collar and begged for the job," he says. Garrett's unbridled zeal and distinctive charm brought him rapid success in his new career. Brooklyn Brewery hired him as brewmaster in 1994; they settled in at their current flagship location in Williamsburg two years later.

Garrett possesses a rare combination of personality traits: intelligence, enthusiasm, and discipline. He is often unable to contain his excitement, and commonly uses phrases like "Shazam!" Meanwhile, he can recite the intricacies of beer history as effortlessly as most people sing along to pop music; he documented his encyclopedic knowledge as editor of the *Oxford Companion to Beer*.

Today, Brooklyn Brewery boasts a beer portfolio that exceeds thirty selections. With standbys like Brooklyn Lager and Brooklyn Pilsner, the brewery also features limited-edition brews from Garrett's Brewmaster's Reserve series, inspired by a range of muses. In 2011, Elevated Wheat was composed in honor of the city's Highline Park, and incorporated local red winter wheat from North Country Farms. It was the first commercially produced beer made with New York State grains in a hundred years. For Eleven Madison Park, Garrett created Nine Pin and Local 1, which are aged in Pappy Van Winkle twenty-year reserve bourbon barrels. With such a diverse repertoire, Garrett finds it difficult to pinpoint a brewing style that he would personify. He says, "It's funny . . . over the years I've turned myself into about eighty different beers!"

Beer-Braised Veal Cheeks

SERVES 4

Braised Veal Cheeks

5 pounds veal cheeks
2 cups diced white onion
1 cup diced carrot
1 cup diced celery
2 sprigs thyme, plus ½ teaspoon thyme leaves
1 bay leaf
1 (750-milliliter) bottle plus ¼ cup Brooklyn Local 2 beer
Salt
1 tablespoon canola oil
2 tablespoons tomato paste
8 cups Chicken Stock (page 499)
2 cups Chicken Jus (page 498)
1 tablespoon butter
Ground black pepper

Trim the veal cheeks of all silver skin. In a large glass bowl, combine the veal cheeks with the onion, carrot, celery, thyme sprigs, and bay leaf. Pour in the bottle of beer, cover, and marinate for 48 hours in the refrigerator. Remove the cheeks from the marinade and pat dry on paper towels. Strain the marinade, reserving both the liquid and the vegetables. In a medium saucepan, bring the liquid to a simmer over medium heat, skimming any fat and impurities that rise to the surface, until it comes to a boil. Strain through a chinois. Preheat the oven to 275°F. Season the cheeks with salt. Heat the oil in a large ovenproof straight-sided sauté pan over high heat. Sear the cheeks on all sides, 1 to 2 minutes per side, and remove from the pan. Drain any excess oil from the pan, lower the heat to medium, and add the reserved vegetables. Sweat until tender, about 10 minutes. Add the tomato paste and cook for 3 minutes. Deglaze the pan with the reserved liquid and reduce by half. Add the stock and chicken jus and bring to a simmer. Return the veal cheeks to the pan, cover, and transfer to the oven. Braise in the oven until the veal is tender and can be easily pulled apart with a fork, 3 to 3½ hours. Remove the pan from the oven and allow to rest, uncovered, for 30 minutes. Gently remove the cheeks from the braising liquid and set aside. Strain the liquid and discard the vegetables. Return the liquid to a saucepan over medium-high heat and skim away any fat and impurities that rise to the surface as it comes to a simmer. Lower the heat to medium-low and reduce the liquid to 3 cups, skimming frequently. Add the remaining ¼ cup of beer and the thyme leaves and whisk in the butter. Season with ground black pepper to taste.

Glazed Vegetables

12 baby carrots, trimmed
12 red pearl onions
2 stalks celery
8 baby spring onions
½ cup Chicken Stock (page 499)
4 tablespoons butter
½ teaspoon salt

Peel each carrot into a smooth cylindrical shape. Peel the pearl onions and the celery stalks. Bring a pot of salted water to a boil and blanch the vegetables until tender, 3 to 4 minutes. Transfer to a bowl of ice water, and, once cool, drain. Cut the celery stalks at 45-degree angles in 2-inch sections. In a medium sauté pan over medium heat, warm together the carrots, pearl onions, celery, spring onions, stock, butter, and salt. Cover and simmer until the vegetables are very tender and glazed, 7 to 8 minutes.

To Finish

Potato Puree (page 501)
4 Bread Crisps (page 498), broken into shards
Parsley leaves
Sauce reserved from making Braised Veal Cheeks

Spoon the potato puree onto 4 plates. Place the veal cheeks on top of the puree and garnish with the glazed vegetables and bread crisps. Top with parsley and finish with the sauce.

Beer-Battered Apples

SERVES 4

Canola oil
2 large Mutsu apples, peeled and cored
5 tablespoons sugar
1 tablespoon ground cinnamon
3 cups flour, plus more for dredging
2 cups Brooklyn Lager
½ cup grapeseed oil
1¼ teaspoons salt
6 egg whites

Pour 3 inches of canola oil into a large saucepan and bring the oil to 375°F over medium-high heat. Slice the apples crosswise into ½-inch-thick rings. Mix the sugar and cinnamon in a bowl and set aside. In a large bowl, mix together the flour, lager, grapeseed oil, and salt. In a separate, very clean bowl, whip the egg whites to soft peaks and fold into the flour mixture. Dredge the apple rings in flour, and then dip them in the beer batter. Fry in batches (2 or 3 at a time) so as to not overcrowd the pan for 2½ minutes, flip, and fry for an additional 3 to 4 minutes or until golden brown. Drain on paper towels and toss while still warm in the cinnamon sugar.

Beets

Satur Farms

Paulette Satur and Eberhard Müller worked in different sectors of the food industry, but after many years, their paths eventually crossed. In 1986, Eberhard opened Le Bernardin with Gilbert Le Coze and quickly joined the ranks of New York City's leading chefs. In 1997, as the chef de cuisine at Lutèce, he met Paulette, who, at the time, was working for a Manhattan wine distributor. "I would come into the restaurant to do a tasting. Surprisingly, Eberhard knew a lot about wine." They immediately bonded over an appreciation for Riesling. The same year they met, they married and bought eighteen acres of land on Long Island's North Fork.

Initially, they started farming so that they could supply Eberhard's kitchen with the finest vegetables, including ones that he simply couldn't find in New York. However, they could not help but lose themselves in the lifestyle. "The farm is a great challenge," Paulette remarks, standing hand-in-hand with her husband. Nodding, he adds, "It's something new every day." Satur Farms' produce is now sold in Manhattan's premier grocery stores and used in the city's top restaurants. Though the farm has expanded to 180 acres, the quality has remained constant, as has Paulette and Eberhard's meticulous attention to detail, which extends to the cleaning and packaging of their produce—it is imperative to them that they provide clean vegetables that are ready to eat straight from the container. Eberhard admits that his tendencies are obsessive, but he knows what it's like to cook in elite restaurants, and he feels that his level of quality control is a function of his respect for his clients and the people they feed. He says, "I sometimes feel jealous because I didn't have this kind of quality produce to work with in my day."

One of Paulette's most beloved crops is her beets. Like all of the vegetables planted at Satur Farms, they are seeded in the nutrient-rich sandy loam soil after it has undergone an intensive cover-crop program. The vegetables enjoy optimal weather conditions as a result of the farm's maritime location. In mid-March, the growing process kicks off when two acres of the land are planted. Ten annual growing cycles follow, with the first batch of beets ready to harvest by June. The baby beets are sized up and bundled together while the rest grow to full size and continue developing their sweetness and earthy flavor. Paulette grows three varieties on Satur Farms: red, golden, and candy striped, avoiding the increasingly popular white beets, which she finds "uninteresting." Even though Eberhard has never been a die-hard fan of this root vegetable, Paulette eats her beets raw, roasted, or prepared in borscht. Smiling, she says, "I am Ukrainian, after all."

Living on the farm full time, the couple believes the change from city life has been beneficial to them. "It is good to have sections in your life," says Paulette. Eberhard, in turn, compares his passions for farming and cooking, and finds a common thread in them. "Over time, there remains a clarity of flavor," he says. Ultimately, it is the quality of the food that matters most to him, a quality that he and Paulette have abundantly achieved at their beloved Satur Farms.

Baby Beet Salad with Chèvre and Fennel

SERVES 4

Raspberry Vinegar

1 cup raspberries
2 cups white balsamic vinegar
1 tablespoon celery leaves
1 teaspoon crushed black peppercorns
½ teaspoon fennel seeds

In a small bowl, crush the raspberries with the back of a spoon. Pour the vinegar over the raspberries. Add the celery leaves, peppercorns, and fennel seeds and transfer to a glass jar. Cover and marinate for 3 weeks at room temperature. Strain out the solids and return the vinegar to the jar. The vinegar will keep for up to 3 months at room temperature. **Note:** This is a great way to utilize raspberries that are really ripe. Use the vinegar during the summer on simple green salads or marinated beets. It is also great in a vinaigrette for fish or seafood.

Roasted Baby Candy-Striped Beets

18 baby candy-striped beets
2 cups olive oil
⅔ cup red wine vinegar
2 tablespoons sugar
Salt

Preheat the oven to 400°F. Wash the beets thoroughly, trim the green tops, and place in a baking dish. Combine the oil, vinegar, sugar, and 2 cups of water. Season the mixture with salt and pour over the beets. Cover the dish with aluminum foil and place in the oven. Roast the beets for 40 to 50 minutes or until tender. Cool to room temperature and then peel. Leave 14 beets whole and quarter the remaining 4.

Beet Vinaigrette

1 cup red beet juice (from 5 cups peeled and diced beets)
¼ cup Raspberry Vinegar
¼ cup orange juice
3 tablespoons olive oil
Salt

In a small saucepan, combine the beet juice and raspberry vinegar with 1 cup of water. Reduce the liquid over high heat to about 1 cup, 10 to 15 minutes. Strain the reduction through a quadruple layer of cheesecloth into a bowl. Cool over an ice bath. Whisk together the strained reduction and the orange juice. Stir in the olive oil and season with salt to taste.

To Finish

2 baby candy-striped beets
2 teaspoons olive oil
1 fennel bulb
6 ounces chèvre
Fennel flowers
Fennel fronds

Wash the beets and shave thinly on a mandoline. Dress the whole and quartered roasted baby beets and the shaved raw beets with the olive oil and arrange on 4 plates. Trim the base of the fennel and remove the outer layers. Set the bulb flat on its bottom and cut it into quarters. Thinly slice the fennel quarters lengthwise on a mandoline and arrange on the plates. Fill in the empty spaces with small mounds of chèvre. Drizzle the beet vinaigrette over the vegetables and chèvre and garnish each plate with fennel flowers and fronds.

Glazed Beets with Bone Marrow and Horseradish

SERVES 4

Roasted Beets in Salt Crust

4 large beets
18 egg whites
7 cups salt

Preheat the oven to 375°F. Thoroughly wash and dry the beets. In a large bowl, whip the egg whites until stiff peaks form. Gently fold the salt into the egg whites and refrigerate the mixture for 30 minutes. Spread half of the egg white mixture in the bottom of a medium baking dish. Arrange the beets in the salt mixture so that they are close together but do not touch. Cover the beets with the remaining egg and salt mixture to cover completely. Bake in the oven until a golden crust develops and the beets are tender, 1¾ to 2 hours. Remove the beets from the salt and peel. **Note:** Use any leftovers as you would roasted beets. They are particularly delicious drizzled with olive oil and seasoned with salt.

Baby Beets

4 baby candy-striped beets
4 baby red beets
4 baby yellow beets
4½ cups olive oil
1 cup red wine vinegar
3 tablespoons sugar
Salt
Ground black pepper
2 tablespoons butter, melted

Preheat oven to 400°F. Wash the beets thoroughly and place in separate baking dishes according to color. Combine the oil, vinegar, sugar, and 4½ cups of water. Season the mixture with salt to taste. Pour one-third of the liquid mixture into each dish. Cover with aluminum foil and roast in the oven until the beets are tender, 40 to 50 minutes. Cool to room temperature, and then peel the beets. Cut into quarters and season with salt and pepper to taste. Drizzle the beets with melted butter and keep warm.

Pickled Beets

4 baby candy-striped beets
¼ cup white balsamic vinegar
¼ cup sugar
Salt
Olive oil

Thinly shave the beets on a mandoline and place in a bowl. In a small saucepan, combine the vinegar and sugar with 2 tablespoons of water. Season the pickling liquid with salt, bring the mixture to a boil, and pour over the beets. Allow to cool to room temperature. Drain the beets and dress with olive oil and salt to taste.

Sautéed Bone Marrow

8 (3- to 4-inch) marrowbones
Salt
Ground black pepper
1 cup flour
¼ cup grapeseed oil

Allow the bones to come to room temperature to soften the marrow. Gently push the marrow out of the bones. Rinse the marrow in ice water to remove the blood and pat dry. Season with salt and pepper, cover with the flour, and let stand for 10 minutes. Shake off the excess flour. In a small sauté pan, heat the oil over medium-high heat. Add the dredged bone marrow and sauté until golden and warm in the center, basting the marrow with the oil and continuously rotating to ensure even color, about 2 minutes.

To Finish

2 raw baby beets
2 ounces fresh horseradish root, peeled
Lovage leaves
Chopped chives
Salt
Ground black pepper
Beef Broth (page 498)

Cut the large roasted beets crosswise into ½-inch slices and punch into rounds using a 4-inch round cutter. Place a beet round in the center of a plate. Arrange the roasted baby beet quarters on top of the large roasted beet round. Position the bone marrow on top of the round. Thinly shave the raw baby beets on a mandoline. Arrange the pickled beets and shaved beets around the plate. Grate horseradish in a small mound onto one place on the plate. Garnish with lovage leaves, chives, salt, and pepper. In a small saucepan, warm the beef broth, and then spoon it around the plate. Repeat with the remaining ingredients, to serve 4.

Berries

Berried Treasures Farm

Berried Treasures Farm turns out produce that is known to stir up a fight at the Greenmarket. Sicilian-born Franca Tantillo oversees her turf both at the farm and at the market, displaying the unique combination of charisma and poise necessary to raise the most perfect berries and control even the most aggressive of customers. Her stand appeals to all, from small children to esteemed chefs, throwing her "can't-get-enough" patrons into a fruit-hungry frenzy.

Before taking residence on her current plot of land in 1986, Franca was a nurse. She realized her agricultural calling during a summer in Pennsylvania when she was employed at an alternative medicine retreat center. While there, if Franca found herself seeking solace, she would tend the grape vines on the property. She began to comprehend what this meant: her family's decades-old farming heritage was beckoning from within. Franca made a new home in Cooks Falls, New York, which is framed by the Catskill Mountains and the rushing Beaverkill River. The farm's landscape can overtake you with its beauty, but working this land can be trying, particularly due to the finicky nature of the fruit. When Franca first began farming, other growers scoffed that the Catskill Mountains would be too cold for strawberries and criticized the odd round shape and small size of the variety she chose to plant. She paid no attention to the naysayers and stuck with her strawberries. Without looking back, without doubting her intuition, she came out on top with crop after crop of thriving fruit, ripened red from end to end.

Now New York City's Greenmarkets are home to one of Franca's most prized gems: the Tristar strawberry. Instead of producing one large crop as the June bearers do, day-neutral varieties like the Tristar produce fruit throughout the growing season, from July until the first frost.

Franca nurtures her strawberries with equal parts zeal and tenacity. She explains, "Not only do berries love my mineral-rich soil, but our cool nights let them relax. In the heat we suffer, and the plants like it cooler too!" Eating one of Franca's Tristars is like tasting the pure essence of strawberry. And the Tristars are only one of Berried Treasures' wonders. They are joined by tart currants; a jewel-toned array of raspberries; and luscious, shirt-staining blackberries.

Franca feels that she has truly found her calling. "I just want to be a farmer," she emphasizes. With a steadfast dedication to her work, she leaves her farm at 4:00 a.m. most days of the week to travel to the city's Greenmarkets where she herself is as beloved as her berries. A nearly perfect attendance means Franca has managed to cultivate cherished friendships with her regular customers. Connecting with people so easily, she has been humorously and lovingly dubbed "Manhattan's Strawberry Shrink." "People confide in me. I am the first to know everything," she says. This comes as no surprise, as her New York sass and wit are as addictive as her local berries.

Salad with Strawberries, Harpersfield Cheese, and Basil

SERVES 4

½ **English cucumber, peeled and thinly sliced**
6 **cups Tristar strawberries, hulled and halved**
2 **tablespoons olive oil, plus more to finish**
1 **tablespoon lemon juice**
Salt
12 **cucamelons, halved**
½ **cup crumbled Harpersfield cheese**
    (a semi-hard, washed-rind cheese)
1 **red onion, thinly sliced**
½ **cup small basil leaves**
Flowering basil
Aged balsamic vinegar
Ground black pepper

Using a ¾-inch round cutter, punch out the seedy core from the cucumber slices. Dress the strawberries with the olive oil, lemon juice, and salt to taste. Divide among 4 plates. Place the cucamelons between the strawberries and sprinkle the cheese on top. Top each plate with 8 or 9 pieces of julienned red onion and 3 cucumber rings. Garnish with basil leaves and flowering basil and finish with additional olive oil and aged balsamic vinegar. Season to taste with salt and pepper.

Raspberry Tart

Sablé Breton

6 egg yolks
1 cup sugar
1 cup butter, at room temperature
2 cups flour
4 teaspoons baking powder
2 teaspoons fleur de sel

In a stand mixer fitted with the whisk attachment, whip the egg yolks with the sugar on high speed until the mixture falls from the whisk in a pale ribbon, about 5 minutes. Add the butter and mix until combined. Change to the paddle attachment and add the flour, baking powder, and salt. Mix on low speed until just incorporated. Divide the dough into 2 portions. Roll out each portion between 2 sheets of parchment paper to just under ¼ inch thick, making sure that the dough measures at least 5 by 14 inches. Place the dough on baking sheets and wrap with plastic wrap. Freeze until solid.

Pastry Cream

2 cups milk
½ cup sugar
¼ cup cornstarch
½ teaspoon salt
4 egg yolks
4 tablespoons butter, at room temperature
2 teaspoons vanilla extract

In a medium saucepan, bring the milk to just under a boil. Stir together the sugar, cornstarch, and salt in a small bowl. Add the egg yolks, mixing until smooth. Slowly whisk the hot milk into the egg mixture, and then return to the saucepan. Cook over medium-high heat, stirring constantly, until the mixture comes to a boil. Simmer for 30 seconds, remove from the heat, and stir in the butter and vanilla. Transfer to a container and lay a piece of plastic wrap directly against the surface of the pastry cream so that a skin does not form. Chill over an ice bath.

Buttercream

1 cup sugar
3 egg whites
1¼ cups butter, cubed and at room temperature
2 teaspoons vanilla extract

Combine the sugar with ¼ cup of water in a heavy-bottomed saucepan over medium-high heat and bring to a boil, stirring to dissolve the sugar. Continue cooking without stirring until the

syrup reaches the soft ball stage (240°F). Meanwhile, place the egg whites in the bowl of a stand mixer fitted with the whisk attachment. When the sugar syrup has reached 230°F, begin whipping the egg whites at medium speed to medium peaks. When the sugar syrup reaches 240°F, gradually pour it into the egg whites with the mixer running on medium speed. As soon as all of the syrup has been incorporated, increase the speed to high and continue to whip until the meringue has cooled to room temperature. Gradually add the butter, 1 cube at a time, mixing after each addition, until it is fully incorporated. Scrape down the sides of the bowl as necessary, and then fold in the vanilla.

Vanilla Puree

Pastry Cream
Buttercream

Recondition the pastry cream by placing it in the bowl of a stand mixer fitted with the paddle attachment and mix on medium speed until smooth. Do the same with the butter-cream. Once they are both smooth, combine them and mix with the paddle attachment until smooth. The two will not emulsify properly if they are not reconditioned before combining.

To Finish

2 pints golden raspberries
2 pints red raspberries

Preheat the oven to 325°F. Cut both of the frozen sablé bretons to fit into the bottoms of 2 rectangular removable-bottom tart pans (4½ by 13½ inches). Line the bottoms of the pans with the cut dough. Bake until golden brown, about 20 minutes. Cool to room temperature, and, once cool, remove the shells from the tart pans. Transfer the vanilla puree to a pastry bag fitted with a #803 piping tip (5/16-inch opening) and pipe the puree into a rectangular shape on top of the tart shells, leaving a narrow border around the edge. Using a small offset spatula, smooth the top of the puree. Refrigerate until cool. Arrange the raspberries on top of the puree.

Black Sea Bass

John Maholey

Years ago, when the young John Maholey was growing up in New York City's Chelsea neighborhood, it was a prominent fishing area, full of fishermen, fishmongers, and butchers. Hooked on the fishing life at an early age, John soon found himself frequenting his parents' second home on Long Island to further pursue his passion. Searching for a fulfilling livelihood, he relocated to Island Park in 1973, procured his first boat, and began to fish regularly, even seeing a professional future in this field. "When I first started, there were no regulations to fishing, and people made 'hobby income' from selling [fish]," he recalls. However, he wanted to be more than just a hobby fisherman, and by 1983, he had secured his paperwork in order to seriously (and legally) work exclusively as a fisherman. It was at that point that he narrowed his focus to black sea bass.

Precision is a requisite for John's minimalist rod-and-reel style of fishery, and the relative elusiveness of sea bass, coupled with the lack of decent sonar equipment, created a challenge for him in his early days. "Business started as a sporadic effort because the navigation tools were totally different than the ones you have today," he says. This problem was solved with the 1970 introduction of a miniature Long Range Navigation system (LORAN-C), which made it possible to accurately find schools of fish within a range of fifty feet. Once John could afford to purchase this system himself in the early 1980s, his business changed completely. He went from being a small-scale hobby fisherman to a large-scale professional one.

John began bringing in significant catches of black sea bass and was feeling very comfortable by the late 1980s. Then suddenly, large commercial fishers started to seek bottom dwellers, particularly the schools of sea bass John was after. "This fish was a highly prized relative to other species and has always been one of the more expensive catches," he explains. After seeking advice from his small pool of restaurant clients, he decided to invest in more technology. "I bought a vessel with a rather sophisticated central basin [in which] to store live fish," he says. The investment expanded his marketability to Asian restaurants in Manhattan and Queens that were seeking quality live fish.

John acknowledges that to be a professional fisherman today, one must constantly pay attention not only to nautical forecasts but also to changes in policy regulation. New maritime laws were enacted in 1986 to prevent overfishing. The rules are intricate and can be frustrating and unpredictable—current decrees allow black sea bass fishing during irregular intervals throughout the year, and catch maximums vary from day to day. John forges ahead, saying, "I've done this for a long, long time."

He fishes through tough conditions—"even if the inlets freeze over, the *Ice Breaker* and I try to keep a clear path"—and admits that it can get lonely out on the water. But John always has his priorities straight, no matter the conditions: "It is all about preserving the black sea bass."

Poached Black Sea Bass with Wild Nettles, Clams, and Squid

SERVES 4

Shellfish

3 tablespoons canola oil
½ cup chopped ginger
½ cup chopped parsley leaves and stems
⅓ cup chopped shallot
1 pound mussels
12 razor clams
1¼ cups white wine
1 bay leaf
1 cup chopped green onion
Salt

In a large straight-sided pot, heat the oil over high heat. Add the ginger, parsley, and shallot and cook for 30 seconds, stirring constantly. Add the mussels and clams and continue cooking for 30 seconds, stirring constantly. Add the wine and bay leaf and cook for 30 seconds, and then cover the pot. Cook over high heat for 4 to 5 minutes. While the shellfish is cooking, blanch the green onion in a pot of boiling salted water until tender, about 2 minutes. Transfer to an ice bath to cool, and then place in a blender. Remove the shellfish from the cooking liquid and strain the liquid through a chinois. Add this stock to the blender. Blend the green onion and stock until smooth and season with salt to taste. Clean the clams and cut the flesh on a bias into 1-inch pieces; reserve for the seafood ragout. Discard the mussels or reserve for another use.

Nettle Bouillabaisse

6 cups tightly packed wild nettles
2 cups tightly packed spinach
Blended green onion and shellfish liquid, reserved from making Shellfish
Salt
Lemon juice

In a pot of boiling salted water, blanch the nettles and spinach until tender, 45 to 60 seconds. Transfer the greens to an ice bath until cool, and then wring out the excess moisture. Blend the nettles and spinach in a blender on high speed with ½ cup of ice water until pureed; pass through a chinois. Combine the strained puree with the green onion and shellfish liquid and season with sea salt and lemon juice to taste.

Seafood Ragout

¼ cup Chicken Stock (page 499)
4 squid (about ¾ pound total), cleaned and scored on the outside
2 tablespoons cold butter
Razor clams, reserved from making Shellfish
Lemon juice
Salt

In a small sauté pan, bring the stock to a simmer over low heat. Add the squid and simmer until cooked through, 1 to 1½ minutes. Add the butter, tossing to glaze the squid. Add the clams and season with lemon juice and salt to taste.

Poached Black Sea Bass

6 cups Chicken Stock (page 499)
10 sprigs thyme
6 cloves garlic, crushed but kept whole
3 tablespoons cornstarch
Salt
Fillets from 1 (2½- to 3-pound) black sea bass, skin on

Preheat the oven to 250°F. Bring the stock to a simmer in a medium stockpot. Add the thyme and garlic and simmer over low heat for 2 minutes. Whisk together the cornstarch and 3 tablespoons of water in a small bowl. Whisk the cornstarch slurry into the seasoned chicken stock and simmer for 5 minutes to thicken and cook out any starchy flavor. Season with salt to taste and strain the liquid into a baking dish. Allow it to cool to 145°F.

Slice the bass fillets into 4 portions total and season with salt. Add the bass, skin side down, to the poaching liquid. Cover with parchment paper, transfer to the oven, and cook for about 15 minutes until the fish is opaque and the tip of a paring knife inserted into the flesh meets little resistance. Remove the fillets from the poaching liquid and allow them to rest for 2 minutes.

To Finish

Red chile flakes
Sea salt

Spoon nettle bouillabaisse onto 4 plates and place a portion of bass on top. Add the seafood ragout and season with chile flakes and sea salt to taste.

Whole Grilled Black Sea Bass

SERVES 4

Salsa Verde

1 tablespoon finely chopped chives
1 tablespoon finely chopped cilantro
1 tablespoon finely chopped parsley
1 tablespoon finely chopped green onion
1 teaspoon finely chopped rinsed salt-packed anchovies
½ teaspoon finely chopped garlic
¼ teaspoon red chile flakes
¼ cup plus 1 tablespoon olive oil
2 tablespoons lemon juice
Salt

Combine the chives, cilantro, parsley, and green onion in a small mixing bowl. Mix in the anchovies, garlic, and red chile flakes. Add the olive oil and lemon juice and stir to combine. Season with salt to taste.

Grilled Black Sea Bass

1 (2½- to 3-pound) black sea bass, scaled, gutted, and gills removed
Sea salt
Ground black pepper
6 (⅛-inch-thick) slices lemon
5 sprigs parsley
5 sprigs thyme
Olive oil

Remove the cooking grate from a charcoal grill and light 5 pounds of charcoal in a chimney starter. When the charcoal is white hot, arrange it in the bottom of the grill. Return the cooking grate to the grill and season the cavity of the fish with salt and pepper. Place the lemon slices, parsley, and thyme inside the cavity of the fish. Brush the outside with olive oil and place the fish on the grill over high heat. Sear for 5 minutes. Flip the fish over, cover the grill, and continue cooking for 7 to 8 more minutes or until the flesh can be flaked from the bones. Remove the fish from the grill and let rest for 5 minutes before serving.

To Finish

2 cups young agretti
2 tablespoons Lemon Vinaigrette (see page 500)
1 lemon, cut into wedges

Toss the agretti with the lemon vinaigrette. Using a fork and a spatula, gently separate and remove the fillets from the bones. Serve the sea bass with lemon wedges, salsa verde, and agretti salad.

Cabbage

Blue Heron Farm

Truly great farmers know that the product their land yields is only as good as the soil. Lou Johns and Robin Ostfeld exemplify this belief. At Blue Heron Farm in Lodi, New York, they grow some of the state's best cabbage in a meticulously managed cover-cropping system, which they have been developing and refining since they moved to this land in 1986.

Fifteen of their 160 acres is under cultivation (Lou, who studied forestry preservation at Evergreen State University in Olympia, Washington, insists that most of their land remain wooded). Robin, who met Lou while they were working on a blueberry farm in Olympia in 1978, explains their method like this: "Because we have heavy soil, Lou designed permanent planting beds framed by grassy strips." The grassy strips provide runways for tractor wheels, keep the soil in the beds from becoming compacted, and anchor the earth. The strips are purposely overgrown with native clover, dandelions, and other beneficial vegetation. This arrangement gives the cabbage at Blue Heron Farm a nurturing environment in which to thrive.

Mini seedlings are transplanted from greenhouses into the nutrient-packed clay loam. "The soil is heavy and slightly alkaline, and gives cabbage plenty of access to water," says Robin. The farmers are usually able to plant multiple times per year. The first planting yields Gonzales cabbages, which are smaller in size than the standard varieties and are ready for harvest in June. According to Robin, "These are nice and tender, and are good for salads or coleslaws." In the fall, the crinkly-leafed red and green Savoys, excellent for blanching and braising, are ready to be harvested. Blue Heron also brings us cabbage in the winter, such as the hearty January King, which is valuable not only because of its ability to persist in cold temperatures, but also for its distinctive taste. "Prolonged exposure to cold makes it the sweetest cabbage of the year," affirms Robin. When the heads are harvested, Lou and Robin place the ones that don't go straight to the market in storage coolers. For the best long-term results, a farmer must know just when to pick: "If you harvest the cabbage when it is too mature, it will not store as well."

Lou and Robin work hard to nurture the ecosystem at Blue Heron Farm, planting repeatedly each year without destroying the soil. Blue Heron keeps its business close to home through markets, a CSA, and food co-ops. Robin and Lou are proud of the local character of their farm, and the reciprocal enthusiasm of their customers keeps them going even when they encounter the hardships that come with being farmers: "Diversity and friendship allow us to keep moving forward, even in the face of great challenge."

Sauerkraut
with Ham Hocks and Potatoes

SERVES 4

Sauerkraut

1 (2- to 3-pound) head green cabbage
2 teaspoons mustard seeds
1 teaspoon coriander seeds
1 teaspoon white peppercorns
3 bay leaves
3 allspice berries
¼ cup plus 2 tablespoons salt

Wearing gloves, remove the outer leaves of the cabbage and discard. It is important to wear gloves when handling the cabbage to keep it uncontaminated. Slice the cabbage into ⅛- to ¼-inch ribbons. Rinse under cold water and transfer to a clean nonreactive container. Using a piece of cheesecloth and butcher's twine, make a sachet containing the mustard seeds, coriander seeds, peppercorns, bay leaves, and allspice. In a large saucepan, combine the sachet and salt with 1 gallon of water and bring to a boil over medium heat. Remove from the heat and chill over an ice bath. Discard the sachet. When chilled, cover the cabbage ribbons completely with the liquid. Lay a quadruple layer of cheesecloth directly against the surface of the cabbage, weigh down with a clean plate, and cover the entire container with cheesecloth. Store the cabbage at room temperature (ideally between 65° and 70°F). Wearing gloves, replace both layers of cheesecloth and skim away any mold every few days for 3 weeks. Drain the cabbage and reserve the liquid. Bring the cabbage liquid to a rolling boil, strain through a chinois, and pour it back over the cabbage. Cool to room temperature and store in the refrigerator. **Note:** A great condiment for sausages and corned beef, sauerkraut will keep in the refrigerator for up to 2 months.

Ham Hock Broth

4 smoked ham hocks
2 cups diced (¼ inch) onion
1 cup diced (¼ inch) carrot
1 cup diced (¼ inch) celery
8 sprigs thyme
2 cloves garlic, crushed but kept whole
1 teaspoon ground black pepper
1 bay leaf

Combine all of the ingredients in a 6-quart stockpot, cover with water, and simmer until the ham hocks are tender, about 3½ hours. Strain the stock through a chinois and reserve. Remove the meat from the bones and reserve.

To Finish

2 tablespoons canola oil
Ham reserved from making Ham Hock Broth
½ onion, thinly sliced
3 cloves garlic, crushed but kept whole
5 sprigs thyme
1 bay leaf
16 baby German Butterball potatoes, peeled
1 cup white wine
4 cups diced (1½ inch) green Savoy cabbage leaves
¾ teaspoon Four-Spice Mix (page 375)
2 tablespoons butter

Heat the oil in a large sauté pan over medium-high heat. Add the reserved ham and sauté for 1 to 2 minutes. Lower the heat to medium-low and add the onion, garlic, 3 sprigs of the thyme, the bay leaf, and potatoes. Sweat for 4 to 5 minutes and add the wine. Add 2 cups of sauerkraut and 3 cups of ham hock broth and simmer until the potatoes are tender, 12 to 15 minutes. Add the cabbage leaves and four-spice mix, cover, and simmer for 5 minutes. Finish with the butter and the remaining 2 sprigs of thyme. Divide among 4 bowls.

Sauerkraut

The word *sauerkraut* comes from the German meaning "sour greens." German immigrants to the United States traveled with barrels of sauerkraut to ward off diseases like scurvy, earning them the nickname "krauts" (just as the British, who warded off scurvy with limes, were called "limeys"). In New York, the immigrants began selling their sauerkraut, along with sausages and rolls, from pushcarts along the Bowery. To this day, you'll find nearly every one of New York's ubiquitous hot dog carts stocked with sauerkraut.

Stuffed Cabbage with Lamb

SERVES 4

Stuffed Cabbage

3 heads Savoy cabbage
1 tablespoon butter
1 cup diced (¼ inch) onion
1 tablespoon minced garlic
2 eggs
2½ cups ground lamb sirloin (about 22 ounces)
1½ cups ground lamb belly (about 11 ounces)
¼ cup cream
3 tablespoons bread crumbs
3 tablespoons chopped rosemary
2 tablespoons ground caraway seeds
2 tablespoons salt

Peel the leaves from the cabbages and discard the tough, dark green outermost leaves and the pale yellow inner leaves, reserving only the pale green middle leaves. Bring a large pot of salted water to a boil and blanch the middle leaves until tender, 6 to 7 minutes, then transfer to an ice bath. Once cool, drain. In a medium sauté pan, melt the butter over medium-low heat. Add the onion and garlic and sweat until tender, 3 to 4 minutes. Remove from the heat and allow to cool. In a large mixing bowl, beat the eggs and combine with the cooled garlic and onion, the ground lamb sirloin and belly, cream, bread crumbs, rosemary, caraway, and salt. Mix thoroughly to combine. Roll a little less than ¼ cup of filling into a ball and wrap in a blanched cabbage leaf; repeat to form 8 stuffed cabbage balls. As you form each ball, place it on a square piece of plastic wrap, bring the corners together and twist tightly to help form the ball. Refrigerate for 1 hour.

To Finish

2 tablespoons canola oil
1 cup red pearl onions, peeled
1 cup white pearl onions, peeled
1 cup diced (½ inch) carrot
1 cup diced (½ inch) celery
1 cup diced (½ inch) onion
4 cloves garlic, minced
Salt
1 tablespoon tomato paste
1 cup red wine
4 cups Chicken Jus (page 498)
2 cups Chicken Stock (page 499)
1 teaspoon ground caraway seeds
2 bay leaves
½ bunch thyme
2 tablespoons butter, softened
Potato Puree (see page 501)

Heat the oil in a large saucepan over medium-high heat. Just before it begins to smoke, add the pearl onions, carrot, celery, onion and garlic and season with salt. Sauté for 3 minutes until the vegetables start to brown. Add the tomato paste and sauté for another 2 minutes. Deglaze with the wine, cooking until the pan is almost dry. Add the jus and stock and bring to a boil. Strain, reserving both the vegetables and the stock. Return the stock to the pan and add the ground caraway, bay leaves, and thyme. Reduce the heat to medium-low, and simmer for 45 minutes until thickened. Season with salt to taste.

Preheat the oven to 400°F. Brush a roasting pan with the butter. Remove the stuffed cabbage from the refrigerator and peel away the plastic wrap. Place the cabbage in the roasting pan and scatter the reserved vegetables around them. Add the reserved liquid, cover with a parchment paper lid, and place in the oven. Roast for 20 minutes. Remove the parchment paper and return to the oven, basting every 5 minutes for 25 minutes until the stuffing in the cabbage is cooked and the tops are golden. Serve the stuffed cabbage with their cooking liquid, the stewed vegetables, and potato puree.

Carrots

Paffenroth Gardens

The simple orange carrot is not the most exciting vegetable. For many, it's eaten as an afterthought and for its health benefits rather than for its flavor. However, for farmer Alex Paffenroth, the carrot is the epitome of a beautiful vegetable. Alex is a fourth-generation farmer in Warwick, New York, working the same land that his great-great-grandfather cleared for farming in the early 1900s. Specializing in root crops, Paffenroth Gardens' unique offerings include white shallots, spicy black radishes, and countless sizes and shapes of potatoes. However, Alex's focus on carrots yields the ultimate root vegetable.

Twenty years ago, Alex started his trips to the Union Square Greenmarket as an onion farmer and saw everybody around him selling the same produce, making it hard to stand out. "In order to get attention, you need to do different things," Alex says. So he looked around at the market to see what was missing and found no one was selling carrots, which just happened to be one of his favorites.

Paffenroth Gardens is a mere fifty miles north of New York City in the Hudson Valley's black dirt region. Alex's farm boasts large concentrations of intensely dark "muck" soil, which radiates with the same life and vigor as compost. "The area is known as a drowned land because it was once the bottom of a lake," explains Alex as he allows the dirt to run through his fingers. "It's like a big nutritious sponge." The farm will occasionally flood after excessive rain, and although this may drown an entire crop of vegetables, it also helps clean and purify the land. Because of the soil's softness, nutrients, and depth—in some areas it's as deep as twenty feet—root vegetables are able to grow to full form. "The land is perfect for growing all root crops—especially my carrots," says Alex. Paffenroth Gardens' carrots range from silky White Satins to bright Yellowstones to two-toned Purple Dragons to the familiar orange carrots—of which, in Alex's world of plenty, there are fifteen varieties from which to choose. These carrots' flavors, textures, and amenity to cooking are what set them apart. Alex's fall carrots reach an unprecedented level of sweetness, giving them intense richness and complexity. The winter carrots are grown larger, making them hearty enough to withstand extended cellaring, loosely packed in charcoal-colored soil, which allows them to be enjoyed even when sweet fall carrots, straight from the earth, are still months away.

Carrot Soup
with Pickled Beets and Radishes

SERVES 4

Chilled Carrot Soup

1 tablespoon olive oil
¼ cup thinly sliced white onion
1 teaspoon minced ginger
½ teaspoon Madras curry powder
¼ teaspoon ground cumin
3 cups peeled and thinly sliced carrots
3 cups carrot juice (from about 12 carrots)
1 cup Granny Smith apple juice (from about 6 apples)
2½ teaspoons salt
2 teaspoons lime juice

In a medium sauté pan, heat the olive oil over medium-low heat. Add the onion and ginger and sweat until tender and translucent, about 4 minutes. Stir in the curry powder and the cumin, and then add the carrots and ¾ cup of water. Sweat until the carrots are tender, adding more water if necessary to keep the pan from drying out, 15 to 20 minutes. Transfer the contents of the pan to a blender, add the carrot juice and apple juice, and puree. Pass through a chinois and season with the salt and lime juice. Chill over an ice bath until cool and refrigerate until ready to serve.

Root Vegetables

4 baby Chioggia beets
4 baby golden beets
4 baby red beets
3 tablespoons olive oil
Salt
½ teaspoon ground black pepper
3 cups red wine vinegar
8 baby red radishes
1 cup white balsamic vinegar
1 tablespoon sugar
8 baby carrots
4 Thumbelina carrots
4 spring onions
1 tablespoon cold-pressed sunflower oil

Preheat the oven to 400°F. Rinse the beets and trim off the tops. Toss them in a mixing bowl with the olive oil, 1 tablespoon of salt, and the black pepper. Divide the beets by their colors into 3 small baking dishes. Add 1 cup of red wine vinegar and ½ cup of water to each baking dish. Cover the baking dishes with aluminum foil and roast the beets in the oven until they are easily pierced with the tip of a knife, 40 to 50 minutes. Let the beets cool in their cooking liquid and then peel.

Trim the radishes, leaving some of the green tops intact, and place in a bowl. Combine the balsamic vinegar, 1 tablespoon of salt, and the sugar in a small saucepan and bring to a simmer. Pour the hot vinegar mixture over the radishes and cover with plastic wrap. Cool the radishes in the pickling liquid to room temperature and drain.

Peel and trim the carrots, leaving some of the green tops intact. Cut the Thumbelina carrots in half lengthwise. Trim off the tops of the spring onions and leave the root ends attached. Bring a pot of salted water to a boil. Blanch the baby carrots for 3 to 4 minutes and transfer to an ice bath. Blanch the Thumbelina carrots until tender, 4 to 6 minutes, and transfer to the ice bath. Blanch the spring onions until tender, 4 minutes, and transfer to the ice bath.

Combine the beets, radishes, carrots, and onions in a mixing bowl and dress with the sunflower oil. Season with salt to taste.

To Finish
Carrot tops
4 teaspoons cold-pressed sunflower oil

Arrange the root vegetables in the bottoms of 4 shallow bowls. Pour the chilled carrot soup around the vegetables. Garnish with carrot tops and finish with sunflower oil.

Roasted Carrots
with Wheat Berries and Cumin

SERVES 4

Carrot-Duck Crumble

1 carrot
1 teaspoon olive oil
¾ teaspoon salt
1½ pounds duck skin
3 shallots
2 cups canola oil
½ teaspoon Madras curry powder
¼ teaspoon ground cumin
Pinch of cayenne pepper

Preheat the oven to 200°F. Peel and thinly slice the carrot on a mandoline. Toss with the olive oil and season with ¼ teaspoon of the salt. Line a rimmed baking sheet with a silicone baking mat and arrange the carrot slices in a single layer. Bake in the oven until dried, about 1 hour. Remove the dried carrot chips from the oven and cool to room temperature. Chop the chips into ¼-inch pieces.

Have your butcher grind the duck skin for you or, to do it yourself, cut the skin into 1- to 2-inch pieces and freeze. Grind the frozen skin with a meat grinder on a small die set-ting. Combine the ground duck skin and 1 cup of water in a medium sauté pan and simmer over medium-low heat until the water has evaporated, about 30 minutes. Drain off half of the rendered duck fat and reserve for the roasted carrots. Return the pan to the stove and continue to crisp the duck skin until golden brown, about 20 minutes. Drain and reserve the rendered duck fat. Transfer the crispy skin to paper towels and cool to room temperature. Once cooled, finely chop the duck skin and combine with the chopped carrot chips.

Peel and thinly slice the shallots on a mandoline. Combine the sliced shallots and canola oil in a large sauté pan and fry over medium heat, stirring constantly until the shallots are golden brown, 12 to 15 minutes. Strain the shallots, drain thor-oughly on paper towels, and cool to room temperature. Chop the shallots into small pieces and combine with the duck skin and carrot chips.

Season the mixture with the curry powder, cumin, cayenne pepper, and remaining ½ teaspoon of salt. Store the crumble in an airtight container at room temperature until ready to serve.

Duck Fat–Roasted Carrots

2 cups rendered duck fat, reserved from making Carrot-Duck Crumble
8 heirloom carrots, such as Purple Haze or Dragon
4 cloves garlic, crushed but kept whole
4 sprigs thyme
2 sprigs rosemary
2 tablespoons butter
Salt

Preheat the oven to 250°F. Melt the rendered duck fat in a large, ovenproof pan over medium heat and add the carrots. Transfer to the oven and roast the carrots for 2 hours, until they are very tender, basting and rotating every 15 minutes. Drain off 1 cup of the duck fat from the pan, transfer the pan to the stove, and continue to cook the carrots over medium-high heat, basting with the remaining duck fat until evenly browned. Add the garlic, thyme, rosemary, and butter, and baste until the butter is browned, 7 to 8 minutes. Remove the carrots and drain on paper towels. Season with salt to taste.

Wheat Berries

1 cup diced (¼ inch) onion
½ cup diced (¼ inch) carrot
½ cup diced (¼ inch) celery
3 cloves garlic, crushed but kept whole
2 strips lemon zest
8 cups Chicken Stock (page 499)
1½ cups wheat berries
¼ cup Lemon Vinaigrette (page 500)
1½ tablespoons salt

Tie the onion, carrot, celery, garlic, and lemon zest in a piece of cheesecloth to make a sachet. In a medium saucepan, combine the sachet, chicken stock, and wheat berries and bring to a simmer over medium heat. Gently cook the wheat berries until they are tender but maintain their shape, 1½ to 2 hours. Drain the wheat berries through a chinois and discard the sachet. While they are still warm, dress the wheat berries with the lemon vinaigrette and season with the salt.

Cumin Oil

¼ cup cumin seeds
½ cup cold-pressed sunflower oil

In a small sauté pan, toast the cumin seeds over medium heat until fragrant, about 10 minutes. In a blender, combine the toasted cumin with the oil and then strain the mixture through a chinois lined with cheesecloth. **Note:** Any leftover cumin oil can be stored in an airtight container in the refrigerator for up to 1 month.

Carrot Sauce

4 cups carrot juice (from about 16 large carrots)
½ cup mascarpone
2 tablespoons Dijon mustard
1½ teaspoons cumin oil
2 tablespoons lemon juice
Salt

Reduce the carrot juice in a small sauté pan until 1½ cups remain, about 30 minutes. Strain the juice through a chinois and transfer to a blender. With the blender running, add the mascarpone, mustard, and cumin oil. Season with the lemon juice and salt to taste. **Note:** Any leftover carrot sauce can be stored in an airtight container in the refrigerator for 2 to 3 days. It is great as a sauce for grilled chicken and fish or it can be spooned over any leftover wheat berries.

To Finish
Carrot tops

Cut 2 of the roasted carrots in half crosswise and place the halves on a plate. Spoon 2 tablespoons of the carrot sauce across the carrots. Spoon ¼ cup of the wheat berries across the top and sprinkle with carrot-duck crumble. Finish with 1 teaspoon of cumin oil and garnish with carrot tops. Repeat with the remaining ingredients, to serve 4. Serve the remaining wheat berries family-style in a bowl.

CAULIFLOWE

Cauliflower

Barber's Farm

Fifth-generation farmer Jim Barber is running a farm on the land that, at one time, fed George Washington and his troops. This earned Schoharie County the title "breadbasket of the American Revolution." Centuries later, the valley is still celebrated, especially for its seventeen feet of healthy topsoil. Each generation of Barbers has judiciously built upon this excellent foundation. Jim's great-grandfather opened a roadside stand, thus establishing a relationship with the community. His son purchased eighty additional acres to raise dairy cows and grow sweet corn. It was Jim who worked with his father to expand the property to four hundred acres. They sold the cows and focused on growing vegetables. One crop in particular pays tribute to the nearby town of Stamford, New York's cauliflower capital.

"A lot has changed with cauliflower," says Jim. "We used to have to hand-tie the leaves to cover the head in order to keep it white. Nowadays, "self-blanching" plants have leaves that naturally form around the crown, protecting the head from the sunlight and keeping the cauliflower white. But beyond the common white cauliflower, Jim is excited about the newer varieties that abound: "Now we grow the purple Graffiti and the green Romanesco, and people are interested in them!"

Jim and his wife, Cindy, are among the pioneers who brought locally grown food to schools in Schoharie. Jim says, "They used to have to buy food for the lowest bid," which explains the poor quality of cafeteria lunches in the past. "We had to have the law changed." With that legal victory, Barber's Farm welcomed school cooks to learn about local produce. Cindy is dedicated to nutrition and education and embraces the opportunity to teach visitors about unique and diverse types of produce. "You may ask why we grow so many types of cauliflower. We do it so people can discover their different flavors and learn how to cook them," she explains.

Jim and Cindy use sustainable practices on Barber's Farm. They cultivate a little less than half of their land at any one time so the soil has a chance to rest under restorative cover crops. They also wholeheartedly believe in continually refining their philosophy and their processes on the farm. The farm has evolved over the past five generations, and these farmers hope to continue to do so for many more to come. Jim says, "We must constantly reinvent ourselves. Anybody who comes to work for the farm, including family, needs to bring new ideas."

Raw Cauliflower Salad

SERVES 4

Whole-Grain Croutons

¾ cup olive oil
2 cloves garlic, crushed but kept whole
½ loaf whole-grain bread, diced (⅛ inch)
4 sprigs thyme
Salt

In a medium sauté pan, heat the oil over medium heat. Add the garlic and cook until light golden brown. Add the bread and stir constantly until it begins to develop color. Add the thyme and continue cooking until the bread is golden. Remove the croutons from the pan and drain on paper towels. Season with salt to taste.

Cauliflower Couscous

1 head cauliflower

With a sharp knife, shave the cauliflower, cutting off only the tips of the florets.

To Finish

6 quail eggs
Salt
12 white anchovies (also called boquerones)
¼ cup capers
Segments from 2 lemons
Parsley leaves
2 small raw cauliflower florets, shaved lengthwise (¹/₁₆ inch)
4 teaspoons Lemon Vinaigrette (page 500)
Sea salt

Bring a small saucepan of water to a boil. Add the quail eggs and simmer for 2 minutes. Immediately transfer the eggs to an ice bath to cool. Peel the eggs and slice in half; the yolks should still be slightly runny. Season with salt to taste. Spoon one fourth of the croutons in the center of a plate. Spoon cauliflower couscous on top and place 3 quail egg halves around the dish. Lay the anchovies between the quail eggs and garnish with capers, lemon segments, and parsley. Arrange shaved cauliflower florets on the plate. Spoon lemon vinaigrette around the edge of the croutons and season with salt to taste. Repeat with the remaining ingredients, to serve 4.

Whole Roasted Cauliflower

SERVES 4

Roasted Cauliflower

1 large head cauliflower
1½ cups Clarified Butter (page 498)
1½ cups canola oil
Salt

Preheat the oven to 350°F. Wash and dry the cauliflower and remove the green leaves. Create an aluminum foil ring large and tall enough to elevate the cauliflower head off the bottom of the pan. In a large ovenproof skillet, heat the clarified butter and oil over high heat. Place the foil ring in the pan and set the cauliflower head in it. Using a small ladle or large spoon, baste the cauliflower with the hot butter and oil until evenly golden brown, 9 to 10 minutes. Transfer the entire skillet to the oven and roast the cauliflower until tender when pierced with a knife, 35 to 40 minutes depending on the size. Transfer to a plate, allow the cauliflower to cool to room temperature, and then transfer to the refrigerator. Once it is cold, slice four ½-inch-thick planks from the center. Reserve 1 cup of roasted cauliflower florets for the ragout.

Cauliflower Puree

3 cups diced (¼ inch) cauliflower
2 cups half-and-half
2 tablespoons Brown Butter (page 498)
Salt

Place the cauliflower and half-and-half in a large saucepan. Bring to a boil over medium-high heat and reduce the heat to low. Simmer the cauliflower until tender, about 25 minutes. Drain the cauliflower, reserving the liquid. Puree the cauliflower in a blender, and then add the cooking liquid 1 tablespoon at a time, until the puree is smooth. You will need about ¼ cup of liquid. Blend in the brown butter and season with salt to taste. Strain through a chinois. **Note:** Leftover cauliflower puree can be refrigerated for 2 to 3 days and makes for a wonderful side dish on its own.

Sweet Pumpkin Seeds

1 cup shelled pumpkin seeds
2 tablespoons honey
Salt

Process the pumpkin seeds and honey in a blender until roughly chopped but combined. Season with salt to taste.

Prune Ragout

2 tablespoons Chicken Stock (page 499)
1 cup pitted prunes, quartered lengthwise
1 cup florets reserved from making Roasted Cauliflower
Sweet Pumpkin Seeds
2 tablespoons cold butter
Salt

In a medium sauté pan, warm the chicken stock over medium heat. Stir in the prunes, roasted cauliflower, and sweet pumpkin seeds. Add the butter, tossing to glaze. Remove from the heat and season with salt to taste.

To Finish

2 tablespoons shelled pumpkin seeds
Olive oil
Salt
Brown Butter (page 498)
Shaved (¹⁄₁₆ inch) raw cauliflower florets
Parsley leaves
Lemon segments

Preheat the oven to 350°F. Toss the pumpkin seeds in olive oil and season with salt. Place the pumpkin seeds on a parchment paper–lined baking sheet and toast in the oven for 6 to 7 minutes until fragrant and lightly browned. Place the roasted cauliflower planks on a baking sheet and brush with brown butter. Heat in the oven until just warm, 7 to 8 minutes. Spoon 2 tablespoons of cauliflower puree in the center of each of 4 plates. Place a roasted cauliflower plank in the center of the puree and top with 2 tablespoons of prune ragout. Garnish with shaved cauliflower florets, parsley leaves, lemon segments, and toasted pumpkin seeds. Repeat with the remaining ingredients, to serve 4.

Celery Root

Farm at Miller's Crossing

Chris Cashen and his daughter, Lael, make the rounds of their celery root fields. The bordering creek rushes by and a brisk wind swipes the leaves from the trees—autumn is in full swing. Lael keeps careful hold of the celery root tucked under one arm while she reaches up with the other to grasp her father's back pocket. Anne-Mae, her older sister, carrying another bundle of vegetables, catches up and walks along on Chris's other side. When they get back to the house, their younger brothers, Christopher-John and Connelly, listen intently as their mother, Katie, conducts the day's lesson in the home classroom. She breaks up the standard curriculum by teaching them about working on the farm. Chris beams. "Our kids know a lot about farming already. They have lived here for their entire lives."

Growing up on a farm in the Hudson Valley, Chris had an interest in agriculture, but pursued a degree in political science and philosophy and ultimately took a journalism job after graduation. He flirted with farming when he came home from college each summer but got more serious about the business when he started dating Katie. As an apprentice on his family's farm, she displayed a work ethic and commitment to farming that inspired him. The pair moved to Chatham in 1995 to manage Kline Kill Organic Gardens. After five years, they returned to the Hudson Valley to establish the Farm at Miller's Crossing and began growing one of their most celebrated crops: celery root.

A slow and deliberate approach is the key to successfully cultivating this gnarly root vegetable. "We start celery root in the greenhouse in February," explains Chris, "yet we won't pick it until October." The farmers cater to this plant's sensitivity by planting it along with peas and other cover crops in heavy loam soil saturated with nutrients. Celery root forms a large root that grows with half of its bulb above the soil's surface. The vegetable's tops resemble conventional celery, but the stalks are significantly shorter and much too fibrous to eat. They are noticeably fragrant, exhibiting the brightest and most vivid celery aroma when snapped. This aroma serves as a lovely introduction to the hearty bulb, which is infused with a distinctly bright flavor. When the Cashens eat celery root at home, they sometimes roast it alongside other root vegetables, but they prefer to eat it raw, grating it and combining it with mustard, mayonnaise, and lemon juice to make a rémoulade.

Five of Chris's nine siblings live on the farm, and he and his wife enjoy having them close by. Katie adds, "Our children are growing up with an appreciation for the land and its relationship with the people living on it." This portion of the Hudson Valley thrives largely because of the support of the Cashen family. The land's fantastic yield is no surprise, given the care that everyone, from the youngest toddler to the oldest elder, put into it.

Celery Root Risotto

SERVES 4

1½ cups Arborio rice
½ cup butter
2 tablespoons diced (⅛ inch) shallot
2 cups diced (⅛ inch) celery root
½ cup white wine
2 teaspoons mascarpone
¼ cup grated Tarentaise cheese (an aged
  cow's milk cheese)
Salt

In a medium saucepan, combine the rice with 6 cups of water. Bring to a boil over medium heat, turn down the heat, and simmer until the rice is overcooked and mushy, about 30 minutes. Strain the rice and discard, reserving only 2 cups of the starchy liquid.

In a medium saucepan, melt ¼ cup of the butter over medium-low heat. Add the shallot and sweat until tender, about 3 minutes. Add the celery root and continue sweating for another 2 minutes. Add the wine, raise the heat to medium, and cook for 2 to 3 minutes. Pour in the 2 cups of reserved rice liquid and cook, stirring frequently, until the celery root is tender, 7 to 8 minutes. Remove the pan from the heat and let stand for 30 seconds. Stir in the remaining ¼ cup of butter and the mascarpone. Fold in the Tarentaise and season with salt to taste.

To Finish
Celery sprouts
Celery
Yellow celery leaves
Olive oil
Amaretti cookies
Tarentaise cheese

Divide the risotto among 4 bowls. Using a mandoline, thinly shave the celery sprouts and celery. Toss the shavings and celery leaves with olive oil and arrange on top of the risotto. Crumble amaretti and Tarentaise over the top to finish.

Roasted Celery Root with Chestnuts

SERVES 4

Whole Roasted Celery Root

2 large celery roots, root tendrils intact
2 tablespoons butter
2 cloves garlic, crushed but kept whole
2 sprigs thyme
Salt

Preheat oven to 375°F. Wash the celery roots thoroughly and place each separately on a large piece of aluminum foil. Add 1 tablespoon of butter, 1 garlic clove, and 1 thyme sprig to each root. Season with salt. Bring the corners of the aluminum foil to the center and seal the packages. Roast on a baking sheet in the oven until tender, 1½ to 2 hours. Cool to room temperature and slice each root into four ½-inch-thick rounds, for a total of 8 rounds. Using a 3-inch cutter, punch out a round from each slice. Reserve the rounds and the roasted root tendrils. **Note:** Any leftovers can be tossed with lemon vinaigrette (page 500) and served chilled.

Chestnut Puree

1 pound chestnuts
1 tablespoon grapeseed oil
½ cup Cognac
2 cups Chicken Stock (page 499)
⅔ cup mascarpone
1½ tablespoons sugar
Salt

Preheat the oven to 350°F. Score the chestnuts with a paring knife and place them on a rimmed baking sheet. Roast in the oven until they are lightly browned and the shells begin to curl, 10 to 15 minutes. Cool to room temperature and peel away the shells and inner skin. Cut the peeled chestnuts into ¼-inch pieces. Heat the oil in a large sauté pan over high heat and add the diced chestnuts. Toast over medium-high heat until deep golden brown, 4 to 5 minutes. Remove from the heat and deglaze the pan with the Cognac. Return the pan to medium heat and reduce the liquid until the pan is almost dry. Pour the stock over the chestnuts and cover with a parchment paper lid. Simmer over low heat until tender, about 45 minutes. Transfer the chestnuts with their cooking liquid to a blender, add the mascarpone, and puree. Blend in the sugar and season with salt to taste. Pass through a chinois.

Celery Root Puree

1 pound celery root, peeled and diced (¼ inch)
1½ cups half-and-half
3 sprigs thyme
½ clove garlic, crushed
2 tablespoons butter
Salt

In a medium saucepan over medium heat, combine the celery root with the half-and-half. Wrap the thyme and garlic in a piece of cheesecloth, tie with butcher's twine, and add to the saucepan. Just before the liquid comes to a boil, reduce the heat to low, and simmer until the celery root is tender, 20 to 25 minutes. Discard the thyme and garlic. Strain the mixture through a chinois, reserving both the celery root and the liquid. Transfer the celery root to a blender and process, gradually incorporating only as much liquid as necessary to make a smooth but not overly thin puree. With the blender still running, add the butter. Season with salt to taste.

Roasted Chestnuts

3 tablespoons butter
16 chestnuts, peeled

Melt the butter in a medium sauté pan over medium heat. Using a paring knife, crumble the chestnuts. When the butter is foamy, add the chestnuts and stir frequently until golden brown, 7 to 8 minutes.

Celery Root Crumble

8 ounces celery root, peeled and diced (½ inch)
8 ounces russet potatoes, peeled and diced (½ inch)
12 cups canola oil
Salt

Place the celery root and potatoes in a blender and fill to the top with water. Blend until the mixture resembles coarse sand. Pour the mixture through a chinois and rinse under cold water to remove any excess starch. Transfer to a kitchen towel and wring out the excess water. In a large, deep pot, heat the oil over medium heat to 220°F. Add the celery root and potato mixture, whisking continuously to prevent it from burning, and fry until golden. Drain in a chinois, and then on paper towels. Season with salt to taste.

To Finish

2 stalks celery, peeled
2 tablespoons butter
1 tablespoon Chicken Stock (page 499)
Salt
Celery leaves

Bring a pot of salted water to a boil and blanch the stalks until tender, 3 to 4 minutes. Cut into 2-inch pieces. Spread celery root puree onto the center of 4 plates. In a small sauté pan, combine the butter and stock and add the roasted celery root and blanched celery pieces. Cook over medium heat to create a glaze. Season with salt to taste. Place a roasted celery root round on top of the puree on each plate and arrange the root tendrils (reserved from making the roasted celery root) around. Spoon a small amount of the chestnut puree on the plate and arrange the roasted chestnuts around. Place a piece of blanched glazed celery on top of the celery root and spoon celery root crumble alongside. Garnish with the celery leaves.

Chamomile

Mountain Sweet Berry Farm

Rick Bishop grew up in Poughkeepsie, the son of a truck driver. When he was in high school, Rick's family moved to Sullivan County, and, to keep himself busy, he began gardening. What began as a simple pastime turned into a lifelong passion. For the past twenty-five years, he has been a fixture at New York City's Greenmarkets, supplying both restaurants and individual customers with some of the markets' most sought-after produce. With his magnetic personality, charm, and enthusiasm, he has built lasting relationships with countless New Yorkers who have come to swear by his strawberries, potatoes, and peas.

Because Rick is so dependable and consistent, his wild side might not be apparent to his urban customers. One day while we were driving around on the farm, he suddenly veered off to the shoulder, rolled down his window, and plucked a sample of the season's first tender pine needles. "Try this," he urged. As the plant released its lemony fragrance, he whipped back onto the road, too eager to wait for the verdict.

We were on our way to see his German chamomile, a wildflower that reveals Rick's unbridled pursuit of all things edible. Rick pointed out a plot that seemed to be nothing more than an overlooked grassy knoll next to a storage barn, and on it we found a strip of land in full bloom. "A chef asked me to grow chamomile, so I just let it come back year after year," he said, collecting a delicate bouquet tinged with white, yellow, and green. The dainty plants can withstand five flushes or harvests per year; however, it is best to stop picking after the third bloom to allow the plants to naturally reseed. Optimally, seeds are sown in the fall, as they benefit from freezing during the winter. The blossoms perfume the air with the faint whiff of honey and apples well into late spring.

Though most of us are acquainted with chamomile only in its dried state—steeped in hot water to make tea—the fresh flowers offer a wide range of culinary potential and release the most intense floral flavor and aroma shortly after harvest. "Chefs always want something new and unique, and I provide that with the chamomile," says Rick. While all of his produce is stellar, it is Rick's constant curiosity, his willingness to grow just about anything, and his desire to continue living off the land that have made him one of New York's most beloved farmers.

Chamomile with Strawberries

Strawberry Chamomile Consommé

16 cups hulled and halved Tristar strawberries
1½ cups sugar
⅔ cup dried chamomile

Place all of the ingredients in a heatproof bowl and cover tightly with plastic wrap. Set over a pot of barely simmering water to create a double boiler, making sure that the simmering water does not touch the bottom of the bowl. Simmer over low heat for 2 hours. Strain through a quadruple layer of cheesecloth, allowing the solids to drain overnight; reserve only the liquid.

Chamomile Frozen Yogurt

1 cup milk
⅓ cup dried chamomile
Zest of ½ lemon
3 sheets gelatin
½ cup sugar
¼ cup honey
3 cups sheep's milk yogurt

In a saucepan over medium heat, bring the milk to a boil. Pour over the chamomile and lemon zest. Steep for 30 minutes. Strain the milk into a measuring cup. Add more milk if necessary to reach 1 cup of liquid. Bloom the gelatin by soaking the sheets in a bowl of ice water for 10 minutes until pliable. Squeeze to remove excess moisture. Return the milk to a saucepan and warm over low heat; add the gelatin, sugar, and honey, stirring until they are all dissolved. Add the yogurt and blend with a hand blender. Strain through a chinois, refrigerate until cold, and freeze in an ice cream machine.

Roasted Strawberries in Gelée

1 pint Tristar strawberries, hulled
Confectioners' sugar
4 sheets gelatin
1 cup Strawberry Chamomile Consommé
2 tablespoons granulated sugar
½ teaspoon citric acid

Preheat the oven to 200°F. Lay the strawberries on a silicone mat–lined baking sheet. Lightly dust with confectioners' sugar and bake for about 1½ hours, until the berries are slightly dried but still tender. Bloom the gelatin by soaking the sheets in a bowl of ice water for 10 minutes until pliable. Warm the consommé in a small saucepan. Squeeze the gelatin to remove excess moisture and dissolve it in the consommé, along with the granulated sugar and citric acid.

Preheat the oven to 350°F. Wrap one end of each of four 2½-inch-wide by ⅝-inch-tall ring molds tightly with plastic wrap. Place the molds on a baking sheet, plastic side up, and warm in the oven for 5 to 10 seconds to tighten the plastic. Arrange the molds, plastic side down, on a flat tray and spray lightly with vegetable cooking spray. Divide the roasted strawberries among the molds, leaving a little space between the berries. Fill the molds just to the top with the strawberry gelée, discarding any extra. Refrigerate overnight.

Strawberry Soup

1 sheet gelatin
1 cup Strawberry Consommé
3 to 4 tablespoons sugar
½ teaspoon citric acid

Bloom the gelatin by soaking the sheet in a bowl of ice water for 10 minutes until pliable. Warm the consommé in a small saucepan over low heat. Squeeze the gelatin to remove excess moisture and dissolve it in the consommé along with sugar to taste and the citric acid.

To Finish

Tristar strawberries, halved
Fresh chamomile flowers

To unmold the roasted strawberries in gelée, set a serving bowl over each mold. Carefully turn the bowl with the ring mold over and then lift the mold to release the gelée. Pour strawberry soup around the gelée and top with a quenelle of chamomile frozen yogurt. Finish with halved strawberries and chamomile flowers. **Note:** Leftover chamomile frozen yogurt can be eaten with any extra roasted strawberries, topped with Strawberry Chamomile Consommé. The consommé can also be served over ice and topped with soda water to make a refreshing non-alcoholic beverage.

Chamomile Vinegar

MAKES 2 CUPS

½ cup fresh chamomile
2 whole cloves, toasted
1 sprig tarragon
2 cups white balsamic vinegar
1 teaspoon honey

Place the chamomile flowers, cloves, and tarragon in a small bowl. Add the vinegar, and then slowly pour in the honey while whisking. Continue whisking until the honey is dissolved. Allow the vinegar to sit for 2 weeks in a jar at room temperature. Strain and reserve for up to 3 months in the refrigerator.
Note: This vinegar goes well with fish, chicken, and salads.

Cherries

Mead Orchards

When farmers decide to employ a "U-Pick" model for harvesting, they open their home to friends and strangers alike, giving guests a glimpse into what it means to be a farmer. At Mead Orchards in the mid Hudson Valley, Chuck Mead mows the grass and surveys his forty acres of outstanding fruit, including sweet and tart cherries. "We like the 'U-Pick' model," he says. "It keeps things interesting around here." He contemplates a car attempting to drive through a narrow path between trees and decides not to intervene: "He'll figure it out."

Mead Orchards began when Chuck's grandfather, Gordon, decided to convert to the agrarian lifestyle. After graduating from Yale, he went to Cornell University for a two-year program tailored to individuals who wanted to farm but didn't have farming experience. After finishing the program in 1916, Gordon knew exactly where he wanted to settle. "We have the letter he sent to my neighbor's grandfather asking about the farm he wanted to purchase," says Chuck. The land was down the road from where Gordon had fulfilled a farming internship. After years of mixed agriculture, Gordon's son Sid slowly grew the holdings to 185 acres and transitioned from animal husbandry to strictly horticulture by 1950.

Inspired by his father's commitment to continually evolve the farm, Chuck attended Cornell to study pomology (the science of growing fruit). He planted the first cherry trees in 1998, saying, "I saw a way to fulfill market requests and broaden our 'U-Pick' operation." Cherries are fickle, and they test the boundaries of Chuck's expertise. After a frost-free spring, cherry trees bloom in April. "The tart cherries are self-fertile and set on their own pollen," says Chuck. Sweet cherries require cross-pollination: "Some sweet cherry varieties can only pollinate certain ones. We plant many together and hope for the best." The puzzle is further complicated by harvest timetables and by Chuck's work to create hearty cultivars suited for the wet Northeast—cherries' flesh is weak and prone to cracking if it rains near harvest time. When the climate is optimal, Mead Orchards produces cherries that are at once firm, sweet, and juicy—in short, ideal for locals who wait all year to hand-pick their own cherries.

Salad with New York Cheddar, Mangalitsa Ham, and Almonds

SERVES 4

Cherry Vinegar

2 cups pitted and halved cherries
2 cups white balsamic vinegar

In a small bowl, crush the cherries with the back of a spoon and pour the white balsamic vinegar over them. Transfer to a glass jar, cover, and leave at room temperature for 3 days. Strain through a chinois before using. Cover and store in the refrigerator for at least 1 month and up to 3 months. **Note:** The vinegar can be used in place of any light vinegar in vinaigrettes.

Cherry Salad

1 cup pitted and halved Bing cherries,
  plus 4 Bing cherries, pitted, with stems on
1 cup pitted and halved Rainier cherries,
  plus 4 Rainier cherries, pitted, with stems on
2 tablespoons olive oil
1 tablespoon lemon juice
1 teaspoon ground black pepper
Salt

Toss all of the cherries in the olive oil, lemon juice, and black pepper. Season with salt to taste.

To Finish

½ cup crumbled Tonjes Farm Dairy Rambler cheese
  (a raw cow's milk cheese similar to aged cheddar)
½ cup toasted blanched whole almonds
8 thin slices Mangalitsa ham (a dry-cured ham
  similar to prosciutto)
Baby mizuna

Divide the cherry salad among 4 plates, distributing one of each kind of whole pitted cherry to each plate. Add the crumbled cheese and toasted almonds. Lay 2 pieces of Mangalitsa ham on each plate. Garnish with the mizuna and drizzle 1 tablespoon of cherry vinegar over each dish to finish.

Sour Cherry Crumble

Almond Crumble

1 cup almond flour
½ cup cold butter, diced (¼ inch)
½ cup plus 2 tablespoons bread flour
⅓ cup granulated sugar
2 tablespoons light brown sugar
1 teaspoon salt

Blend all of the ingredients together in a stand mixer fitted with the paddle attachment until the mixture becomes crumbly. Refrigerate until ready to use.

Cherry Filling

4 cups pitted sour cherries
½ cup sugar
3 tablespoons flour
2 teaspoons lemon juice
2 teaspoons vanilla extract
½ teaspoon salt
Zest of ½ lemon
3 tablespoons butter

Preheat the oven to 325°F. In a large bowl, mix together all of the ingredients except the butter using a rubber spatula. Transfer the cherry mixture to a 10 by 7-inch baking dish. Dot the top of the mixture with the butter. Cover with the almond crumble and bake until golden brown and bubbly, 45 minutes to 1 hour.

Whipped Ricotta

½ pound ricotta
½ teaspoon lemon juice
½ teaspoon vanilla extract
¼ teaspoon salt

In the bowl of a stand mixer fitted with the whisk attachment, whip the ricotta with the lemon juice, vanilla, and salt until light and smooth. Serve alongside the warm crumble.

Chèvre

Lynnhaven Goat Dairy

"No matter how bad things are, if you hug a baby goat, all of your troubles go away." Lynn Fleming is in her own world as she rocks a newborn kid in her arms. In 1989, Lynn fell in love with goats at first sight. She abandoned horse farming and has been raising champion show goats on Lynnhaven, her farm in Pine Bush, ever since.

The boundaries that separate Lynn's house and barn are blurry, as each is just an extension of the other. Large metal containers in her dining room function as makeshift pens for baby goats. "For me, it's all about the goats . . . if the lights are on and the goats are fed, then I'm happy," she says. While some of Lynn's goats are sold to other dairy farms or competition herds, 120 top show goats—purebred Nubians and Lamanchas—stay at Lynnhaven for milking. They live in the backyard under large tents and in open barns: "Exposing the goats to the elements year-round makes them stronger," Lynn explains.

The goats' milk goes into the world-class cheeses Lynn began making in 2006. Her goal was never to make award-winning cheese; however, what started as casual experimentation at the kitchen stove has won her high culinary acclaim. After perfecting her method, she began selling her cheese at farmers' markets, despite her initial apprehension: "I was too shy." She is still humble, but her confidence has grown alongside her success. Market-goers now know Lynn as a lighthearted, dependable, convivial farmer committed to the production of some extraordinary cheeses, in a range of styles from classic chèvre logs to crumbly blocks of feta. Lynn also works directly with customers to design cheeses that are tailored to their specific needs, like the dense ricotta required for ethereal *gnudi*. Her willingness to experiment harkens back to her earliest days as a goat farmer in the 1980s.

Lynn's cheeses exhibit a simplicity and purity that are a testament to her methods. "Milk is only a day or two old when we make cheese," she says, maintaining that a minimal delay between milking and cheese-making preserves the full expression of the milk's flavor. Beyond meticulous technique, what truly distinguishes her goat cheeses is on ready display at Lynnhaven: unbounded affection. "Why does my cheese taste different?" Lynn asks. "Because my goats are loved!"

Chèvre Soufflé

SERVES 4

Goat's Milk Pastry Cream

7 egg yolks
1 cup goat's milk yogurt
5¼ ounces fresh chèvre
¼ cup sugar
5 teaspoons cornstarch

Puree all of the ingredients in a blender until smooth. Transfer to a saucepan and cook over medium-high heat, stirring constantly, until the mixture comes to a boil. Simmer for 30 seconds, and then remove from the heat. Pour into a bowl and lay a piece of plastic wrap directly against the surface of the pastry cream so a skin does not form. Chill over an ice bath. **Note:** Any leftover pastry cream can be stored in the freezer, covered, for up to 1 month. Use as you would any pastry cream, for example, in the Raspberry Tart (page 82).

Goat's Milk Frozen Yogurt

2 sheets gelatin
14 ounces fresh chèvre
2 cups goat's milk yogurt
½ cup sugar
⅓ cup glucose syrup
3 tablespoons lemon juice

Bloom the gelatin by placing the sheets in a bowl of ice water for 10 minutes until pliable. Puree the remaining ingredients in a blender. Warm 1 cup of the mixture in a small saucepan over medium heat. Squeeze the gelatin to remove excess moisture and stir it into the warm mixture. Add back to the blender and blend again. Strain through a chinois, then chill over an ice bath. Freeze in an ice cream machine. **Note:** Keep any leftover frozen yogurt in the freezer for up to 1 month.

To Finish

4 tablespoons butter, at room temperature
⅓ cup granulated sugar, plus more for dusting soufflé cups
8 egg whites
¼ teaspoon cream of tartar
Confectioners' sugar

Preheat oven to 350°F. Brush four 4-ounce soufflé cups with the butter. Dust with granulated sugar and shake out any excess. In a medium mixing bowl, stir 1 cup of the goat's milk pastry cream with a spatula until smooth. In the bowl of a stand mixer fitted with the whisk attachment, whip the egg whites on medium speed until foamy. Add the cream of tartar and continue whipping until you can just begin to see the whisk marks, then add the ⅓ cup of granulated sugar. Whip to stiff, glossy peaks. Fold the egg whites into the pastry cream to lighten, noting that the mixture will be slightly loose. Fill each prepared soufflé cup to the rim with batter and level with an offset spatula. Tap the soufflé cups to remove excess air. Run your thumb around the inside of the rim of each soufflé cup to ensure even rising. Place on a baking sheet and bake for 12 minutes.

As soon as the soufflés are done baking, remove from the oven and lightly dust with confectioners' sugar. Drop a quenelle of goat's milk frozen yogurt into the center of each soufflé and serve immediately.

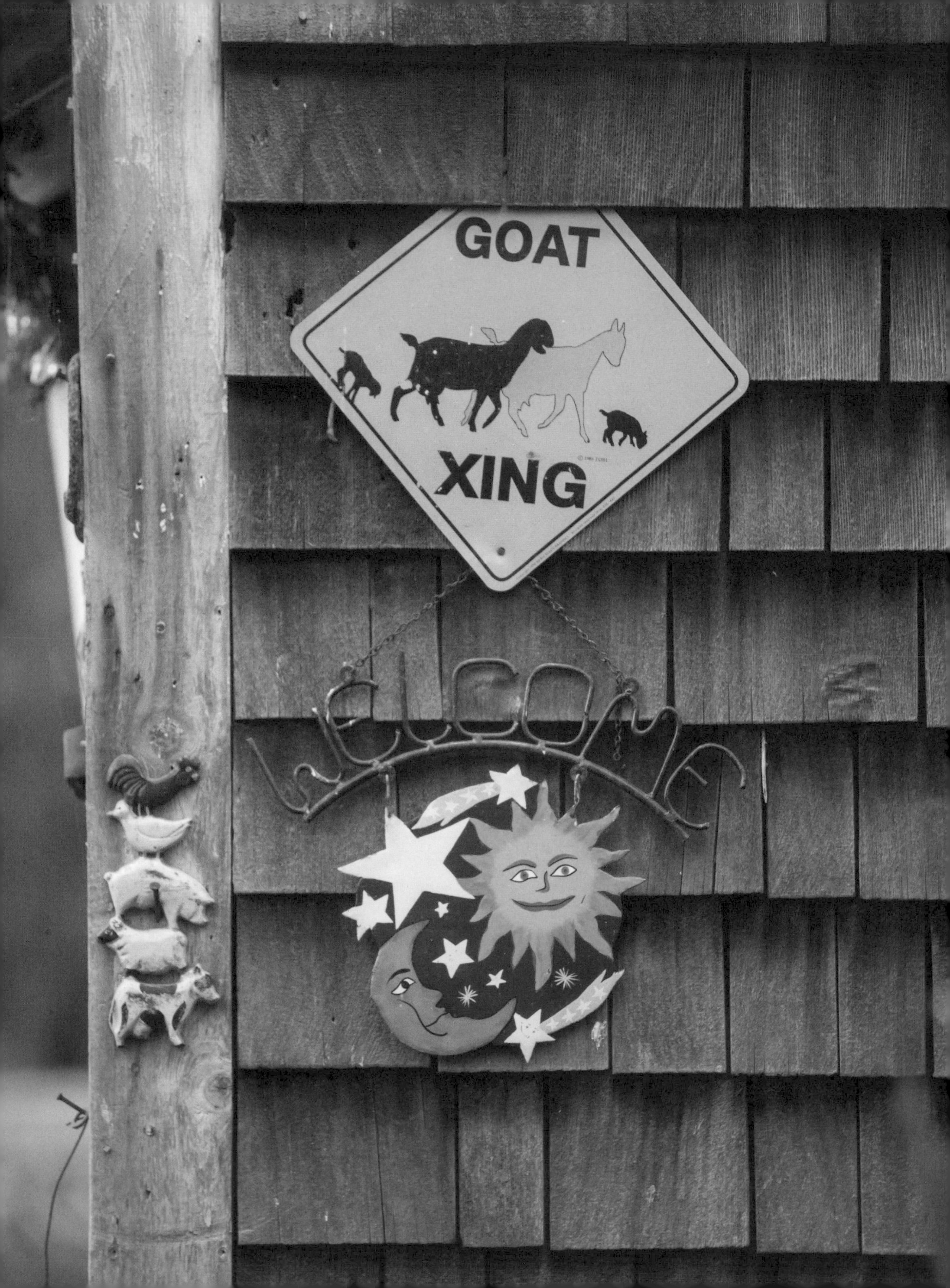
GOAT
XING
WELCOME

Fresh Goat's Milk Curd with Summer Berries and Beets

SERVES 4

Roasted Baby Beets

7 baby beets
2 cups olive oil
⅔ cup red wine vinegar
2 tablespoons sugar
Salt

Preheat the oven to 400°F. Rinse the beets and place them in a small baking dish. In a bowl, combine the oil with the vinegar, sugar, and 2 cups of water. Season with salt. Pour the mixture over the beets and cover the baking dish with aluminum foil. Place in the oven and roast the beets until tender, 40 to 50 minutes. Remove from the oven and cool to room temperature. Peel the beets. Leave 4 of them whole and quarter the remaining 3.

Fresh Goat's Milk Curd

4 cups goat's milk
2 cups cream
Salt
2 tablespoons lemon juice

In a medium saucepan, combine the milk and cream and bring to 183°F over medium heat. Season with salt to taste. Add the lemon juice and allow the temperature to climb to 190° to 195°F. It will take 15 to 20 minutes for the curds to develop. Gently stir the mixture with a spatula until the curds separate from the whey. Remove from the heat and carefully drain the curds in a colander lined with a quadruple layer of cheesecloth. Set over a large bowl and drain overnight. Transfer to a container, cover, and refrigerate.

To Finish

1 baby beet
Raspberries
Blackberries, halved
Red currants
Strawberries, halved
Olive oil
Salt
Flowering mint
Cracked black pepper

Shave the baby beet on a mandoline into ¹⁄₁₆-inch slices. Spoon fresh goat's milk curd into the middle of each of 4 plates. Gently toss the shaved beet, raspberries, blackberries, red currants, whole and quartered roasted baby beets, and strawberries with olive oil and salt to taste. Arrange around the curd along with the flowering mint. Finish with additional olive oil and pepper.

Chicken

Violet Hill Farm

Farmers bear an enormous responsibility: to cultivate the earth for their children and subsequent generations. This is a responsibility that Paul Dench-Layton chose to take on at Violet Hill Farm, located in the stunning Catskills National Park. A first-generation farmer, Paul was driven to this lifestyle after being diagnosed with stage-four cancer at the age of thirty. Fearful of not "leaving something behind, like chickens and eggs, for [his] family to live off of," Paul established Violet Hill Farm, where he created a breed of chicken that he calls Belle Rouge. With members of his family, he raises his beloved birds and lives cancer-free.

Paul's quest to sustainably raise poultry is inspired by France's Label Rouge program, wherein poultry is raised using traditional, free-range methods that also protect the environment. Paul crosses ancient breeds of chickens that live exclusively on foraging. By creating a lifestyle and diet that promote the Belle Rouge's natural maturation, he raises birds that "subsist on nutrition closer to what's found in their natural habitats." Paul's practices appeal to a variety of customers, which include some of the best restaurants in New York. Even his wife, Mary, paid him the ultimate compliment. A self-described former "chicken hater," she was defenseless against his poultry; they married in 2010.

Balance—in both personality and biodiversity—characterizes Violet Hill Farm. Paul is reserved and Mary gregarious, full of youthful energy and humor. Their farm, Mary says, resembles "a wild petting zoo." They have six children of their own plus an extensive Farm Babies program, with a growing flock of piglets, ducklings, and chicks. Even the family exhibits a wild side, foraging together in the surrounding woods for mushrooms, berries, and herbs, and they share their land's bounty with their customers. Beyond selling their goods to the general public at the Greenmarket, Violet Hill Farm hosts an annual summer camp where urbanites trade briefcases for shovels and immerse themselves in pastoral life to get a glimpse into a world that is foreign to so many. And that is the Violet Hill Farm way—always welcoming, always innovating, always thinking of the future. With an eye toward the responsibility that they have chosen to bear as farmers, Paul and Mary have created a farming legacy that will sustain their children and grandchildren.

Schnitzel Sandwich with Capers, Tomato, and Basil

SERVES 4

Chicken Schnitzel

4 boneless, skinless chicken breast halves
2 eggs
1 cup flour
2 cups diced baguette, crust removed,
dried and finely ground
Salt
1 cup canola oil
4 tablespoons butter
4 sprigs thyme
2 cloves garlic, crushed but kept whole

With a mallet, gently pound each piece of chicken between 2 sheets of plastic wrap until the breasts are about 1/8 inch thick. In a mixing bowl, beat together the eggs and 2 teaspoons of water to make an egg wash. Put the flour and the bread crumbs in 2 separate dishes. Season the chicken with salt on both sides and dredge in the flour, coating evenly. Dust off any excess flour and submerge in the egg wash. Transfer the chicken to the bread crumbs and coat evenly on both sides. Place the breaded chicken breasts on a baking sheet lined with parchment paper.

Heat 2 large sauté pans over medium heat. Divide the canola oil between the pans. Set a wire cooling rack in a baking sheet. Add 2 breaded chicken breasts to each pan and fry on one side for 1 to 2 minutes, until lightly golden, continuously moving the chicken in the pan to ensure even coloring. Flip the chicken and add 2 tablespoons of butter, 2 thyme sprigs, and 1 garlic clove to each pan. Raise the heat to high and continue to fry, basting the chicken for 1 to 2 minutes, until evenly browned. Transfer the schnitzel to the wire rack to drain and cool.

Caper Mayonnaise

1 tablespoon capers, finely chopped
1 cup Mayonnaise (page 500)

In a small bowl, fold the capers into the mayonnaise. **Note:** Any leftover caper mayonnaise can be stored, covered, in the refrigerator for up to 1 week and be served alongside grilled fish, spread on sandwiches, or used in lieu of conventional mayonnaise in tuna or chicken salad.

Marinated Tomatoes

2 ripe tomatoes
¼ cup olive oil
1 teaspoon salt
½ teaspoon ground black pepper

Cut the tomatoes into ¼-inch slices and lay them out on a rimmed baking sheet. Season with the olive oil, salt, and pepper and marinate for 15 minutes.

Fingerling Potato Chips

¼ cup salt
5 fingerling potatoes, scrubbed
Canola oil

Bring the salt and 2 quarts of water to a boil. Using a mandoline, thinly slice the potatoes lengthwise. Place the slices in a large bowl, pour the seasoned boiling water over them, and allow to cool to room temperature. Pour 3 inches of canola oil into a large saucepan and bring the oil to 325°F over medium-high heat. Remove the potato slices from the water with a slotted spoon, pat dry, add to the oil, and fry in batches until crisp, 3 to 4 minutes. Drain on paper towels and cool to room temperature.

To Finish

1 loaf focaccia
Basil leaves

To make 1 large sandwich, split the focaccia lengthwise. Spread caper mayonnaise on each cut side of the focaccia. Arrange basil leaves and half of the marinated tomatoes on one side and place the chicken schnitzel on top. Top with the remaining marinated tomatoes and more basil leaves. Top with the other half of focaccia. Cut the sandwich into 4 equal pieces and serve with the fingerling potato chips.

Fried Chicken with Potato-Cucumber Salad

SERVES 4

Potatoes

2 pounds Yukon Gold potatoes
2 quarts Chicken Stock (page 499)
1¼ cups whole-grain mustard
2 tablespoons red wine vinegar
½ teaspoon salt

Rinse and scrub the potatoes. With an apple corer measuring ¾ inch in diameter, punch out cylinders from the potatoes. Trim the ends of the cylinders so that they are flat on both ends. Set the potatoes aside in a bath of cold water. In a large pot, reduce the stock to 1 quart. Stir in the mustard, red wine vinegar, and salt. Drain the potatoes, add them to the stock, and simmer over medium heat until they are almost cooked through, about 15 minutes. Remove the pot from the heat and allow to cool to room temperature. The potatoes will finish cooking in the hot stock as it is cooling. Transfer to a container, cover with plastic wrap, and store the potatoes in the stock in the refrigerator overnight.

Marinated Chicken

4 cups milk
1 cup Frank's RedHot sauce
1 cup thinly sliced onion
1 cup thinly sliced seeded jalapeño chile
1½ tablespoons salt
1 pound boneless chicken thighs, cut into 1-inch pieces

In a large stainless steel mixing bowl, stir together the milk, hot sauce, onion, jalapeño chile, and salt. Add the chicken and marinate for at least 2 hours and up to 8 hours in the refrigerator.

Seasoned Flour

3 cups flour
1½ tablespoons smoked paprika
1 tablespoon chopped rosemary
1 tablespoon thyme leaves
1½ teaspoons coarsely ground black pepper

In a mixing bowl, stir together all of the ingredients.

Buttermilk Dressing

¼ cup buttermilk
¼ cup Mayonnaise (page 500)
2 teaspoons sliced chives
2 teaspoons chopped dill
Pinch of coarsely ground black pepper
1 teaspoon salt

In a small bowl, whisk together all of the ingredients. **Note:** Any leftover dressing can be stored in the refrigerator, covered, for up to 1 week and can be used to dress green salads.

To Finish

2 quarts canola oil
1 English cucumber, peeled
4 teaspoons Pickled Mustard Seeds (page 500)
Dill sprigs

Heat the oil in a large saucepan to 300°F. Take 3 or 4 pieces of chicken from the marinade and dredge in the seasoned flour. Do not dust off the excess flour. Gently add the dredged chicken to the hot oil and fry until golden, 4 to 5 minutes. Carefully remove the chicken from the oil with a slotted spoon and drain on a cooling rack. Repeat with the remaining chicken. Drain the potato cylinders, slice each in half on the bias, and place in a bowl. Thinly slice the cucumber lengthwise on a mandoline, avoiding the seeds; add to the bowl. Toss the cucumber slices and the potato cylinders with ¼ cup of the buttermilk dressing. Arrange the cucumber and potatoes on each of 4 plates and garnish with 1 teaspoon of pickled mustard seeds and dill sprigs. Arrange the fried chicken pieces around the plate. Aerate the remaining buttermilk dressing with a hand blender and spoon the frothy dressing onto the plates.

Roasted Chicken with Apples, Chestnuts, Garlic, and Herbs

SERVES 4

Stuffed Chicken

1 teaspoon canola oil
2 tablespoons finely diced shallot
1 cup peeled and diced (⅛ inch) raw chestnuts
½ peeled and diced (⅛ inch) Granny Smith apple
1 cup rye bread crumbs
1 cup butter, at room temperature
2 tablespoons minced parsley
1 teaspoon salt
1 (3- to 3½-pound) chicken

In a medium sauté pan, heat the oil over low heat. Add the shallot and sweat until translucent, 3 to 4 minutes. Add the chestnuts and apple and sweat for 8 to 10 minutes. Transfer to a bowl and fold in the bread crumbs, butter, parsley, and salt, stirring to thoroughly combine. Transfer the mixture to a piping bag and keep at room temperature until ready to stuff the chicken.

Open the cavity of the chicken and pull out any excess fat. To butterfly the chicken, begin by placing it breast side down on a cutting board. Insert a sharp knife or shears into the cavity and cut down both sides of the backbone and remove it from the chicken. Flip the chicken so that the breast side is up and use your hands to crack the sternum and flatten the chicken. Remove the wings. Using a boning knife, scrape the meat and skin from the ends of the legs to expose about 1 inch of the bone. Make a small incision on each side of the breast. Cross the legs, tucking them under the skin to hold them in place. Carefully work your fingers under the skin to create space for the stuffing. Pipe the apple and chestnut stuffing under the skin of the legs and breasts. The stuffing should be distributed evenly to maintain the shape of the chicken. Chill the chicken in the refrigerator until the stuffing is set, about 2 hours.

To Finish

2 tablespoons canola oil
8 Lady apples, halved
2 heads garlic, halved crosswise
¼ cup peeled raw chestnuts
¼ cup peeled and halved cipollini onions
¼ cup peeled pearl onions
Salt
1 bunch rosemary
1 bunch thyme

Preheat the oven to 475°F. In a large cast-iron pan, heat the oil over high heat. Add the apples and garlic, cut sides down, along with the chestnuts and onions, and cook until golden, 3 to 4 minutes. Move the apples, garlic, chestnuts, and onions to the outer edges of the pan and place the chicken in the center, skin side up. Season with salt and sear the chicken for 2 minutes on the stove before transferring to the oven. Roast for 35 minutes, add the rosemary and thyme, and continue roasting for another 10 to 15 minutes until the skin is golden and the temperature of the thickest part of the breast close to the bone is 150°F. Transfer the chicken to a wire rack and let rest for 15 minutes before carving. Serve the chicken with the roasted apples, garlic, chestnuts, and onions.

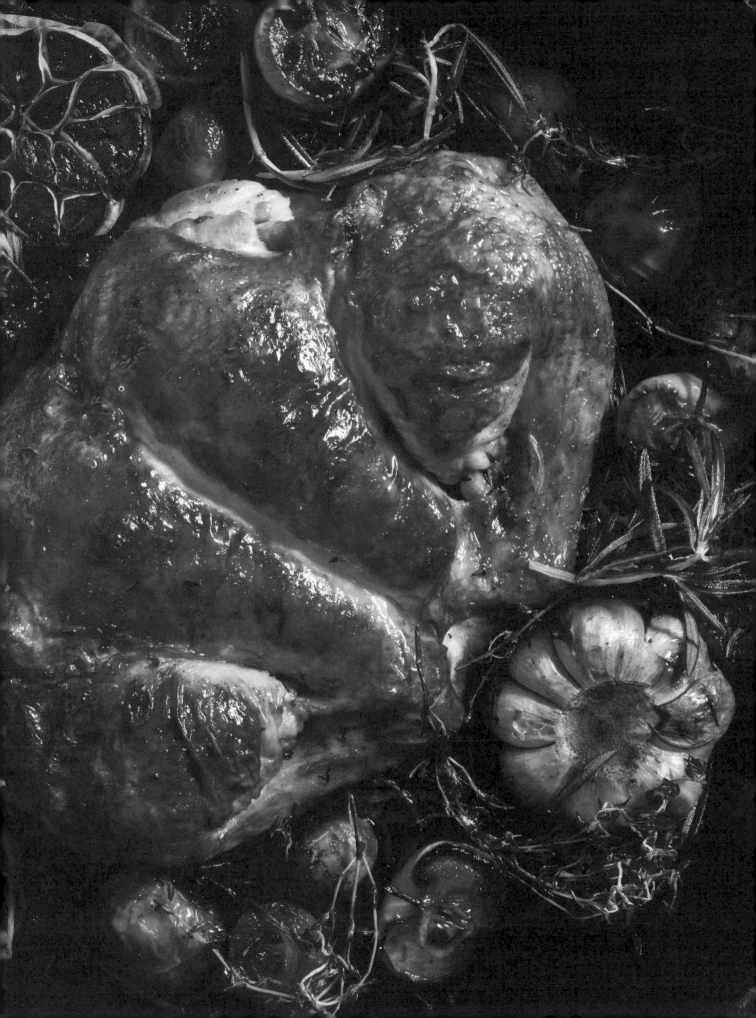

Chocolate

Mast Brothers Chocolate

"Chocolate is food, not candy," states Rick Mast, half of the eponymous duo at Mast Brothers Chocolate in Brooklyn. He and his brother, Michael, joined forces with the goal of making "the best tasting chocolate in the world." Initially, they had separate careers: Rick worked in various New York kitchens and Michael was in film production. Both enjoyed their vocations, but their true passion was practiced off the clock at home. "We started making chocolate in our Greenpoint apartment six or seven years ago," remembers Rick. "The cacao bean represented a new frontier," adds Michael, "something that encompassed our desires to create." They quit their day jobs in 2007, grew out their beards, and began a life dedicated to chocolate.

Situated in the Williamsburg section of Brooklyn, their establishment is part factory and part retail store. "We are in an urban area, and chocolate is grown in tropical regions," says Rick. "There is nothing local about chocolate, but we do everything we can to connect people to the process." Demonstrating how chocolate is made allows customers to truly understand the product. A pallet of burlap sacks filled with cacao beans from around the world sits in the middle of the sales room. "We are one of the only chocolate makers in New York City that receives cacao in this form," states Michael, running his fingers through the beans in one of the bags. The cacao at Mast Brothers Chocolate comes from farms with which the company works directly, forging connections with their suppliers as well as their New York customers.

These farmer relationships translate to better quality beans and the opportunity for the Masts to highlight regional expressions of cacao. Uninterested in making products that yield the same flavor time and time again, Michael believes that "chocolate should be particular and distinct and taste like where it comes from." Artificial flavors never come near their chocolate. Instead, the brothers gently coax the beans to display their own distinctive flavors.

At Mast Brothers Chocolate, every detail is considered and executed thoughtfully. Their bars are beautifully packaged in recycled paper showcasing local artists' designs. In an homage to historic cacao transportation, the company recently worked with Captain Eric Loftfield to sail twenty tons of organic cacao from the Dominican Republic to New York in a seventy-foot, three-masted schooner called the *Black Seal*. This was just one means by which the brothers hope, as Michael puts it, to help "people realize that chocolate is exotic and not a commodity. It should be cherished."

Chocolate Egg Cream

SERVES 4

Chocolate Sauce

1 cup sugar
3 ounces Mast Brothers Madagascar chocolate, chopped
6 tablespoons cocoa powder
2 tablespoons cornstarch

In a small saucepan over medium heat, melt together the sugar and chocolate with ⅓ cup of water. In a mixing bowl, whisk together the cocoa powder and cornstarch with ⅓ cup of water. Add to the melted chocolate mixture and bring to a boil. Cook for 2 minutes to cook out the starch. Strain through a chinois and chill over an ice bath. Refrigerate until ready to use. **Note:** Any leftover chocolate sauce can be stored in the refrigerator for up to 1 week and used to make hot chocolate or chocolate milk.

To Finish

¾ cup milk
Seltzer water

Pour 3 tablespoons of chocolate sauce into each of four 8-ounce glasses. Top with 3 tablespoons of milk. Add enough seltzer to almost reach the top of the glass. Stir vigorously and drink immediately.

You can count on almost one hand how many places there are left in New York where you can get an egg cream, but once upon a time they were available on nearly every block. One of the staples of the classic soda fountains that became the city's gathering places during Prohibition, the egg cream is a uniquely New York creation whose origins are wildly debated. People from Brooklyn claim it's from Brooklyn, people from Manhattan say it's from Manhattan, and so on. It may have been created at Louis Auster's soda fountain, where he capitalized on the popularity of sweet fountain drinks made with eggs. Or it may have come about when soda fountains were publicizing their use of Grade A milk. A "chocolate A cream" then became "chocolate egg cream" due to the phonetics of the name. And yet another story centers around the corruption of the German word *echt*, meaning genuine, by soda fountains publicizing their use of good cream. Another possible creator of the egg cream was Uncle Hymie, owner of a Second Avenue candy shop during the 1920s. He made a very popular drink using flavored syrup, cream, seltzer, and eggs to emulsify it. With the onset of the Great Depression, he had to cut back on the use of the most expensive ingredients, resulting in the eggless, creamless version of the egg cream. Who invented it and where doesn't really matter; we're just happy it exists.

Mast Brothers Chocolate Cookies

MAKES ABOUT 21 COOKIES

**8¾ ounces plus 6⅓ ounces Mast Brothers
    70 percent chocolate, chopped**
3 tablespoons butter, at room temperature
⅔ cup plus 2 tablespoons granulated sugar
2 eggs
2 teaspoons vanilla extract
¼ cup flour
1½ teaspoons baking powder
1 teaspoon salt
Confectioners' sugar, optional

Line two baking sheets with parchment paper. Preheat the oven to 325°F. Place the 8¾ ounces of chocolate in a heat-proof bowl and set over a pot of barely simmering water to create a double boiler, making sure that the simmering water does not touch the bottom of the bowl. Heat until melted. Set aside to cool. In the bowl of a stand mixer fitted with the paddle attachment, beat the butter with the granulated sugar until light and fluffy. Add the eggs, one at a time, and then the vanilla. In a medium bowl, mix together the flour, baking powder, and salt until just combined. Incorporate the melted chocolate, and then fold in the remaining 6⅓ ounces of chopped chocolate.

Using a 40-millimeter (2¾-inch) scoop, scoop the dough onto the baking sheets, leaving 1 inch between cookies, as they will spread. Bake for 10 minutes, rotating the pans after 5 minutes. The cookies should be cracked and slightly shiny. Cool on the baking sheets. **Note:** Dust the cookies with confectioners' sugar if desired.

Chocolate Truffle Tart

MAKES TWO 8-INCH TARTS; EACH SERVES 8

Tart Shell

1 cup butter, at room temperature
½ cup sugar
1 egg
Zest of 1 orange
½ vanilla bean, split lengthwise and scraped
¼ teaspoon salt
3 cups flour

In a stand mixer fitted with the paddle attachment, cream together the butter and sugar on medium speed until light and fluffy. Add the egg and continue mixing until thoroughly combined. Add the orange zest, vanilla bean seeds, and salt. Incorporate the flour, 1 cup at a time, and mix until the dough comes together. Divide into 2 equal portions and roll out the portions between 2 sheets of parchment paper to ⅛ inch thick. Refrigerate for 30 minutes. Remove the parchment paper from the dough. Line two 8-inch tart pans with removable bottoms with the dough, molding it into the pans and gently pressing it into the edges with your fingers. Make sure that the dough is of even thickness throughout to ensure even baking. With a paring knife, trim away excess dough from the pans' edges. Chill in the refrigerator for at least 30 minutes before baking or freeze, tightly wrapped, for up to 1 month.

Preheat the oven to 350°F. Place the tart pans on a baking sheet and bake until the shells are golden brown, about 15 minutes. Remove from the oven and cool to room temperature.

Chocolate Truffle Filling

10 ounces Mast Brothers Brooklyn Blend chocolate, chopped
½ cup butter, at room temperature
4 eggs
½ cup sugar
⅓ cup glucose syrup
¼ teaspoon salt

Place the chocolate in a heatproof bowl and set over a pot of barely simmering water to create a double boiler, making sure that the simmering water does not touch the bottom of the bowl. Heat until melted, and then stir in the butter until fully incorporated. Remove the melted chocolate mixture from the double boiler and cool to room temperature. Meanwhile, warm the eggs, sugar, glucose syrup, and salt in a double boiler to 100°F. Transfer the warmed egg mixture to the bowl of a stand mixer fitted with the whisk attachment and whip until tripled in size. Whisk one-third of the whipped egg mixture into the melted chocolate and mix until completely incorporated and emulsified. Using a rubber spatula, gently fold the remaining whipped eggs into the chocolate until fully incorporated. The resulting mixture will be mousselike.

To Finish

¼ cup cocoa powder

Preheat the oven to 325°F. Divide the chocolate truffle filling between the baked tart shells and smooth with an offset spatula. Bake for 6 minutes, and then cool to room temperature. Cover with plastic wrap and refrigerate for 2 hours. Before serving, allow to come to room temperature. Using a strainer, sift a thin layer of cocoa powder over the tarts.

Clams

Ed Warner

When most people think of raking, they think of the autumn chore to rid their yard of leaves. Ed Warner has a completely different idea and relationship to this pastime. It relates to harvesting wild clams that inhabit his underwater backyard on Long Island. For Ed, a fifth-generation fisherman in Southampton's Cold Spring Pond, raking is not a chore. "Most baymen like me consider this a lifestyle, not a job," he says with conviction.

Growing up near Hampton Bay, Ed discovered his destiny at a young age: "In high school, I used to wake up early to gather scallops and clams and still make it to class before the first bell." Upon graduation, he started doing it full time, working ten-hour days, dedicating his life to hauling home loads of the native quahogs, or hard-shelled clams. Two decades later, this labor-intensive career keeps the forty-year-old bayman looking youthful. He works solo from his boat, saying, "I like working alone because it's peaceful."

Ed begins his work at daybreak, reversing his small wood and fiberglass sharpie into the brackish water of Cold Spring Pond inlet. He explains how tidal signs or other wildlife can hint at the clams' whereabouts. Although he knows well that they prefer to burrow in muddy areas on the inlet's floor, he relies mostly on his instinct. "There are plenty of tall tales about what I do," he says while peering at the water's surface, "but, ultimately, I just know where to look."

Ed uses three rakes for harvesting—each with different basket attachments and lengths varying from fifteen to thirty feet. Knowing the underwater topography like the back of his hand, he chooses a rake; five-inch teeth are better for digging in the mud, whereas one-inch spikes are better for harder surfaces. Ed grips the handle with both hands, completely submerges the instrument, and vigorously digs. Clams that are less than one inch in size fall through the teeth and remain in the water to mature. Ed depends on his sixth sense for all things related to harvesting shellfish. "I know when there are clams in the rake," he asserts while hauling them to the surface. "Even if I've never clammed somewhere, I can tell if the land is productive or fallow." He substantiates his confidence as he loads and separates a plentiful catch.

These clams are some of the best, in part because the waters in which they grow are heavily protected. Ed himself acts as one of Southampton's trustees who oversee the town's twenty-six thousand areas of underwater real estate and promote sustainable fishing practices in the greater Peconic Bay and its tributaries. Ed's lifelong dedication to this one product has allowed him to get to know it better than anyone else, and the succulent Long Island clams that he pulls up are a testament to generations of a commitment to tradition.

Marinated Clams with Basil

SERVES 4

Basil-Apple Gelée

2 cups packed basil leaves
2 cups Granny Smith apple juice (from about 12 apples)
6 sheets gelatin
1 teaspoon salt

Bring a pot of salted water to a boil. Add the basil and blanch for 20 seconds. Transfer to a bowl of ice water. When chilled, wring out any excess water and puree in a blender with 1 cup of ice and 1 cup of water. Blend until smooth and strain through a chinois. In a small saucepan, bring the apple juice to a boil, skimming off any impurities that rise to the top. Strain through a quadruple layer of cheesecloth and cool in the refrigerator. Bloom the gelatin by placing it in ice water for 10 minutes until pliable. Wring out any excess moisture and combine with 1 tablespoon of the apple juice in a small saucepan. Over low heat, melt the gelatin until smooth. In a bowl, combine 1 cup of strained basil water, 3 tablespoons of the cooled apple juice, and the melted gelatin. Reserve the remaining juice for the basil-apple vinaigrette. Season with the salt. Spray a 13 by 18-inch plastic tray with nonstick vegetable cooking spray and wipe away any excess spray with a paper towel. Pour the mixture into the tray and refrigerate until set, about 1 hour.

Basil-Apple Vinaigrette

1 tablespoon grapeseed oil
1 cup peeled and diced (¼ inch) Granny Smith apple
¼ cup finely diced shallot
2 cups basil leaves
Salt
2 teaspoons lemon juice
2 tablespoons olive oil

Heat the grapeseed oil in a medium saucepan over medium heat. Add the apples and shallots and sweat for 1 minute. Add 1½ cups of water and simmer over medium-low heat until the apples are tender, 7 to 8 minutes. While the apples are simmering, bring a pot of salted water to a boil and blanch the basil for 20 seconds. Transfer to a bowl of ice water. When chilled, wring out any excess water. Blend the cooked apples and shallots with the basil on high speed until smooth. Strain through a chinois and season with salt. Chill over an ice bath. When ready to serve, add 3 tablespoons of the reserved apple juice and the lemon juice, stirring to combine, and top with the olive oil. **Note:** Any leftover vinaigrette can be refrigerated for up to 1 day and be used to dress grilled fish or salads.

Clam Salad

20 littleneck clams
4 sea scallops
¼ cup diced (¼ inch) Granny Smith apple
1 tablespoon finely diced shallot
1 tablespoon Lemon Vinaigrette (page 500)
Salt

Slide a clam knife into the front of each clam, move the knife toward the hinge, and pry the shell open. Remove each clam from the shell and cut away and discard the mantle, leaving only the belly. Slice the scallops about ⅛ inch thick. In a medium bowl, combine the clams, scallops, apple, and shallot. Toss with the vinaigrette and season with salt to taste.

To Finish

¼ cup diced (⅛ inch) apple
Basil leaves
Flowering basil

With a 3-inch cutter, punch out 4 rounds of the basil-apple gelée. Work quickly after cutting to prevent the gelée from turning brown. Divide the clam salad among 4 plates. Top each with a round of gelée. Spoon basil-apple vinaigrette around the plate and garnish with the diced apple, basil leaves, and flowering basil.

Clam Toast

Clams

5 pounds littleneck clams
¼ cup flour
3 tablespoons canola oil
½ cup sliced shallot
¼ cup sliced ginger
1 cup white wine
1 bunch parsley

Thoroughly scrub and rinse the clams under cold running water. In a large pot, heat the oil over high heat until very hot. Add the clams and stir for 10 seconds. Add the shallot and ginger and continue stirring for an additional 15 to 20 seconds. Add the white wine and parsley and cover. Continue cooking over high heat until most of the clams have opened, 1½ to 2 minutes. Transfer the clams to a bowl and cool over an ice bath, reserving the cooking liquid and discarding any unopened clams. When cool, remove the clams from the shells and cut away and discard the mantles, keeping only the bellies.

Dill Aioli

5¾ cups bottled clam juice
Cooking liquid reserved from making Clams
1 egg
1½ tablespoons lemon juice
1½ cups grapeseed oil
1 tablespoon chopped dill

In a medium saucepan, combine the clam juice and the reserved clam cooking liquid. Reduce over high heat until ¼ cup remains. Allow to cool slightly. Combine the reduced clam juice with the egg and lemon juice in a blender on high speed. Slowly stream in the oil, blending until emulsified. Transfer to a bowl and fold in the chopped dill. **Note:** Any left-over aioli can be stored in the refrigerator, covered, for up to 1 week and can be served alongside grilled fish, with gravlax or crudité, or on sandwiches.

To Finish

2 tablespoons olive oil
1 baguette, sliced on the bias into eight ¼-inch pieces
1 small fennel bulb
2 tablespoons Lemon Vinaigrette (page 500)
1 bunch dill
Dill flowers
Fennel flowers

Heat the oil in a large sauté pan over medium-low heat. Add the baguette slices and cook on one side until golden brown, 3 to 4 minutes. Remove and pat with a paper towel to remove excess oil. Using a mandoline, thinly slice the fennel, and then dress with the vinaigrette. Spread dill aioli on the toasted side of the baguette slices and top with the shaved fennel. Arrange 7 or 8 clams on each slice and garnish with the dill, dill flowers, and fennel flowers.

Manhattan Clam Chowder

SERVES 4

Clam Chowder Sauce

5¾ cups bottled clam juice
5 pounds littleneck clams
¼ cup flour
3 tablespoons canola oil
3 shallots, sliced (¼ inch)
2 ribs diced (¼ inch) celery
2 heads garlic, halved
1 tomato, quartered
1 bunch parsley
¼ cup tomato paste
1 cup white wine
2 tablespoons butter
3 sprigs thyme
Lemon juice

In a medium saucepan over high heat, reduce the clam juice to 2 cups. Thoroughly scrub and rinse the clams under cold running water. In a large pot, heat the oil over high heat. Add the shallots, celery, garlic, tomato, parsley, and tomato paste and stir constantly for 30 seconds. Add the clams and stir for 30 seconds. Add the wine, cover, and continue cooking over high heat until most of the clams have opened, 1½ to 2 minutes. Transfer to a bowl and cool over an ice bath; discard any unopened clams. Reserve about 2 cups of cooking liquid. Remove all but 8 clams from the shells and cut away and discard the mantles, keeping only the bellies. In a medium saucepan, combine the reduced clam juice with the clam cooking liquid and bring to a simmer. Remove from the heat and stir in the butter until emulsified. Add the thyme sprigs, season with lemon juice to taste, and steep for 10 minutes. Remove and discard the thyme sprigs.

Clam Ragout

¼ cup Chicken Stock (page 499)
2 tablespoons diced (⅛ inch) shallot
1 cup fresh corn kernels
¼ cup diced (¼ inch) celery
Clams, reserved from making Clam Chowder Sauce
Confit Cherry Tomatoes (page 499)
¼ cup green celery leaves
12 cherry tomatoes, halved
2 tablespoons cold butter
Salt

In a medium sauté pan, bring the chicken stock to a simmer over medium-low heat. Add the shallot and simmer until tender, about 2 minutes. Add the corn kernels and simmer until cooked, 1½ to 2 minutes. Add the celery and cook until tender,

2 to 3 minutes. Add the clams, confit cherry tomatoes, and celery leaves. Continue simmering until the celery leaves have wilted and the cherry tomatoes and clams are warm. Add the halved cherry tomatoes and the butter. Swirl the pan to melt the butter into the ragout and season with salt to taste.

To Finish

Celery leaves
Olive oil

Divide the clam chowder sauce among 4 bowls, reserving ¼ cup for finishing. Divide the clam ragout among the bowls. Aerate the reserved clam chowder sauce with a hand blender and spoon the foam on top of each dish. Garnish with celery leaves and 2 clams in their shells and finish with olive oil.

With the rise of the Italian and Portuguese populations in Rhode Island's fishing communities in the middle of the nineteenth century came the introduction of the tomato into traditional clam chowder. By the twentieth century, this new version came to be called Manhattan clam chowder (some historians say that it was also called Coney Island clam chowder and Fulton Market clam chowder). It is believed that distainful New Englanders named the red-stained chowder after Manhattan because they believed New Yorkers were the only ones crazy enough to add tomato to a pristine white chowder.

Corn

Sycamore Farms

Shuffling through his lush corn fields, Kevin Smith of Sycamore Farms dismisses the belief that corn must be cooked. He pulls an ear off the stalk, peels away the husk and silk, and takes a bite. At the market, he encourages everyone to do the same, hawking raw samples to woo even the staunchest of skeptics. Amused by the naivete of some of his clientele, he says, "Some people ask me how the butter will melt on cold corn, but that's before they taste my sweet kernels."

In 1979, Kevin's parents, Henry and Sue, purchased land in Middletown, New York. Henry had left his job as a teacher to learn corn farming from his own father. Today, Henry continues to seed Sycamore's thirty-five acres, while Kevin manages the other duties in the field. Most of the corn they plant is Butter and Sugar, which combines the sweetness of white corn with the starchy richness of yellow varieties.

The vigorous early-harvest corn varieties persevere through spring's cool weather and are picked in ninety days. Summer varieties, like the Providence (Kevin's favorite), bask in the heat for eighty-two more days. When four weeks remain in the growing cycle, pollen-coated tassels top the grasses at their maximum height. The pollen comes into contact with the silk on the tops of each ear, causing every silk strand to form a single kernel of corn over the course of the next few weeks. To ensure crop growth throughout the season, harvesting begins on the fourth of July, which is fitting because, as Kevin points out, "Everybody wants corn on the cob on Independence Day!"

While driving around the hilly expanse of his 237 acres, Kevin tells us, "Corn is in our DNA. You take what your dad did, and put your own twist on it." Undoubtedly, though, those twists can bring conflict. He thinks back to one of the first disagreements between his father and grandfather—it was about harvest distribution. Wholesalers were always used in the business, but Henry eventually convinced Walter to eliminate the middleman by setting up a roadside produce stand. Shortly thereafter, in 1981, Henry secured a table at Manhattan's Greenmarket. Kevin explained how gratifying it is for him to continue doing business at the market: "There is a certain nicety about people telling you that they like your products."

Kevin recently started a Ready To Eat Program at Sycamore's Greenmarket stand. Because corn immediately starts transforming tasty sugars into chalky starches as soon as it's picked, Kevin devised a system to guarantee that every sale is made at peak flavor. The crew arrives at the market early in the morning with eighty bags of fresh-picked corn. In the afternoon, another delivery arrives, so that all patrons are given an equal opportunity to taste his corn's purest expression of summer.

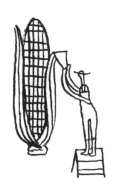

Corn Pizza with Bacon

SERVES 4

Pizza Dough

7 cups flour
3 tablespoons olive oil
2 tablespoons plus 2 teaspoons salt
1 packed tablespoon fresh yeast

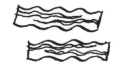

Combine all the ingredients with 2¾ cups of warm water (about 75°F) in the bowl of a stand mixer fitted with the dough hook and mix for 4 minutes on low speed. Transfer the dough to an oiled 18 by 13-inch plastic tray. Cover and let rest at room temperature for 2 hours. Refrigerate for 4 hours or until the dough is completely cool. Portion the dough into 4 equal pieces. Form each piece into a *boule*: hold the dough in both hands and gently stretch the surface of the dough around all sides, pulling the ends to the bottom and pinching them together. Add a little more flour as needed to keep the dough from sticking to your hands. Wipe the tray, re-oil it, and place the *boules* on the tray, leaving enough room for them to rise without touching. Wrap the tray with plastic wrap and refrigerate overnight.

To Finish

Corn Pudding (page 499)
¼ cup mascarpone
1 cup fresh corn kernels
½ cup diced (⅛ inch) uncooked bacon
Red chile flakes
4 ounces grated Tonjes Farm Dairy Rambler cheese (a raw cow's milk cheese similar to aged cheddar)
Olive oil

Remove the pizza dough from the refrigerator and allow it to proof for 1 hour at room temperature. Remove the cooking grate from a charcoal grill. Light 5 pounds of charcoal in a chimney starter and, when it's white hot, arrange the coals in the bottom of the grill. Return the cooking grate to the grill and place a pizza stone on top. Dust a work surface with flour and stretch one of the pieces of dough into an 8 by 12-inch oval. Combine the corn pudding and mascarpone in a medium bowl and spoon ¾ cup of the mixture onto the stretched pizza dough. Sprinkle ¼ cup of corn kernels, 2 tablespoons of bacon, and chile flakes onto the pizza. Flour the back of a baking sheet and use it to transfer the pizza to the stone. Close the lid and grill the pizza for 3 to 4 minutes until the dough is cooked. Remove the pizza from the pizza stone and sprinkle grated cheese on top. Finish with olive oil. Repeat with the remaining ingredients, to make 4 pizzas.

Corn Salad with Bulgur and Purslane

Crispy Polenta

½ cup polenta
Canola oil
Salt

Preheat the oven to 175°F. Combine the polenta with 2½ cups of water in a medium saucepan and cook over medium heat until thickened and tender, 35 to 40 minutes. Allow the polenta to cool to room temperature, and then roll between 2 sheets of parchment paper to 1/16-inch thickness. Transfer to an 18 by 26-inch baking sheet and dehydrate in the oven until dry, about 8 hours. Pour 2½ inches of canola oil into a saucepan and bring the oil to 400°F over medium-high heat. Break the dried polenta into 1½- to 2-inch shards and fry in the oil until crispy, 2 to 3 seconds. Remove from the oil with a slotted spoon and pat dry on paper towels. Season with salt to taste.

Corn Salad

1 cup bulgur
Canola oil
1 cup fresh corn kernels
8 baby corn
1 cup White Balsamic Pickling Liquid (page 501)
2 tablespoons chopped chives
1 tablespoon finely diced shallot
2 tablespoons Lemon Vinaigrette (page 500)
Salt

Preheat the oven to 175°F. Place the bulgur in a heatproof bowl. Bring 2 cups of salted water to a boil and pour over the bulgur. Cover with plastic wrap and let steep at room temperature until the bulgur has absorbed all the water and has cooled to room temperature, about 20 minutes. Divide the cooked bulgur in half. Place one half of the cooked bulgur on a 13 by 18-inch baking sheet and dehydrate in the oven until dry, about 2 hours. Reserve the remaining cooked bulgur. Pour 2½ inches of oil into a saucepan and bring the oil to 350°F over medium-high heat. Fry the dried bulgur for 20 to 30 seconds until crispy. Remove from the oil with a slotted spoon and pat dry on paper towels. Bring a saucepan of salted water to a boil. Add the corn kernels and cook until tender, 2 to 3 minutes. Transfer with a slotted spoon to a bowl of ice water. Add the baby corn to the boiling salted water and cook until tender, 3 to 4 minutes. Transfer to the ice water. Cut 4 of the baby corn into rounds and cut the remaining 4 baby corn in half lengthwise. Place the rounds in a bowl. Bring the pickling liquid to a boil and pour it over the rounds. Cool to room temperature, making sure the rounds are completely submerged in the liquid. Drain the rounds, discarding the liquid. Combine the cooked bulgur, crispy bulgur, cooked corn kernels, blanched baby corn halves, and pickled baby corn in a medium bowl. Add the chives and shallots and toss with the vinaigrette. Season with salt to taste.

To Finish

Lemon Buttermilk Dressing (page 318)
Olive oil
Purslane
Amaranth leaves
Corn shoots
Freeze-dried corn

Arrange the corn salad on each of 4 plates. Drizzle lemon buttermilk dressing around the plate and finish with olive oil. Garnish with crispy polenta, purslane, amaranth, corn shoots, and freeze dried corn.

Corn Soup with Buttermilk

SERVES 4

Corn Soup

**8 cups Tomato Water from about 20 pounds of tomatoes
  (page 231)**
2 tablespoons butter
½ cup fresh corn kernels
¼ cup finely diced shallot
4 cups corn juice (from about 8 quarts of corn kernels)
½ cup loosely packed basil leaves
Lime juice
Cayenne pepper
Salt

In a medium saucepan over medium-high heat, reduce the tomato water to 4 cups. In a separate saucepan, melt the butter and sweat the corn and shallot until tender, 4 to 5 minutes. Add the reduced tomato water and bring to a boil. Add the corn juice and simmer for 5 minutes. Remove from the heat, bruise the basil leaves with the back of a knife, and add to the soup. Let stand for 10 minutes, and then strain through a chinois. Chill in the refrigerator before seasoning with lime juice, cayenne, and salt to taste. **Note:** Any leftover soup can be refrigerated for 2 to 3 days.

Buttermilk Espuma

5 sheets gelatin
2 teaspoons lemon juice
2 cups buttermilk
Salt
Cayenne pepper
6 egg whites

Bloom the gelatin by placing it in ice water for 10 minutes until pliable. In a small saucepan, warm the lemon juice over low heat. Remove the gelatin from the water and squeeze out any excess moisture. Whisk the gelatin into the warm lemon juice. Season the buttermilk with salt and cayenne pepper. Whisk the gelatin mixture and buttermilk and transfer to a whipped cream dispenser. Add the egg whites and charge the dispenser with 2 cartridges of nitrous oxide (N_2O). Shake vigorously and chill in an ice bath until ready to use.

To Finish

Freeze dried corn
Nasturtium flowers
Nasturtium leaves

Expel buttermilk *espuma* into 4 bowls. Garnish with freeze dried corn, nasturtium flowers, and nasturtium leaves. Pour chilled soup around the outside of the *espuma*.

Cranberries

Joseph J. White

Only three fruits that are native to North America are grown commercially in the United States. Concord grapes are still widely planted on the East Coast and blueberries are in market stands all summer long. However, just like the wetlands in which they work, cranberry growers are somewhat of an endangered species. Two fifth-generation farmers, Joe Darlington and Brenda Conner, have a long legacy in cranberries, one they've committed to keeping alive. In 1857, Joe's great-great-grandfather, James A. Fenwick, established the family business: "Cranberries were originally harvested by natives, and one day, my great-great-grandfather simply put a fence around a plot and started farming on his own. Years later, his son-in-law, Joseph J. White, designed his own bogs and expanded the company tenfold."

The Joseph J. White estate is bordered by coniferous trees, which grow well in the nutrient-poor, highly acidic, sandy soil. Like the trees that surround them, cranberries are a species of evergreen that thrives in New Jersey's Pine Barrens, content in an environment where most other plants cannot survive. And, as Joe explains, they have a particular set of needs when it comes to moisture. "In nature, they grow in low-lying areas next to streams," says Joe as he steps down into one of the farm's bogs. The water table should be shallow and accessible to the cranberries' roots, but the plants should not be submerged, and the soil should have good drainage. "These bogs have water one foot below the surface," explains Brenda, crouching down to the plants. Their six-inch roots draw the water upwards through capillaries, just as they do in their wild habitat. "You see, this is native agriculture!" she exclaims.

In June, the highly fertile plants launch into a blooming frenzy, with a single acre producing up to 25 million flowers. The flowers give way to fruit that ripens to a deep red during the late summer's cool nights. Once harvested, much of the fruit is destined to be juiced or canned. Some snacking varieties are dry-farmed to protect their shelf life; these include the teardrop-shaped Ben Lear and the large, rounded Scarlet Knight. Both are pleasant, their light sweetness spiked with the puckering tannins that are unique to cranberries. For the wet harvest, the low-lying, levee-ringed bogs are flooded with water. Cranberries have air pockets that cause them to float, making it easy to pluck them from the surface: "In the river, this phenomenon happens naturally, too," says Joe.

Ordinarily, tractors are used to drag specialized pickers through the bog, but Joe is working on developing a floating harvester to lessen the damage to the vines—even after thirty years, he continues to reinvent his practice. Once the berries are released from the plant, a net gathers them to one end of the bog, creating a brilliant crimson blanket on the water's surface. The farm's eighty bogs are submerged in water for the entirety of winter; the ice layer that forms protects them for the following season.

Cranberry Bread Pudding

SERVES 8

8 cups diced (½ inch) brioche, crusts removed
1½ cups (6 ounces) fresh cranberries
8 ounces white chocolate chunks
4 cups cream
2 vanilla beans, split lengthwise and scraped
5 egg yolks
3 eggs
½ cup sugar
2 teaspoons salt
4 tablespoons butter, softened

Preheat the oven to 275°F. Grease a 9 by 13-inch baking dish or a 3-quart gratin dish with butter. Place half of the bread, the cranberries, and half of the white chocolate chunks in the dish. Cover with the rest of the bread. In a saucepan, warm the cream to just below a simmer. Remove from the heat, add the vanilla bean seeds and pods, and steep for 10 minutes. Whisk together the egg yolks, eggs, sugar, and salt. Bring the cream to a boil and add the remaining white chocolate. Remove the saucepan from the heat. Making sure the chocolate is melted, whisk in the egg mixture. Strain through a chinois and pour over the bread. Allow to stand for 30 minutes. Dot the top with the butter and cover with aluminum foil. Set the baking dish in a large roasting pan and add enough boiling water to come halfway up the sides of the baking dish. Bake for 45 minutes to 1 hour, until the custard is set. Remove from the bath, remove the foil, and increase the oven temperature to 350°F. Return the pudding to the oven and bake until golden brown, about 30 more minutes.

Cranberry Soup with Cinnamon Ice Cream

SERVES 4

Candied Cranberries

6 cups sugar
2 cups (½ pound) fresh cranberries

In a large saucepan over medium heat, combine the sugar with 6 cups of water. Once the sugar is completely dissolved, remove from the heat, allow to come to room temperature, and then refrigerate. Pierce each cranberry with a cake tester and place in a large saucepan. Cover with water and place over high heat. When the first wisp of steam appears, remove from the heat and discard any cranberries that have burst. Drain the cranberries and add them to the cold simple syrup. Chill the berries in the syrup over an ice bath. Once completely chilled, heat the berries in the syrup until very hot but not boiling. Cool the berries in their syrup over an ice bath. Once cooled, store in an airtight container in the refrigerator for 2 days before using. **Note:** Any leftover candied cranberries can be eaten over ice cream or stirred into pancake batter.

Cranberry Soup

2 cups unsweetened cranberry juice
4 cups (1 pound) fresh cranberries
1 sheet gelatin
3 tablespoons sugar

In a small pot, combine the cranberry juice with the fresh cranberries. Bring to a simmer over medium heat, simmering until all of the cranberries have burst, about 15 minutes. Remove from the heat and steep for 30 minutes. Strain through a quadruple layer of cheesecloth overnight in the refrigerator.

Bloom the gelatin by soaking the sheet in cold water for 10 minutes until pliable. In a small saucepan, warm 1 cup of the enriched cranberry juice with the sugar, stirring until the sugar is dissolved. Squeeze the gelatin to remove excess moisture and stir into the juice mixture until dissolved. Transfer to a container, cover, and refrigerate overnight.

Glühwein Granité

1 (750-milliliter) bottle red wine
1 navel orange, quartered
2 cinnamon sticks
1 vanilla bean, split lengthwise and scraped
1 tablespoon cardamom pods
1 tablespoon allspice berries
1 tablespoon black peppercorns
½ cup sugar

Place the wine, orange, and spices in a saucepan over medium heat and reduce by half. Strain and measure the liquid. If you have less than 2 cups, add enough water to yield 2 cups. Add the sugar, stirring until dissolved. Pour into a 9 by 9-inch baking dish, cover with plastic wrap, and freeze overnight. The next day, scrape the frozen wine with a fork. **Note:** Any granité that you don't use can be kept in the freezer for up to 1 month. Fluff with a fork again before serving.

Poached Apples

1 (750-milliliter) bottle off-dry Riesling
1½ cups sugar
Zest and juice of 1 lemon
4 large Mutsu apples, cored

In a large saucepan over medium heat, bring the wine, sugar, lemon zest, and lemon juice to a boil. Remove from the heat and steep for 30 minutes. Slice one of the apples horizontally ¼ inch thick. Using a small round cutter (about ¾ inch in diameter), punch at least 16 small rings out of the apple slices, avoiding the skin. Using a 25-millimeter (1-inch) Parisian scoop, scoop large balls with skin from the remaining 3 apples. Bring the syrup to a simmer, add the apple rings and balls, and poach until fork tender, 25 to 30 minutes. Store in their syrup in the refrigerator for up to 1 day until ready to serve.

Cinnamon Ice Cream

2 cups cream
1 cup milk
½ cup powdered milk
1½ teaspoons ground cinnamon
6 egg yolks
⅔ cup sugar
1 teaspoon salt

In a medium saucepan over medium heat, warm the cream, milk, powdered milk, and cinnamon, stirring frequently so as to not scorch the mixture. In a bowl, whisk together the egg yolks, sugar, and salt. Slowly pour the hot cream into the egg mixture, whisking constantly. Return the mixture to the saucepan and cook to 184°F, stirring constantly. Strain through a chinois, and then chill over an ice bath. Freeze in an ice cream machine. **Note:** Store any leftover ice cream in the freezer for up to 1 month.

To Finish

In the center of each of 4 bowls, place a large pile of Glühwein granité. Drain the candied cranberries and arrange them, along with the poached apple s, around the granité. Pour just enough of the cranberry soup into the bowls to come up halfway up the apples. Finish with a large quenelle of cinnamon ice cream.

Raw Cranberry Chutney

MAKES 4 CUPS

3 cups (¾ pound) fresh cranberries
1¾ cups sugar
2 teaspoons orange zest

Combine all ingredients in the bowl of a stand mixer fitted with the paddle attachment. Mix on low speed for 1 hour, and then transfer to a bowl, cover, and refrigerate until ready to serve, up to 1 week. **Note:** Use this chutney with turkey, game, or pork, or serve it over vanilla ice cream.

Cucumbers

Windfall Farms

At the age of sixteen, Morse Pitts was already passionate about gardening, and so it was a big moment for him when his family inherited 150 acres of land in Montgomery, New York. "My father called the place 'Windfall,' not as something that is good or bad, but instead something that just falls across your path." Despite his father's neutrality, Morse felt as though they had won the lottery, and he eventually inherited the land himself in 1979.

Over thirty years later, Windfall Farms is very different than it used to be. The dirt road that ran past the front yard has been paved over and now functions as a thruway for trucks heading to nearby industrial complexes. As Morse explains, "My land is zoned for industrial purposes." Yet he continues to farm on his land—with unbelievable results—always experimenting with organic crops, including an incredible array of cucumbers.

Morse's cucumbers come in myriad shapes and sizes. Knobby and plump Kirby cucumbers make a crisp pickle, as do the miniature gherkins, which have a snap that even curing won't kill. Morse cannot seem to get enough: "We pick the gherkins small, and I love eating them in the field."

Then there are the unconventional varieties, like baseball-sized heirloom lemon cucumbers and the pale Boothby's Blondes, neither of which look like cucumbers at all. Both have thin skins and are incredibly juicy. One of the most peculiar varieties is an heirloom called sandita, also known as cucamelon. Morse points out toward a farmer in the field and says, "See Jessica? She is the rogue farmer that brought us the sanditas." Unbeknownst to Morse, Jessica planted the sanditas at Windfall Farms; it was only when the plants were in full bloom that Morse, delighted, caught sight of them. Unlike standard ground-creeping cucumber vines, these are trellised to climb upwards. The fruits look like watermelons that have been shrunk to the size of marbles and their thick skin even tastes like pickled watermelon rind. But the pulpy flesh tastes like cucumber—the plant to which they are most closely related. Morse warns, "They are sweet when they're young, but they develop an enhanced sour quality when they mature."

Morse credits his success to his employees, who in turn praise him for being overwhelmingly generous and creative. "We are always trying something new at my farm," he says. For example, his former high school classmate, Hubert, introduced him to biodiesel, and now a Windfall resident, Darren, produces the eco-friendly fuel on site to power the farm's ubiquitous green bus. This kind of move epitomizes Morse's relentless experimental spirit. Without any children of his own to whom he can pass along the windfall that fell into his lap so many years ago, Morse enjoys helping aspiring farmers, empowering them one cucumber at a time.

Salad of Cucumbers

SERVES 4

Garlic Pickles

6 to 8 large Kirby cucumbers, halved lengthwise
4 cups white vinegar
4 heads garlic, cloves separated and peeled
½ cup salt
1 tablespoon coriander seeds
1 tablespoon mustard powder
1 teaspoon red chile flakes
1 teaspoon ground turmeric

Divide the cucumbers between 2 clean 2-quart glass jars. Combine the remaining ingredients with 4 cups of water in a medium stockpot. Bring the liquid to a boil and pour over the cucumbers. Allow the cucumbers and pickling liquid to cool to room temperature before covering. Refrigerate for at least 1 week; keep for up to 1 month.

Hot Pickles

10 to 12 medium lemon cucumbers, halved
4 cups white vinegar
½ cup salt
3 tablespoons red chile flakes
1 tablespoon black peppercorns
1 tablespoon coriander seeds
1 tablespoon sugar
1 teaspoon tomato paste
4 allspice berries
2 bay leaves
2 whole cloves

Divide the cucumbers between 2 clean 2-quart glass jars. Combine the remaining ingredients with 4 cups of water in a medium stockpot. Bring the liquid to a boil and pour over the cucumbers. Allow the cucumbers and pickling liquid to cool to room temperature before covering. Refrigerate for at least 1 week; keep for up to 1 month.

Dill Pickles

6 to 8 large Kirby cucumbers
4 cups white vinegar
2 cups loosely packed dill
½ cup salt
2 tablespoons dill seeds
1 tablespoon coriander seeds
1 tablespoon red chile flakes
2 cloves garlic, peeled

Divide the cucumbers between 2 clean 2-quart glass jars. Combine the remaining ingredients with 4 cups of water in a medium stockpot. Bring the liquid to a boil and pour over the cucumbers. Allow the cucumbers and pickling liquid to cool to room temperature before covering. Refrigerate for at least 1 week; keep for up to 1 month.

Bread and Butter Pickles

10 to 12 medium lemon cucumbers
5 cups cider vinegar
4 cups sugar
1 cup salt
2 tablespoons coriander seeds
1½ tablespoons celery seeds
2 teaspoons mustard powder
2 teaspoons ground turmeric

Divide the cucumbers between 2 clean 2-quart glass jars. Combine the remaining ingredients with 2 cups of water in a medium stockpot. Bring the liquid to a boil and pour over the cucumbers. Allow the cucumbers and pickling liquid to cool to room temperature before covering. Refrigerate for at least 1 week; keep for up to 1 month.

continued >

Buttermilk Dressing

⅓ cup Crème Fraîche (page 499)
¼ cup buttermilk
2½ tablespoons White Balsamic Vinaigrette (page 501)
½ garlic clove, minced
1 teaspoon salt

In a small bowl, combine the crème fraîche and buttermilk, whisking until smooth. Add the vinaigrette, garlic, and salt, mixing until combined. **Note:** Any leftover dressing can be stored in the refrigerator, covered, for up to 1 week. Use it to dress green salads.

Cucumber Relish

1 English cucumber, peeled and finely diced
1 teaspoon salt
White balsamic vinegar

Season the cucumber with salt and hang it in a quadruple layer of cheesecloth for 1 hour. Discard the liquid. Season the drained cucumber generously with vinegar.

To Finish

Boothby's Blonde cucumbers
Burpless cucumbers
Cucamelons
Lemon cucumbers
Spiky cucumbers
Pickled Mustard Seeds (page 500)
Borage flowers
Flowering cucumbers
Purslane
Olive oil
Ground black pepper

Slice and arrange garlic, hot, dill, and bread and butter pickles on 4 plates. Do the same with the different varieties of cucumbers and the cucamelons. Add 2 teaspoons of cucumber relish to each plate. Spoon pickled mustard seeds around the cucumbers. Aerate the buttermilk dressing with a hand blender and spoon the foam onto the salad. Garnish with borage flowers, flowering cucumbers, and purslane. Finish with olive oil and pepper to taste.

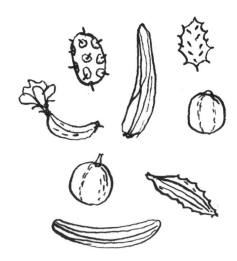

Cucumber Dressing

MAKES 2 CUPS

1 English cucumber
⅓ cup white balsamic vinegar
1 cup grapeseed oil
¾ cup loosely packed dill
Salt

Cut the cucumber in half lengthwise and remove the seeds. Roughly chop the cucumber and place in a blender with the white balsamic vinegar. Slowly stream in the oil while blending on high speed. Add the dill and continue blending until smooth. Strain through a chinois and season with salt to taste. **Note:** Serve alongside grilled or smoked fish and as a dressing for summer salads. Keeps in the refrigerator for 1 to 2 days.

Duck

Duck Farm at Stone Church

"I was born and raised in New York City, but I always felt like an outsider," says duck farmer Robert Rosenthal. In the 1970s, Robert went to his parents' home country of Argentina, seeking a change of pace and perspective. There he found work in a vineyard—and unexpectedly developed a passion for agriculture. When he returned to the states, he chose to settle in the farmlands of upstate New York rather than in the city he had left behind four years earlier. Together with his wife, Noelia, Robert renovated a derelict nineteenth-century stone church, started growing vegetables, and eventually began raising free-range chickens. But he saw an opportunity when he realized that there was an unmet demand for heirloom birds in the area. Lacking the knowledge or experience to meet that demand, he traveled to France, where he lived for three and a half years, learning as much as he could about raising heritage breeds of poultry.

In France, Robert discovered a farming method that really resonated with him—and it hardly felt like farming at all. It involves a hands-off approach whereby the farmer would find out what the birds (in Robert's case, ducks) needed to survive before creating a nurturing environment in which they could thrive on their own. Upon his return to New York, Robert reopened his farm to feature the black-and-white feathered Duclair duck, a breed native to Normandy. He overhauled his property, expanding from a churchyard with a natural pond to a flourishing, two-hundred-acre wetland with two additional manmade ponds. He planted oak trees full of acorns rich in omega-3 fatty acids and diverse greenery including Japanese millet, buckwheat, and clover. "[The ducks] choose their own diet—like at a salad bar," Robert says. The ducks eat what they want when they want, and roam and swim freely across the expansive grounds. Despite the lack of fences and enclosures, the ducks never leave the farmland. "Ducks only fly for one reason," explains Robert, "because they are seeking what they need to sustain themselves."

In this prolific ecosystem, the birds mature to full size naturally, carrying the majority of their weight in their breasts, a desirable trait to consumers. The meat is tender and vibrant in color, while the flavor is at once meaty and gamey. People who try Stone Church ducks for the first time wonder if they've ever *really* tasted duck before. Of this unconventional approach to duck farming—a fenceless environment where the birds can come and go as they please and where they choose their own diets—Robert says, "What I'm doing in my field is the future of food."

Braised Duck Legs

SERVES 4

1 cup salt
½ cup plus ¼ cup sugar
5 sprigs thyme
4 duck legs
¼ cup coriander seeds
¼ cup cumin seeds
¼ cup dried lavender flowers
¼ cup Szechuan peppercorns
1 cup duck fat
1 cup diced (½ inch) onion
3 cloves garlic, crushed but kept whole
1 cup red wine
1 star anise
1 cup orange juice
½ cup lemon juice
½ cup lime juice
4 cups Duck Stock (page 500)
1 cup Chicken Jus (page 498)
Zest of 1 orange, 1 lemon, and 1 lime
Segments from 1 orange, 1 lemon, and 1 lime
Dried lavender sprigs

Combine the salt, the ½ cup of sugar, and the thyme in a bowl. Arrange the duck legs in a glass or plastic container and coat evenly with the mixture. Cover the dish with plastic wrap and refrigerate for 4 hours. Preheat the oven to 325°F. Rinse the duck legs under cold water and pat dry. Combine the coriander, cumin, lavender flowers, and Szechuan peppercorns and grind to a fine powder in a spice grinder. Coat both sides of the duck legs with the spice powder. In a large, ovenproof skillet, melt the duck fat over high heat. Add the duck legs, skin-side down, and sear until evenly browned, 7 to 10 minutes. Remove the legs and set aside. Drain all but 2 tablespoons of fat from the skillet. Reduce the heat to medium-low, add the onion and garlic, and sweat until tender, 5 to 6 minutes. Deglaze the pan with the red wine, raise the heat to high, and reduce the liquid by half. Add the remaining ¼ cup of sugar, the star anise, and the orange, lemon, and lime juices and reduce the liquid by half. Add the duck stock and chicken jus and bring to a simmer. Return the legs to the skillet, skin side up, and transfer to the oven. Cook the duck legs uncovered until the meat pulls away easily from the bone, 1¾ to 2 hours. Remove the legs with a slotted spoon and reserve. Strain the liquid and skim the fat from the top. Reduce the liquid over medium heat until thick enough to coat the back of a spoon. Garnish the duck legs with the citrus zest and segments and lavender sprigs and serve with the reduced braising liquid.

Duck Sausage

15 feet of hog casings
¾ pound pork belly
9 ounces diced (¾ inch) boneless duck legs
6 ounces diced (¾ inch) boneless pork shoulder
1½ tablespoons salt
2¼ teaspoons fennel seeds
2¼ teaspoons mustard seeds
⅜ teaspoon pink curing salt
1½ teaspoons minced garlic
½ teaspoon ground black pepper
2 cups packed stemmed kale
½ cup diced (⅛ inch) carrot
1 tablespoon canola oil

Thoroughly rinse the hog casings under cold running water. In a large bowl, combine the pork belly, duck legs, and pork shoulder with the salt, fennel seeds, mustard seeds, pink curing salt, garlic, and black pepper. Cover and marinate in the refrigerator for 2 hours. Pass through a meat grinder on a medium die. Bring a pot of salted water to a boil and blanch the kale until tender, 4 to 5 minutes, and then transfer to the ice bath. Blanch the carrots until tender, 2 to 3 minutes, and transfer to the ice bath. Dry the blanched vegetables on paper towels and slice the kale into ribbons. Fold the kale and the carrots into the ground meat. Using a sausage stuffer, fill the casings with the meat mixture and twist into 5-inch links.

Bring a pot of salted water to 175°F and poach the sausages until cooked to 145°F, 14 to 15 minutes. Remove the sausages and cool in the refrigerator. Heat the oil in a sauté pan over high heat and brown the sausages, 1 to 2 minutes on each side. As an alternative, you can grill the poached sausages. **Note:** The uncooked sausages can be tightly wrapped and frozen for up to 1 month. Serve them with roasted potatoes, Pickled Plums (page 362), and braised winter greens.

Pan Roasted Duck Breast

SERVES 4

4 duck breasts
Salt
2 tablespoons canola oil

Trim the excess fat from the duck breasts and remove any silver skin, leaving as much skin intact as possible. Season the breasts with salt and sandwich 2 breasts together with the skin sides facing out and the thick ends of the breasts at opposite ends. Truss the breasts together tightly with butcher's twine. Chill the breasts uncovered in the refrigerator for 1 hour.

Heat the oil in a medium sauté pan over high heat. Season the breasts with salt and sear in the pan, beginning on the seams to seal the breasts together. Then turn the breasts, searing the skin sides until evenly browned, about 2 minutes per side. Reduce the heat to medium-low and continue cooking to medium doneness (an internal temperature of 130° to 135°F), turning to brown evenly and rendering the duck fat until crispy, 17 to 20 minutes. Allow to rest 10 to 15 minutes before slicing. Serve alongside grilled apricots.

Eggs

Flying Pigs Farm

Jen Small could not stand the sight of farmland in the town of Shushan, New York, being turned over to developers. Jen's father was raised there, and he introduced her to the unspoiled Battenkill River Valley at a young age. She could not help but become attached. So in 1999, fresh out of grad school with a degree in public health, Jen convinced her husband, Mike Yezzie, to buy the property where her father grew up to ensure that new development would not take over the land. Mike, a newly minted lawyer with a deep interest in social issues, was intrigued by the idea. They scraped together what money they could to buy the property. A playful housewarming gift christened their farm: "We received a pair of pigs with wings, meaning that our project would be done when pigs would fly." Overjoyed with their acquisition, they were unsure of what to do with their property until a brilliantly practical idea occurred to them. "We raised three pigs to help pay the taxes on the land. In 2001, we had more pork than we could eat!" Jen exclaims. What started as an emotional attachment to the farm and its land turned into a successful business. Jen and Mike established Flying Pigs Farm with heritage-breed pigs and developed their agricultural prowess with good old-fashioned trial and error.

But Jen had an idyllic farm picture in mind, one where chickens roam free around the land. To fulfill her picturesque ideal of the farming lifestyle, they bought a dozen Rhode Island Red chickens. "There is something wonderful about seeing them roam around the grass, streams, flowerbeds, and woods." And, Jen adds, "Everybody eats eggs, right?"

Immediately, the benefits began to abound. "I stopped buying eggs from supermarkets," Jen says, recalling how their home quickly began filling with farm-fresh eggs. As she began cooking with them in her home, she realized that these weren't ordinary eggs. With custardy, bright orange yolks, these eggs, she decided, were the most delicious she had ever tasted.

At the farm, exceptional quality is a result of expert breeding and care. Each of their hens takes thirty hours to produce a single egg. Jen says, "I found a new respect for eggs. I never waste them, and now I take better care of each one." The brown shells are noticeably denser than the market average due to the chickens' diets. "We grind up oyster shells and sprinkle it on their feed," reveals Mike. "The extra calcium makes them stronger." The birds are also encouraged to forage for their own sustenance—and they happily oblige, feasting on bugs and plants. Every couple of weeks, the entire pen is relocated within the sprawling field. Mike affirms that their chickens' varied nourishment affects the flavor profile of their eggs. "When the chickens have access to fresh grass, the eggs are more flavorful and rich. Plus, the land benefits from dethatching and natural fertilizer."

Mike and Jen offer their customers eggs of all different shapes and sizes, each carton its own perfectly imperfect parcel. Pigs have yet to fly at Flying Pigs Farm, but Jen and Mike's incredible pork, chicken, and eggs make any dish they are used in soar.

Baked Egg with Spinach, Mushrooms, and Cheese

SERVES 4

Mushroom Duxelles

3 tablespoons butter
4 cups diced (⅛ inch) cremini mushrooms
½ cup diced (⅛ inch) shallot
2 sprigs thyme
2 tablespoons sherry
Salt

Melt the butter in a medium sauté pan over medium-high heat. Add half of the mushrooms and cook, stirring frequently, until the mushrooms are golden brown, 10 to 12 minutes. Add the rest of the mushrooms and continue cooking until golden brown, another 10 to 12 minutes. Add the shallot and cook until softened, 2 to 3 minutes. Add the thyme and sherry and cook, stirring frequently, about 5 minutes. Season with salt to taste.

Sautéed Spinach

2 teaspoons butter
1 teaspoon diced (⅛ inch) shallot
4 cups spinach, stems removed
Salt

In a medium sauté pan, melt the butter over medium heat. Add the shallot and sweat until softened, 2 to 3 minutes. Add the spinach and sauté until wilted. Season with salt to taste.

To Finish

8 slices deli ham
**½ cup crumbled Tonjes Farm Dairy Rambler cheese
    (a raw cow's milk cheese similar to aged cheddar)**
8 eggs

Preheat the oven to 375°F. Line 8 of the wells of a muffin pan with the slices of ham, treating them like muffin liners. Divide the sautéed spinach among the 8 wells and top with the mushroom duxelles. Distribute the cheese evenly, and then crack an egg into each well. Bake in the oven until the whites are set but the yolks are still runny, 11 to 13 minutes. Rest for a few minutes before gently removing the baked eggs from the muffin pan with a small offset spatula.

Ham and Egg Sandwich

SERVES 4

8 slices rye bread, ¼ inch thick
1 pound sliced Consider Bardwell Farm Rupert cheese (an aged raw cow's milk cheese made in the style of Gruyère)
1 pound thinly sliced smoked ham
½ cup butter, at room temperature
1 tablespoon canola oil
4 eggs

Preheat the oven to 350°F. Build each sandwich by starting with a piece of bread, followed by cheese, ham, and then more cheese. Using a 2¼-inch round cutter, punch a hole through the layers of ham and cheese and the bottom piece of bread; remove the circle of ham, cheese, and bread. Top with an unpunched slice of bread. Spread butter on both sides of the sandwiches. Heat the oil in a large cast-iron skillet over medium-low heat (use two skillets if necessary to hold all 4 sandwiches). Place the sandwiches, hole-side down, in the skillet, and reduce the heat to low. Cook until golden brown, 3 to 4 minutes. Flip the sandwiches and crack the eggs into the holes. Transfer the skillet to the oven and bake until the egg is cooked and the cheese is melted, 10 to 12 minutes.

Fluke

The Lester Family

In Long Island's East End, the shores of Napeague Harbor are scattered with primitive-looking nets fastened to large whitewashed posts—a baffling sight to most passersby. These basic traps, mostly unchanged from their original Native American design, are still the most commonly used apparatus to catch Long Island fluke. But there is one major change: assembled in waist-high water, the original traps had a capacity to hold about six fish, whereas the modern version has the capacity to secure upwards of 13,000. The Lester siblings, Danny, Kelly, and Paul, work to preserve traditional fluke fishing and are proud that "the family's been doing it this way for a hundred years."

Planting a trap is surprisingly complicated, considering its basic structure and design, but every March, the Lesters consult the family blue prints and begin building. Young oak trees are plunged into the shallow water's sand every twenty-five feet and are connected with a net. The staves cause fluke schools to retreat from the shallows, only to be intercepted and grouped by a funnel in the "heart" or "inner pound." The fluke pass through a three-foot entrance to their destination—a pen framed by netting on the bottom and all sides, in which they swim around freely. "The one great thing about this type of fishery is that the catch stays alive," says Danny, as he assures us that his practices are gentle. "It's like a big fish tank."

Given the frenetic nature of their work, it is ironic that the Lesters work off the banks of a town called Lazy Point. At dawn, everyone strategically splits up, taking small wooden boats called sharpies toward the full traps. First, the nets are hauled up from the bottom of the harbor, bringing the fluke with them. Then, using smaller hand nets, the fishers transfer the catch into the boat. Some of the fluke are sold live to a local shop, while the rest are cut, bled, and sent to the New Fulton Fish Market at Hunts Point in the Bronx.

Weather variations are a significant challenge between April and November. Wincing, Danny recalls one season: "Back to back nor'easters destroyed our traps. We made $5,000 all year." A frozen bay can freeze activity, and the fishermen cannot make up for the lost time. But periods of calm help keep the nets full, allowing the Lesters to reach their daily goal of 120 pounds of fluke with ease.

Even though time-honored practices so often trump technological innovations in terms of quality and sustainability, old-fashioned fluke fishing, like many artisan endeavors that require time, patience, and care, is nearly obsolete. The Lesters' preservation of a traditional method is a rare treasure and one that provides the market with extraordinary Long Island fluke.

Fish and Chips

SERVES 4

Chips

3 Russet or other starchy potatoes
Canola oil

Wash the potatoes leave the skins on. Cut lengthwise into thin fries about ¼ inch thick. Place the cut potatoes in water while you work to avoid oxidation. In a large stockpot, heat 3 inches of canola oil to 300°F over medium-high heat. Thoroughly rinse the potatoes of any starch and pat dry. Drop the potatoes in the oil and fry until tender, 3 to 4 minutes. They should achieve no color. Remove the fries from the oil and drain on paper towels. Reserve the oil for the second round of frying. Place the fries on a baking sheet lined with parchment paper and freeze until solid, about 2 hours.

Tartar Sauce

2 eggs
¼ teaspoon mustard
1½ teaspoons lemon juice
¾ cup grapeseed oil
1 teaspoon finely chopped rinsed salt-packed anchovy
1 teaspoon finely chopped capers
1 teaspoon finely chopped parsley
1 teaspoon finely chopped shallot
¼ teaspoon caper juice
Salt

Place 1 egg in a saucepan and cover with at least 1 inch of cold water. Bring to a boil over high heat, and then remove from the heat. Cover the pan and let the egg rest for 12 minutes before transferring it to an ice bath. When cool, peel and finely chop the egg. Combine the remaining egg with the mustard and lemon juice in a blender. While the blender is running, slowly stream in the oil to emulsify. Fold in the chopped egg, anchovy, capers, parsley, shallots, and caper juice. Season with salt to taste.

Fish Batter

3 cups flour
¾ cup cornstarch
2 teaspoons baking powder
Salt
1 cup plus 1 teaspoon beer

Combine the flour, cornstarch, and baking powder in a medium bowl. Season with salt. In a separate bowl, combine 1 cup of the flour mixture with the beer and whisk to combine. Reserve the remaining flour mixture for dredging the fish.

To Finish

Salt
3 pounds fluke, cleaned, filleted, and skinned

Reheat the chip frying oil over medium-high heat, adjusting as necessary to maintain it at 375°F. Lower the frozen chips into the oil. Fry until golden brown, 3 to 4 minutes. Drain on a cooling rack and season with salt to taste. Bring the oil to 400°F. Cut the fluke into strips 4 inches long and ½ inch thick. Dredge the fish in the reserved flour mixture, shake off the excess, and dip in the batter. Drop the fish strips into the hot oil and fry until golden brown, about 2 minutes. Remove from the oil, drain on a cooling rack, and season with salt to taste. Serve immediately with the tartar sauce and hot chips.

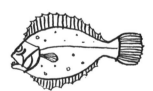

Raw Fluke with Cherry Tomatoes

SERVES 4

Tomato Water

5 pounds ripe tomatoes
½ bunch basil
1 tablespoon salt

Rinse the tomatoes under cold running water and remove the cores. Cut into quarters and place in a mixing bowl with the basil and salt. Line a colander with 10 layers of cheesecloth. Dampen the cheesecloth with cold water and press out any excess moisture. Place the prepared colander in a deep bowl to catch the liquid as it drains. In three batches, puree the tomato mixture in a blender on high speed for 30 seconds and pour into the cheesecloth. Cover, refrigerate, and drain overnight.

Reserve the strained tomato water, discarding the solids. You should have about 2 cups, depending on the ripeness of your tomatoes. To intensify the flavor of the tomato water, it can be reduced in a saucepan over medium heat. **Note:** Any extra tomato water can be frozen in ice cube trays. The individual cubes can then be defrosted and used in vinaigrettes or to season soups in lieu of lemon juice or vinegar. They can also be used as ice cubes in cocktails and savory sodas. Tomato water can also be seasoned with salt and herbs and enjoyed warm as a consommé.

Tomato Vinaigrette

⅓ gelatin sheet
⅓ cup Tomato Water
½ cup olive oil
1 teaspoon lemon juice
Salt
Cayenne pepper

Bloom the gelatin by placing it in ice water until pliable, about 10 minutes. In a saucepan, warm the tomato water. Squeeze the gelatin to remove excess moisture and melt it into the tomato water. Stirring frequently, chill the liquid over an ice bath until it thickens slightly. Combine the thickened tomato water, olive oil, and lemon juice. Season with salt and cayenne pepper to taste.

To Finish

28 heirloom cherry tomatoes, halved
Olive oil
Salt
Ground black pepper
1 pound fluke fillets
Bush basil leaves
Flowering basil

Toss the cherry tomatoes with olive oil and season with salt and pepper to taste. Slice the fluke diagonally against the grain into ⅛-inch slices. Brush the fluke with olive oil and season with salt and pepper to taste. Divide the fluke among 4 plates and arrange the tomatoes around the fluke. Spoon tomato vinaigrette onto the plate and garnish with basil leaves and flowers.

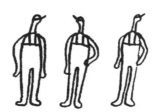

Poached Fluke
with Radishes and Favas

SERVES 4

Herb Fumet

1 pound fluke bones
1 tablespoon canola oil
¼ cup diced (⅛ inch) celery
¼ cup diced (⅛ inch) celery root
¼ cup thinly sliced shallot
2 tablespoons diced (⅛ inch) button mushroom
¼ cup dry vermouth
¼ cup white wine
8 cups ice cubes
1 cup cream
¼ cup Crème Fraîche (page 499)
3 sprigs mint
3 sprigs tarragon
2 sprigs lemon verbena
Lime juice
Salt
Cayenne pepper

Rinse the fluke bones of any blood and cut into 2-inch pieces. Dry the bones on paper towels. In a large straight-sided pan, heat the oil over high heat. Add the bones to the pan and sear for 30 to 45 seconds on each side. Remove from the pan and set aside. Reduce the heat to low and add the celery, celery root, shallot, and mushroom. Cover with a parchment paper lid and sweat the vegetables until tender, about 5 minutes. Uncover, raise the heat to medium, and deglaze with the dry vermouth. Reduce until the pan is almost dry. Add the white wine and reduce until almost dry, but be careful not to brown the vegetables. Return the bones to the pan and add the ice cubes. Bring to a simmer, skimming off any fat and impurities that rise to the top. Remove from the heat and cover with a lid; steep for 30 minutes. Strain the liquid through a chinois and return to the pan. Add the cream and bring to a simmer. Whisk in the crème fraîche and add the mint, tarragon, and lemon verbena. Let steep for 4 to 5 minutes and strain. Season with lime juice, salt, and cayenne pepper to taste.

Poached Fluke

6 cups Chicken Stock (page 499)
10 sprigs thyme
6 cloves garlic, crushed but kept whole
3 tablespoons cornstarch
Salt
1 (3-pound) fluke, filleted and skinned

Preheat the oven to 250°F. Bring the chicken stock to a simmer in a medium stockpot and add the thyme and garlic. Simmer over low heat for 5 minutes. In a small bowl, whisk together the cornstarch and 3 tablespoons of cold water. Whisk the cornstarch slurry into the chicken stock and allow it to simmer and thicken, about 5 minutes. Season with salt to taste and strain the liquid through a chinois into a baking dish. Allow it to cool to 145°F. Slice the fluke fillets into 4 portions and season with salt. Place the fillets in the liquid. Cover with parchment paper and transfer to the oven. Cook for about 15 minutes until the fish is opaque and the tip of a paring knife inserted into the flesh meets little resistance. Remove the fillets from the poaching liquid and allow them to rest for 2 minutes.

To Finish

½ cup shelled fava beans
24 baby radishes, green tops intact
2 tablespoons cold butter
Olive oil

In a medium saucepan, blanch the fava beans in boiling salted water until tender, 1 to 1½ minutes. Shock in ice water, and then peel away the outer skins. Blanch 16 of the baby radishes in the same water until tender, 4 to 5 minutes. Shock in ice water, trim the green tops, and then slice them in half. Hold the remaining 8 baby radishes by their greens and blanch only the radish in the boiling water until tender, 2 to 3 minutes. During the last 10 seconds of cooking, let the radish greens drop into the water. Transfer the blanched fava beans and all of the blanched radishes to a small sauté pan over low heat and add 2 tablespoons of herb fumet. Add the butter to the pan, tossing to glaze. Place each portion of poached fluke in the center of a plate. Evenly distribute the glazed fava beans and halved baby radishes on the plates. Place 2 blanched baby radishes with greens on each plate. Aerate the remaining herb fumet with a hand blender to create a foam and spoon onto each plate. Finish each dish with a drizzle of olive oil.

Foie Gras

Hudson Valley Foie Gras

The story of Hudson Valley Foie Gras spans over twenty years and encompasses the lives of two very different men who came together in a very fortuitous way. The tale begins with co-proprietor Michael Ginor, who graduated with an MBA from New York University before beginning his professional career on Wall Street. He left his corporate job in 1988 to serve in the Israeli Defense Forces. During his time in the Middle East, he was introduced to foie gras as simple street food, grilled on skewers over glowing coals; it was a snack that ultimately turned into an obsession. He came back to New York and began a tireless search for a match to the foie gras he had tasted in the Middle East. As he scoured the city, all he found were failed attempts. Even Manhattan's best restaurants were not serving good-quality foie gras. So eventually Michael decided to take it upon himself to become a world-class foie gras producer. But without any experience of his own raising geese, he knew he needed a partner.

Michael's business partner-to-be, Izzy Yanay, got his start working at an Israeli goose farm in the 1970s. The farm's mission was to produce an alternative to pork fat, but some aspects of its decentralized business model bothered Izzy. He sought first to improve upon the disease-prone geese, and began experimenting with ducks. Eventually, he cross-bred Muscovy and Peking ducks to yield hearty Moulard ducks that produced some of the most stunning foie gras he had ever seen.

Up until this time, low-quality goose livers had been regarded as peasant food and were given away to the farmers. However, Moulard ducks produced huge livers with obvious foie gras marketing potential. This left Izzy with a big question: "I had the material to bring every aspect of this business to one location, but where was I going to go?" With lingering apprehension, he emigrated from Israel to New York, found business partners, and settled upstate in an abandoned chicken coop. He found reassurance in Manhattan's flourishing restaurant scene, where chefs and diners alike demonstrated an appreciation for quality ingredients . . . but not yet for good foie gras.

And then along came the matchmaker. In 1985, Izzy was introduced to New York chef Ariane Daguin, whose father, André, was a famous chef in France and arguably the world's most influential connoisseur of foie gras. When Ariane tasted Izzy's domestic foie gras, she felt as though she had finally found a product that was on par with the one that her father cooked with in France. She left her job and launched D'Artagnan—a groundbreaking specialty meat and game purveyor based in New Jersey—with Izzy's foie gras as her initial product.

When Izzy had a falling out with his initial business partners in 1989, Ariane introduced him to Michael, whose financial strengths and unbridled enthusiasm for foie gras made him an ideal match. They continued to work with Moulard ducks and established Hudson Valley Foie Gras. Today, Izzy works behind the scenes while Michael's personality shines on the front line. Widely revered in the culinary world, the pair is rightfully proud of their trajectory. They make an unmatched local product with international appeal. Michael beams as he says, "Izzy and I will forever be known for introducing American chefs to foie gras."

Foie Gras Terrine with Red Wine

MAKES ONE 11 BY 3-INCH TERRINE, TO SERVE 8

1 (750-milliliter) bottle port
1 (750-milliliter) bottle red wine
3 Grade A Hudson Valley foie gras, about 1¾ pounds each
2 tablespoons salt
1 teaspoon sugar
¼ teaspoon ground white pepper
Brioche, sliced and toasted

Combine the port and red wine in a saucepan and reduce over medium-high heat by almost half to about 3½ cups. Transfer to a bowl and chill over an ice bath. Meanwhile, allow the foie gras to come to room temperature. Clean the foie gras by separating the lobes and removing the network of veins with a knife and a pair of tweezers, leaving the lobes as whole as possible. Place the cleaned foie gras in the reduced wine. Cover and marinate for 24 hours in the refrigerator. Remove the foie gras from the marinade, pat dry with paper towels, and season with the salt, sugar, and white pepper. Pack the seasoned foie gras into an 11 by 3-inch terrine mold, placing the largest pieces on the bottom and filling any gaps with the smaller pieces. Much of the fat will render off as it cooks, so the foie gras should be mounded high in the terrine. Cover with the lid and place the mold in a large, deep pan.

Preheat the oven to 275°F. Pour enough water into the pan to come halfway up the sides of the terrine. Transfer to the oven and bake the terrine for 40 to 45 minutes, rotating every 10 to 15 minutes. When the temperature in the center of the foie gras reaches 100°F and the temperature around the edges of the terrine reaches 120°F, remove the terrine from the oven and the water bath and allow it to cool to room temperature. Every 10 to 15 minutes while the terrine is resting, pour the fat out of one corner into a bowl and reserve. Before the foie gras has cooled completely, cut a piece of cardboard the same size as the terrine mold's interior and wrap it tightly in plastic wrap. Place the wrapped cardboard on top of the foie gras and evenly apply pressure. Weigh down the terrine by placing canned goods on top of the cardboard. Pour off any liquid that rises to the top. Transfer to the refrigerator and chill for 24 hours. Cover the bowl of rendered foie gras fat and refrigerate.

When the terrine has been weighted down for 24 hours, remove the weights and the cardboard and clean up the edges of the terrine with a paring knife and paper towel. At this point, the terrine should be solid and level. Return the terrine to the refrigerator if it has softened. Punch a hole down the edge of the hardened rendered foie gras fat. Pour any settled liquid out of the hole and discard. Rinse the block of solid fat under cold water, pat dry on paper towels, and transfer to a small saucepan. Bring the fat to a simmer over medium heat to clarify. Strain the liquid fat through a linen napkin or a quadruple layer of cheesecloth to remove any impurities. Allow the fat to cool to room temperature but do not let it solidify. Pour the clarified foie gras fat over the pressed terrine, creating a ⅛-inch layer. Transfer the terrine to the refrigerator and allow it to set for another 48 hours before serving. Serve slices of the foie gras terrine with toasted brioche. **Note:** This dish is also excellent accompanied with poached pears, Pickled Plums (page 362), and figs.

Smoked Foie Gras

SERVES 8

Smoked Foie Gras

1 Grade A Hudson Valley foie gras, about 2 pounds
1 pound salt

Completely bury the foie gras in the salt and allow to cure for 6 hours in the refrigerator. Rinse the salt off the foie gras and pat dry with paper towels. Allow the foie gras to dry, uncovered, in the refrigerator for 2 to 3 hours.

Put 2 cups of applewood chips in a bowl and cover with water. Remove the cooking grate from a charcoal grill and light 1 pound of charcoal in a chimney starter. When the coals are white hot, arrange them in a pile on one side of the grill bottom. Drain the wood chips and place on top of the hot charcoal. Return the cooking grate to the grill. Place the foie gras in a pan and set it over a pan of ice. When the chips begin to smoke, position the pan with the foie gras on the cool side of the grate (that is, not on top of the coals). Cover the grill and smoke for 20 to 25 minutes. Check frequently and add more wood chips if necessary to maintain heavy smoke. Remove the pan with the foie gras, wrap tightly with plastic wrap, and refrigerate for 3 hours before slicing and serving. **Note:** Any extra foie gras can be tightly wrapped and frozen for up to 1 week.

Peanut Puree

1 cup shelled roasted unsalted peanuts
¼ cup brown sugar
1 tablespoon sherry vinegar
Salt

Preheat the oven to 300°F. Place the peanuts on a baking sheet lined with parchment paper and toast lightly, 5 to 7 minutes. Cool to room temperature and transfer to a blender. Add the brown sugar, vinegar, and ½ cup of water to the blender and puree until smooth. Season with salt to taste. **Note:** Any leftover puree can be stored in the refrigerator, covered, for up to 1 week. Use as you would peanut butter, noting that this is a little sweeter and more acidic than conventional peanut butter.

Sherry Vinaigrette

1 cup olive oil
⅓ cup sherry vinegar
Salt

In a medium bowl, whisk together the olive oil and vinegar. Season with salt to taste. **Note:** Any extra sherry vinaigrette can be refrigerated for 1 to 2 days and used to dress greens.

To Finish

Sea salt
Ground black pepper
1 pound mixed market greens such as butterhead lettuce, green frill mustard, green and red kales, Lolla Rossa, and frisée
Pickled Red Pearl Onions (page 501)

Place the smoked foie gras in the freezer for 30 minutes, and then slice 12 thin sheets and roll the sheets into cylinders. Place 3 cylinders on each plate and season to taste with salt and pepper. Spoon 1 tablespoon of peanut puree onto each plate. Dress the greens with sherry vinaigrette and place the salad on the plates. Garnish with pickled red pearl onions and finish with sherry vinaigrette.

Foie Gras Torchon with Maple Syrup and Apples

MAKES 1 TORCHON, TO SERVE 8

Foie Gras

1 Grade A Hudson Valley foie gras, about 2 pounds, at room temperature
1 tablespoon salt
2 teaspoons Madeira
1 teaspoon Cognac
1 teaspoon sugar
½ teaspoon pink curing salt
½ teaspoon white pepper
4 teaspoons maple syrup

Separate the lobes and clean the foie gras by removing the network of veins with a knife and tweezers. Pass the foie gras through a tamis to remove any remaining veins. Place in a bowl and mix in the salt, Madeira, Cognac, sugar, curing salt, and white pepper with a spatula. Cover tightly with plastic wrap and refrigerate overnight.

Remove the foie gras from the refrigerator and allow it to soften at room temperature. Whip with a rubber spatula to re-emulsify the foie gras. Cut two 2½-foot by 12-inch pieces of plastic wrap. Overlap them on a flat work surface to create one 2½-foot by 18-inch piece with the long side facing you. Leaving 2 inches of clean plastic wrap at the bottom, spread the foie gras into a rough rectangle measuring 11 inches long by 3½ inches wide along the width of the plastic wrap, near the bottom. Using the plastic wrap, tightly roll the foie gras into a cylinder, pressing in the sides to compress them. The cylinder should now measure about 7½ by 2¾ inches. Tie the ends and pierce all over through the plastic wrap with a cake tester to remove any air pockets. Submerge in ice water and refrigerate for 5 hours to solidify. When the foie gras has set, unwrap the *torchon*. Working quickly, slice four ½-inch-thick discs from the *torchon*. Transfer these discs to a tray lined with wax paper and place in the freezer. Cut four ¼-inch-thick discs from the torchon and transfer them to the tray in the freezer. Remove one of the ½-inch discs from the freezer and scoop out a small cavity using a 25-millimeter (1-inch) Parisian scoop, being careful not to cut through to the bottom of the disc. Fill the cavity with 1 teaspoon of maple syrup and top with one of the ¼-inch discs. Return to the freezer. Repeat with the remaining discs. When all discs have been carved, filled, and topped, use a 2¼-inch round cutter to punch out the center. Remove the outer section of foie gras from the cutter and transfer the centers to the refrigerator until ready to serve. **Note:** Any leftover foie gras trimmings can be stored in the refrigerator for 2 to 3 days and spread on toast as a snack.

Gingerbread Crumble

1 cup butter
1 cup granulated sugar
½ cup dark brown sugar
2½ cups flour
1½ teaspoons ground ginger
1 teaspoon baking soda
1 teaspoon ground cinnamon
1 teaspoon ground cloves

Preheat the oven to 350°F. In a stand mixer fitted with the whisk attachment, cream together the butter and the sugars. Slowly add the dry ingredients. Once fully incorporated, roll the dough ¼ inch thick between 2 pieces of parchment paper. Transfer to a baking sheet, remove the top piece of parchment paper, and bake until golden brown, 12 to 14 minutes. Cool to room temperature. Break into pieces, and then grind in a food processer until the mixture resembles coarse sand. **Note:** Any leftover crumble can be stored in an airtight container at room temperature for up to 1 week and eaten with any leftover foie gras or used in lieu of graham cracker crumbs for cheesecake or pumpkin pie crusts.

Apple Puree

5 tablespoons grapeseed oil
5 Granny Smith apples, peeled, cored, and diced (¼ inch)
½ cup white wine
Salt

Heat 3 tablespoons of the oil in a sauté pan over medium-high heat. Add the apples, stirring to prevent them from achieving any color. Add the wine and cook for 2 minutes. Add ½ cup of water, cover with a parchment paper lid, and lower the heat. Checking frequently, cook until tender, 4 to 5 minutes. Transfer to a blender and puree until smooth, streaming in the remaining 2 tablespoons of oil. Pass the puree through a chinois, chill over an ice bath, and season with salt to taste.

To Finish

1 cup port
1 cup red wine
5 whole cloves
1 stick cinnamon
½ cup sugar
½ cup red wine vinegar
1 teaspoon salt
2 Gala apples
Baby mizuna
Sea salt

In a saucepan, combine the port and red wine with the cloves, cinnamon, sugar, vinegar, and salt. Reduce over high heat to ½ cup. Using a 20-millimeter (¾-inch) Parisian scoop, scoop 12 balls from the apples. Add the apples to the wine syrup and lower the heat to medium-low. Simmer for 1 minute, remove from the heat, and cool to room temperature in the poaching liquid. Spread apple puree on each of 4 plates and place 1 disc of foie gras on top. Spoon the crumble onto the plate. Place 3 apple balls around the foie gras and garnish with the baby mizuna. Finish with a few grains of sea salt.

Garlic

Keith's Farm

Born and raised in New Zealand, Keith Stewart had always been enamored with New York City. So immediately after obtaining an English degree in 1967, he packed his bags, jumped on a plane, and moved to America. He wasted no time taking on New York, driving a cab, playing poker in the city's clubs, and beginning a career as a writer. Keith enjoyed this eclectic lifestyle for ten years before he met Brooklyn-born art teacher Flavia Bacarella. They married in 1986 and moved to their current home in Orange County without yet knowing where the next twenty years would take them.

Keith's affair with garlic began on an ordinary day over two decades ago, when an unfamiliar variety called Rocambole was presented to Flavia as a gift. It was from an elderly Italian neighbor who had smuggled it in from Calabria. As documented in the couple's farming memoir, Keith explains that many garlic growers "learn that they have entered into a relationship with a plant that will not be easily cast off." Immediately attracted to the plant's "stately appearance in the field . . . its hardiness, its ancient lineage, and the way it comports itself in this world," Keith knew that he had found his passion. These strong feelings could not be inspired by ordinary garlic varieties—only the unique Rocambole warranted such devotion.

An extraordinary allium, the Rocambole has a very specific structure. The stalk is a working of eleven layered leaves that form the bulb's exterior, which is thick and nearly woodlike—ideal for prolonged storage. In late October, Keith studs his mineral-rich field with the sweet, spicy, and pungent cloves. They are the source of the following year's harvest, resting underground during the winter and sprouting in the spring. Keith explains that after the summer solstice, as the days begin to get shorter, the leaves finish growing. The plant, sensing this, turns its focus to bulb formation. Harvesting occurs one month later, when half of the leaves turn yellow. Once gathered, the garlic is cured so it can be readily available for use throughout the winter. As in the Italian countryside, Keith's garlic is braided and then hung in the barn's dark lower cellar so it can dry into a sort of woven mosaic, creating an inviting fragrance that permeates the air.

Flavia explains with a girlish smile how much the couple enjoys garlic farming together. Keith says, "the organic life keeps you young," as he shoots a smile toward his wife. Keith's gift for growing garlic is as enchanting as this heirloom variety itself. He says, "Once bitten by the garlic bug, many growers develop a lifelong attachment . . . these are living things, and they respond to external forces." In fact, a variety of energies act on his garlic: the land's serenity, Flavia's lightheartedness, and Keith's patience.

Baked Garlic with Fresh Curd and Peas

SERVES 4

Baked Garlic

4 heads garlic
3 tablespoons butter

Preheat the oven to 325°F. Cut each head of garlic in half horizontally. Melt the butter in a medium sauté pan over medium-high heat until foamy. Turn down the heat to medium and add the garlic, cut side down. Sauté until golden brown, 2 to 3 minutes. Turn the garlic over so the seared side is facing up, and transfer the sauté pan to the oven. Bake until the garlic is tender, 16 to 19 minutes. Reserve the garlic and the browned butter.

To Finish

1 cup shelled English peas
¼ cup sugar snap peas
2 tablespoons Chicken Stock (page 499)
2 tablespoons cold butter
1 cup Fresh Milk Curd (page 305)
Bread Crisps (page 498)
Garlic flowers
Pea tendrils

Bring a medium saucepan of salted water to a boil. Add the English peas and cook until tender, 2 to 3 minutes. Transfer to a bowl of ice water. Blanch the sugar snap peas until tender, 3 to 4 minutes, and transfer to the ice water. Once the English and sugar snap peas are cool, drain them. In a sauté pan, bring the peas and the chicken stock to a simmer. Add the butter and reduce the liquid to glaze the peas. Spoon fresh curd onto each of 4 plates. Place the baked garlic on top of the curd and arrange the peas around the garlic. Garnish with bread crisps, garlic flowers, and pea tendrils. Spoon the reserved browned butter onto the plate to finish.

Garlic Soup with Prawns and Favas

SERVES 4

Garlic Soup

1 cup peeled garlic cloves
2 teaspoons butter
1 tablespoon diced (⅛ inch) celery root
1 tablespoon diced (⅛ inch) fennel
1 tablespoon diced (⅛ inch) shallot
⅓ cup white wine
1 cup diced (⅛ inch) fingerling potatoes
¾ cup half-and-half
2 sprigs thyme
¼ cup cream
Lime juice
Salt
Cayenne pepper

Place the garlic cloves in a small saucepan and cover with cold water. Bring to a boil, and then pour off the water. Cover again with cold water, bring to a boil, and then pour off the water. Repeat this process 4 more times to reduce the bitterness of the garlic.

In a medium stockpot, melt the butter over medium-low heat. Add the celery root, fennel, and shallot and sweat for 5 minutes. Add the garlic cloves and continue to sweat for 3 minutes. Add the white wine and raise the heat to high. Reduce the wine by half, to just under 3 tablespoons. Add the potatoes, half-and-half, thyme, and 2½ cups of water. Lower the heat to medium-low and simmer until the vegetables and potatoes are tender, 25 to 30 minutes. Remove and discard the thyme and transfer the soup to a blender. Blend on high, and then pass through a chinois. Whisk in the cream and season with lime juice, salt, and cayenne pepper to taste.

Fava Bean and Prawn Ragout

2 cups shelled fava beans
½ cup Chicken Stock (page 499)
12 colossal (U-10) prawns (just over 1 pound total), shelled and deveined
4 tablespoons cold butter
Salt

Bring a medium saucepan of salted water to a boil. Add the fava beans and blanch until tender, 1 to 1½ minutes. Shock in ice water and peel away the outer skins. In a medium sauté pan over medium-low heat, bring the stock to a simmer and add the prawns. Add the butter and glaze the prawns, cooking for 45 seconds to 1 minute. Flip the prawns, add the fava beans, and cook for another 45 seconds to 1 minute. Season with salt to taste.

To Finish

Garlic flowers
Mint leaves

Divide the fava bean and prawn ragout evenly among 4 bowls. Aerate the garlic soup with a hand blender until frothy and pour over the ragout. Garnish with garlic flowers and mint leaves.

Grains

Cayuga Pure Organics

Waist-high in a field of wheat, Erick Smith picks a stalk of grain, chews on the end, and determines that it is underripe. As he launches into an explanation of how moisture impacts the harvest, his bookish charm makes it easy to imagine Erick as a professor or scholar. In fact, he did have vacillating courtships with both academia and farming, resulting, as he says, in a "schizophrenic feeling" as he wavered between the two professions. Ultimately, after eight years of teaching at the University of Illinois, he decided to pursue farming. Now well into his sixties, Erick's success with wheat and other grains promises to keep him in the fields for the foreseeable future. He is, quite simply, "thrilled to be part of the local food movement," working with crops that have been part of this area's history for hundreds of years. New York has long been densely sown with a wide variety of cereal grains. In the late 1700s, Rochester was dubbed the "Flour City," and New York farmers, including Erick, are celebrating that history by replanting heirloom grains and creating locally ground flours.

Erick and his wife, Debora, began farming when they relocated to the Finger Lakes and posted a "U-Pick" sign in their strawberry field. In 2003, after seventeen years of growing strawberries, Erick connected with another academic-turned-farmer, Dan Lathwell, and launched Cayuga Pure Organics. They addressed the shortage of local grains by growing pesticide-free feed for New York cattle. Two years later, Ithaca's GreenStar Cooperative Market approached the duo in search of local beans. Erick was intrigued, saying, "This really got us interested in producing more than cattle feed." In 2008, Manhattan's Greenmarket invited them to sell their beans, grains, and flours. "It was a big step as well as an exciting step. But it required a lot of change," Erick remembers. It was around that same time that Greg Mall joined the team to run Farmer Ground, the milling arm of the operation.

Seasonal chills make the Northeast ideal for growing hard red wheat. Of Cayuga's spring and winter varieties, Erick was particularly drawn to the heirloom Red Fife, America's first bread wheat. Its flavor makes up for its small and inconsistent yields. This ground-to-order flour is ideal for artisan baking: "A small-scale baker can feel our product and know what to do with it. Large scale bakeries that only run on formulas cannot use it." Cayuga's portfolio also includes unique whole-grain products like Arabic freekeh, which is produced by roasting wheat while it's still green, or underripe, for an uncommonly earthy and smoky result. However, Erick's all-time favorite is emmer, or Italian farro, a hulled wheat native to the Middle East that grows beautifully in the Finger Lakes region. The revival of these grains is a testament to Cayuga Pure Organics' commitment to revitalizing a historical wheat culture that has its roots firmly planted in New York.

Wheat Berry Salad with Yogurt, Cucumber, and Melon

SERVES 4

Labne

2 cups plain Greek-style yogurt
Sea salt
Ground black pepper
2 cups olive oil

Place the yogurt in a quadruple layer of cheesecloth and suspend over a container in the refrigerator for 48 hours, allowing moisture to drain from the yogurt. Remove the yogurt from the cheesecloth. Using your hands, roll it into 1-inch balls and place in a single layer in a container. Season with sea salt and black pepper to taste. Cover with the olive oil. **Note:** Labne can be stored in the refrigerator for up to 1 month. It can be eaten alongside grilled lamb or with cucumber salads.

Wheat Berry Salad

1 cup wheat berries
¼ cup sliced chives
1 tablespoon diced (⅛ inch) shallot
2 tablespoons Lemon Vinaigrette (page 500)
1 teaspoon lemon juice
Salt

Rinse the wheat berries thoroughly. In a medium saucepan, cover the wheat berries with 4 cups of water and bring to a simmer over low heat. Cook until the wheat berries are tender, 2 hours. Drain any excess water and cool to room temperature. Transfer the cooked wheat berries to a medium mixing bowl and add the chives and shallot. Dress with the lemon vinaigrette and lemon juice and season with salt to taste.

Cucumber Relish

1 English cucumber, peeled and finely diced
1 teaspoon salt
White balsamic vinegar

Season the cucumber with salt and hang in a quadruple layer of cheesecloth for 1 hour. Discard the liquid. Season the drained cucumber generously with vinegar.

To Finish

2 Easter egg radishes
¼ cantaloupe, peeled and seeded
¼ honeydew, peeled and seeded
¼ cup plain Greek-style yogurt
Salt
Confit Cherry Tomatoes (page 499)
4 baby radishes
4 cucamelons, halved
Flowering cucumbers
Flowering mint
Red-veined sorrel

Using a mandoline, thinly slice the Easter egg radishes, the cantaloupe, and the honeydew. Season the yogurt with salt and spoon 1 tablespoon onto each of 4 plates. Divide the wheat berry salad among the plates. Arrange the radish, cantaloupe, and honeydew slices around the salad, as well as the confit cherry tomatoes, baby radishes, and cucamelon halves. Garnish each plate with 3 balls of labne, flowering cucumbers, flowering mint, and sorrel.

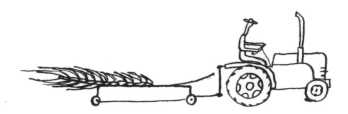

Farro with Corn, Cockscomb, and Chicken Oysters

SERVES 4

Farro

1 cup farro
4 cups Chicken Stock (page 499)

Rinse the farro thoroughly and place in a medium saucepan. Cover with the stock and bring to a simmer. Cook until the farro is tender and the stock is absorbed, 40 to 45 minutes.

Shallot Confit

3 tablespoons diced (⅛ inch) shallot
½ cup olive oil

Place the shallot in a small saucepan and cover with the oil. Bring to a simmer and lower the heat. Cook the shallot until tender, about 10 minutes.

Cockscombs

6 cockscombs
Salt
5 sprigs thyme
1 clove garlic, crushed but kept whole
4 cups duck fat, melted

Preheat the oven to 250°F. To cure the cockscombs, submerge them in salt for 30 minutes. Rinse the cockscombs thoroughly and pat dry. Place in a baking dish with the thyme and garlic and cover with the duck fat. Cover the dish with aluminum foil and transfer to the oven. Cook until tender, about 3 hours. Cool to room temperature. Remove the cockscombs from the dish with a slotted spoon. Reserve the duck fat for another confit preparation or to make French fries. Pat the cockscombs dry on paper towels. Cut 2 cockscombs into ¼-inch pieces; leave the remaining 4 whole.

Corn Foam

1 tablespoon grapeseed oil
1 cup fresh corn kernels
3 tablespoons diced (¼ inch) shallot
¼ cup plus 1 tablespoon white wine
½ cup Chicken Stock (page 499)
1 cup Corn Pudding (page 499)
2 cups cream
Lime juice
Salt
Cayenne pepper

Heat the oil in a medium saucepan over medium heat and add the corn and shallot. Sweat until the corn is tender and the shallot is translucent, 3 to 4 minutes. Add the white wine and reduce until the pan is almost dry. Add the chicken stock and reduce by half. Add the corn pudding and bring to a boil. Add the cream and bring to a gentle simmer before removing from the heat. Strain through a chinois and season with lime juice, salt, and cayenne pepper to taste. **Note:** Any leftover corn foam can be used to garnish summer soups. Simply aerate it with a hand blender just before using.

Farro and Corn Ragout

1 cup White Balsamic Pickling Liquid (page 501)
1 cup plus 4 teaspoons sweet corn kernels
Farro
2¼ cups Chicken Stock (page 499)
½ cup Corn Pudding (page 499)
Shallot Confit, drained
Diced cockscomb from making Cockscombs
2 teaspoons sliced chives
Salt

In a small saucepan, bring the white balsamic pickling liquid to a boil. Pour it over the 4 teaspoons of corn kernels and allow to come to room temperature. Drain, reserving 2 teaspoons of the pickling liquid. Place the remaining 1 cup of corn kernels, the farro, and the chicken stock in a medium saucepan and cook over medium heat until the corn is tender, 3 to 4 minutes. Add the corn pudding, shallot confit, and diced cockscomb. Continue cooking over medium heat until the consistency resembles a risotto, about 5 minutes. Remove from the heat and fold in the pickled corn, reserved 2 teaspoons of pickling liquid, and the chives. Season with salt to taste.

To Finish

2 teaspoons canola oil
16 chicken oysters, skin on
Salt
Purslane
Young agretti

Heat the oil in a large sauté pan over high heat. Add the chicken oysters skin side down and sear for 2 minutes, pressing gently. Pour off the rendered fat, turn down the heat to low, and continue cooking until the skin is crispy, 2 to 2½ minutes. Flip the chicken oysters and cook for 1 minute. Remove from the heat and allow to rest for 1 minute. Season with salt to taste. Divide the farro and corn ragout among 4 bowls and top each with 4 chicken oysters and 1 whole cockscomb. Aerate the corn foam with a hand blender and spoon around the dish. Garnish with purslane and agretti.

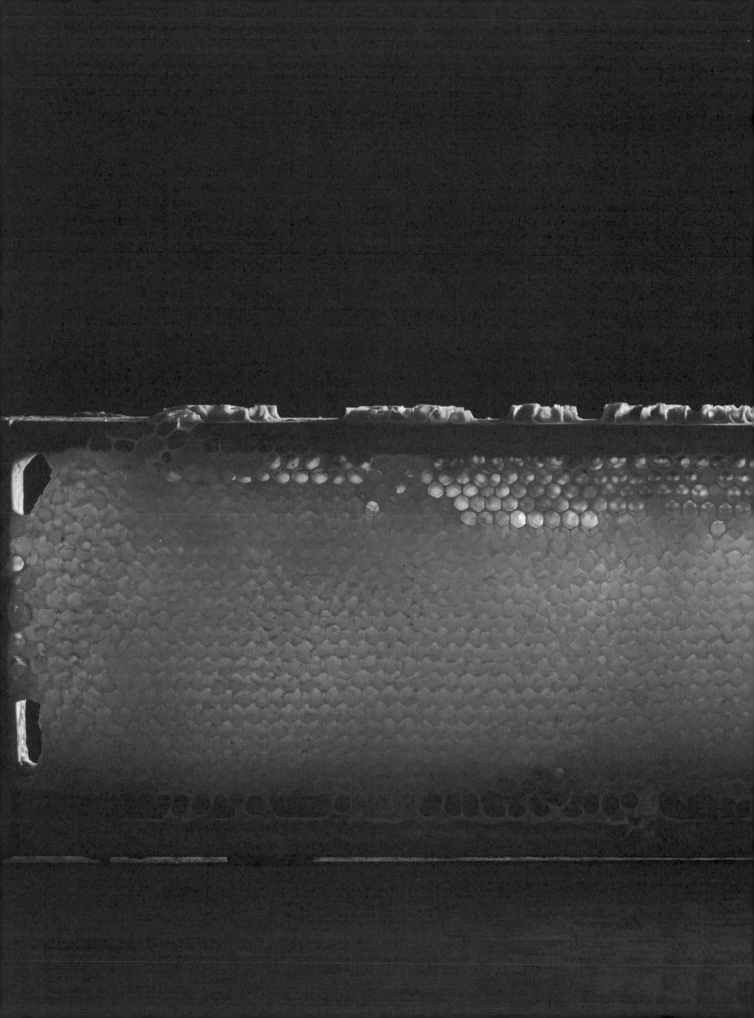

Tremblay Apiaries

"Bees make their combs by secreting a waxy substance from their sides, chewing on it, and then creating perfect equilateral triangles from their antennae and mouths." That is enough to impress most, but Al Tremblay continues in awe, "They do it in total darkness, and it is perfect. Perfect!" Bees exchange plants' nectar in a back-and-forth pattern, essentially swapping nectar amongst each other to make a more saturated liquid. Then the hive's natural airflow further evaporates the moisture. The ultimate result is one of nature's most amazing gifts: honey.

Al's bee yards, home to a diverse array of native New York flora, are scattered throughout the thirty-mile radius that surrounds his honey processing center in the Finger Lakes. "Monoculture does not work for bees. Just like humans, they need variety," Al says. As a seasoned apiculturist, Al finds it hard to not get lost in his work. He explains, "It's one of those things that, if you have the interest, you catch it with your fingers, and then it crawls right up your sleeve."

Al's interest was caught when he was eighteen years old. He had a conversation with a man who had left his position as a school principal to work as a custodian so that he would have more time to focus on his passion—bees. "I was fascinated with what he had to say. I was hooked." That semester, at Cornell University, Al spent all of his time at the Dyce Laboratory for Honey Bee Research. Now, forty years later, he is still at it.

Al's total colony population, spread across hundreds of hives, fluctuates from twenty thousand in the winter to over fifty thousand in the summer. Dressed in a white suit and mesh hat and armed with a cold smoker, Al's hands remain uncovered. He supports glove-free beekeeping, saying, "You just need to be stubborn in this business." Knowledge of the hives' complex ecosystems is just as necessary as protective gear to successful beekeeping. Al puffs smoke into the hives, which resemble stacked wooden crates, each with removable honeycombed panels. The smoke frightens the bees, which makes them eat, and in turn, their mood mellows. This allows Al to check on his bees and harvest their honey.

Tremblay Apiaries' products are stunning. Single-flower dominant offerings are made from linden tree flowers, goldenrod, and locust blooms. Raspberry honey is mildly fruity, while multiflora rose honey is seductively fragrant. One of Al's most invigorating blends is Ambrosia, which combines several beneficial bee-related tonics: fall flower honey, pollen, tree propolis, and royal jelly, a nutrient consumed only by the young and the queen.

Although bees are governed by a matriarchal system, Al Tremblay is the king of this apiary. He is as ardently caring and supportive as he is demanding. But his values are transparent, as illustrated by a rule of conduct that is posted on a pegboard at the apiary. It reminds his team to work with pride and in harmony with one another other, a principle derived directly from his bees, one that has made the little creatures such a successful and productive species.

Honey Marshmallows

YIELDS 48 MARSHMALLOWS

10 sheets gelatin
1½ cups sugar
½ cup plus 2 tablespoons honey
½ cup glucose
3 egg whites
Confectioners' sugar
Bee pollen

Spray a 9 by 13-inch baking pan with nonstick vegetable cooking spray. Bloom the gelatin by soaking the sheets in a bowl of ice water for 10 minutes until pliable. Combine the granulated sugar, honey, and glucose with ½ cup of water in a heavy-bottomed saucepan over medium-high heat and bring to a boil, stirring to dissolve the sugar. Continue cooking without stirring until the mixture reaches the soft-ball stage (240°F.) Meanwhile, place the egg whites in the bowl of a stand mixer fitted with the whisk attachment. When the sugar syrup has reached 230°F, begin to whip the egg whites at medium speed to medium peaks. When the sugar syrup reaches 240°F, gradually stream it into the egg whites with the mixer running on medium speed. As soon as all of the syrup has been incorporated, increase the speed to high. Squeeze the gelatin to remove any excess moisture, add to the warm meringue, and continue to whip until the mixture is slightly cool but still spreadable. Pour into the prepared pan and smooth with an offset spatula. Cool at room temperature. Wrap with plastic wrap and store overnight at room temperature, keeping the marshmallow away from moisture. The next day, spray a knife with nonstick vegetable cooking spray and cut the marshmallow into 1½-inch pieces. Turn out the marshmallows onto a cutting board dusted with confectioners' sugar. Coat on all sides with confectioners' sugar, and then sprinkle with bee pollen.

Milk and Honey

SERVES 4

Milk Ice

3¼ cups milk
½ cup plus 1 tablespoon cream
½ cup plus 1 tablespoon powdered milk
⅓ cup sugar
2 tablespoons glucose syrup
1 teaspoon salt

In a small saucepan over medium-low heat, reduce 2 cups of the milk to ⅔ cup. Combine the reduced milk with the remaining ingredients in a blender and blend until smooth. Strain through a chinois then chill over an ice bath. Freeze the mixture in an ice cream machine. **Note:** Store in the freezer for up to 1 month.

Honey-Oatmeal Crumble

½ cup plus 2 tablespoons butter, softened
⅓ cup sugar
¼ cup honey
1 teaspoon salt
½ teaspoon vanilla extract
1 cup plus 1 tablespoon flour
½ cup old-fashioned rolled oats
¼ teaspoon baking soda

Preheat the oven to 300°F. In a stand mixer fitted with the paddle attachment, cream together the butter, sugar, honey, salt, and vanilla. Add the flour, oats, and baking soda, mixing until just combined. Turn the dough out onto a piece of parchment paper and roll to ¼ inch thick. Transfer to a rimmed baking sheet and bake until golden brown, about 15 minutes. Lower the oven temperature to 150°F and continue to dry for 30 minutes, checking the dough to make sure it does not get too dark. Cool to room temperature, and then break it into small pieces. Store in an airtight container for up to 2 days.

Honey Brittle

1 cup sugar
¼ cup butter
2 tablespoons honey
1½ teaspoons salt
½ teaspoon baking soda

Line a 13 by 18-inch rimmed baking sheet with parchment paper. In a medium straight-sided sauté pan bring the sugar, butter, honey, and ¼ cup water to a boil. Cook over medium-high heat to a light caramel, 2 to 3 minutes. Add the salt and baking soda and mix well. Pour the brittle in a thin layer onto the prepared baking sheet. Allow to cool completely to room temperature, and then break into small pieces. Store in an airtight container for up to 2 days.

Dehydrated Milk Foam

2 cups milk
5 tablespoons glucose syrup

Preheat the oven to 150°F. Line a 9 by 13-inch rimmed baking sheet with acetate or a silicone baking mat. In a medium saucepan, heat the milk and glucose to just under a boil. Remove from the heat and froth with a hand blender. With a large spoon, scoop the foam onto the prepared baking sheet, discarding any liquid. Dry in the oven for 8 to 9 hours. Allow the foam to cool, and then break it into small pieces. Store in an airtight container for up to 2 days.

To Finish

Buckwheat honey

Place a small amount of the dehydrated milk foam, honey brittle, and honey-oatmeal crumble in each of 4 small bowls. Spoon a large quenelle of milk ice on top. Drizzle lines of buckwheat honey across the top of the quenelle.

Lamb

Sheep Meadow Farm

The winding roads of Fort Ann, New York, culminate in a hamlet surrounded by mountains offering an epic view of nearby Black Mountain. Here in Fort Ann, perched on a hilltop, sits Sheep Meadow Farm. From this vantage point, Paul Paulsen and his wife, Cindy, keep a keen eye out for visitors making their way up to the farm. With a hearty handshake and a genuinely warm smile, Paul and Cindy greet their guests.

Before starting Sheep Meadow Farm, Paul and Cindy had a thriving flower company in Connecticut. Upon selling it in 1987, they discovered an overgrown two-hundred-acre expanse in Fort Ann covered in ten years' worth of weeds. It would be a perfect new home for the couple seeking a change. They looked beyond the barn's dilapidated condition and were inspired. Cindy is still surprised at their late-blooming ambition: "We were old when we started this. We thought about having dairy cows but decided lambs were more manageable." They took an entrepreneurial risk, and it paid off. Sheep Meadow Farm has now been producing lamb of extraordinary quality for nearly a quarter of a century.

The Paulsens' panoramic view from their hilltop allows them to oversee their flock of 150 ewes. Dorset purebreds or crosses give birth in late winter—just the right timing for spring lamb. Newborns remain in the barn consuming mother's milk, grain, and hay until they are sold, at which time the ewes go to pasture. Paul explains this practice, saying, "You don't want the babies in the field only eating grass because they will not develop the correct muscle structure." When young lambs achieve the optimal weight of approximately 54 pounds, they are entrusted to Vermont Quality Meats to be delivered to the high-end kitchens of chefs who value Paul and Cindy's lamb for its exceptional flavor.

Lamb Meatballs

SERVES 4

Tomato Confit

4 Roma tomatoes
2 tablespoons olive oil
5 sprigs thyme
2 cloves garlic, peeled and thinly sliced
Salt

Preheat the oven to 200°F. Bring a pot of salted water to a boil. Using a paring knife, score the tomatoes with shallow Xs on the bottom. Add the tomatoes to the boiling water and cook for 10 seconds. Transfer to an ice bath. When cool, peel the skin from the tomatoes, remove the core, slice in half, and remove the seeds. Combine the olive oil, thyme, garlic, and salt in a bowl. Toss the tomatoes in the oil mixture and place them cut side down on a rimmed baking sheet lined with parchment paper. Bake in the oven for 1½ hours, and then flip over and return to the oven for an additional 1½ hours. They should be the texture of soft raisins.

Garlic Chips

1 clove elephant garlic, peeled
1 cup milk
Canola oil
Salt

Trim off the top and bottom of the garlic clove. Thinly slice the garlic on a mandoline. In a saucepan, bring the garlic and the milk to a simmer. Remove from the heat and steep for 10 minutes. Strain the garlic and discard the milk. Rinse the garlic under cold water and pat dry. In a small sauté pan, heat the oil to 275°F over medium-high heat. Fry the garlic until pale blond, about 45 seconds. Remove the chips with a slotted spoon and drain on paper towels. Season with salt to taste.

Spiced Lamb Sauce

2 tablespoons olive oil
1 tablespoon coriander seeds
1 teaspoon cumin seeds
1 teaspoon paprika
1 cup Lamb Jus (page 500)
Salt
Sugar

In a medium saucepan, heat the oil over medium-high heat. Add the coriander and cook for 20 seconds. Add the cumin and cook for 20 seconds. Add the paprika and cook for 20 seconds. Add the lamb jus and bring to a simmer. Remove from the heat, cover, and steep for 20 minutes. Strain through a chinois and season with salt and sugar to taste.

Lamb Meatballs

6 teaspoons olive oil
3 sprigs thyme
3 cloves garlic, crushed but kept whole
¼ cup diced (⅛ inch) onion
¼ cup diced (⅛ inch) red pepper
¼ cup diced (⅛ inch) zucchini
12 ounces ground lamb belly
4 ounces ground lean lamb meat
2 eggs
½ cup bread crumbs
3 tablespoons grated Sprout Creek Farm Ouray
**   (a raw cow's milk cheese similar to a dry cheddar)**
2 teaspoons thinly sliced mint
1½ teaspoons salt
Pinch of cayenne pepper

Preheat the oven to 300°F. In a small sauté pan, heat 2 teaspoons of the oil over medium heat. Add a thyme sprig and garlic clove. Add the onion and cook until soft, 2 to 3 minutes. Repeat with the red pepper and zucchini, using the remaining oil, thyme, and garlic, in separate sauté pans. Remove the vegetables from the pans and cool in the refrigerator. Remove the thyme and the garlic and combine the sautéed vegetables with the remaining ingredients, mixing thoroughly. Roll the mixture into 8 meatballs measuring 1½ inches in diameter. Line a 9 by 13-inch rimmed baking sheet with parchment paper and arrange the meatballs in even rows ½ inch apart. Bake for 20 to 25 minutes.

To Finish

4 small to medium-sized Italian eggplants
¼ cup olive oil
Salt
8 Taggiasca olives
Flowering mint
Mint leaves

Slice a ½-inch plank from the center of each eggplant. In a large sauté pan, heat the oil over high heat. Add the eggplant planks and cook until caramelized, 2 to 3 minutes. Flip the planks over and cook for an additional 2 to 3 minutes. Season with salt to taste, cut each plank in half lengthwise, and place 2 halves on each of 4 plates. Place 2 lamb meatballs on the eggplant and position 2 pieces of tomato confit between the meatballs. Arrange 2 olives on the plate and spoon the spiced lamb sauce over the eggplant and the meatballs. Top the meatballs with the garlic chips and garnish with flowering mint and mint leaves.

Lamb Rack with Cucumber Yogurt

SERVES 4

Cucumber Yogurt

1½ cups plain Greek-style yogurt
2 cucumbers
Salt
2 teaspoons lemon juice
1 tablespoon olive oil
½ clove garlic
1½ tablespoons chopped dill

Line a colander with a quadruple layer of cheesecloth and pour the yogurt into the cheesecloth. Suspend over a large bowl and refrigerate for 48 hours, allowing the moisture to drain from the yogurt.

Peel and grate the cucumbers on a box grater. Season with 1 teaspoon of salt and hang in a quadruple layer of cheesecloth to drain excess moisture, about 1 hour. Measure 1 cup of the drained yogurt and reserve the rest for another use. Combine the cup of yogurt and the drained cucumbers in a medium bowl. Stir in the lemon juice and olive oil. Grate the garlic on a Microplane grater into the mixture and fold in the chopped dill. Mix well and season with salt to taste.

Roasted Lamb Rack

1 tablespoon canola oil
1 lamb rack (about 2¼ pounds), frenched and tied
Salt
2 tablespoons butter
5 sprigs thyme
1 clove garlic, crushed but kept whole

Preheat the oven to 300°F. Heat a large cast-iron skillet over high heat. Season the lamb rack generously with salt. Place the rack in the skillet fat side down and sear over high heat until browned, 2½ to 3 minutes. Turn and sear the bottom for 1 minute. Turn the rack back onto the fat side and add the butter, thyme, and garlic. Baste the rack with the butter for 2½ to 3 minutes. Transfer the lamb rack fat side up to a wire rack set in a rimmed baking sheet and roast in the oven for 10 minutes. Turn the lamb rack over, baste with butter, and return to the oven for another 10 minutes. Remove the lamb rack from the oven, turn it back over, and baste once more. Roast in the oven for another 10 to 15 minutes, until the internal temperature reaches 130° to 135°F. Let the lamb rack rest for 10 to 15 minutes before slicing. Serve with the cucumber yogurt and heirloom tomatoes.

Lettuce

Blue Moon Acres

Jim and Kathy Lyons of Blue Moon Acres are passionate about lettuce's potential beyond its usual second-fiddle status. They honor each leafy green's individual character—the bite of arugula, the zest of sorrel, the snap of fresh romaine—and see each type as able to both stand on its own and complement a wide variety of flavors and preparations. As Kathy weeds a patch of intensely sweet sucrine lettuce, she talks about her perspective on the direction of attitudes toward food: "There is a new trend for simple and real food." Blue Moon Acres is riding the momentum of that movement with extraordinary success. Focused on just a sliver of the world of produce, they strive to perfect their craft and deliver the most impeccable greens to some of the most demanding restaurants, caterers, and home cooks in the greater New York area.

Jim met Kathy while studying natural healing at the Kushi Institute in Massachusetts. Kathy was trying to break from her family's farming tradition and follow a different career path. "I never wanted to farm," she explains, "but that's all Jim wanted to do." In 1992, with forty subscribers and one greenhouse, the couple established their CSA in Buckingham, Pennsylvania. Initially, they focused on microgreens but soon added full-grown lettuces to their repertoire. In 2008, they expanded to Pennington, New Jersey, giving them more land to accommodate an expanding portfolio of all things leafy and green.

Jim, who has the demeanor of a mad scientist and a deep familiarity with macrobiotics, shares some of his farming philosophy: "Farming is like cooking. You want some creativity but first you need to get the systems down." For example, he explains that at larger farms, soil is seen as secondary to the plants themselves. But Jim knows that in order for lettuces to develop proper flavor, they require nutrient-rich soil: "Organic matter is the living portion of soil. You need to feed it to feed the plants." The Lyons are committed to a unique and sophisticated compost program; a mixture of homemade fertilizer, peat, nitrates, and sulfates is tailor-made for their delicate plants. And the benefits of this attentive approach to farming are obvious: statuesque red romaine, tightly compacted Bibb, and tiny Baby Gem lettuces thrive in topsoils that are markedly vibrant, even to the untrained eye. The harvested results resonate with a singular combination of personality and brawn that is matched by the farmers who nurtured the greens to life.

Braised Lettuce Salad

SERVES 4

Lettuce Puree

24 large romaine lettuce leaves
2 tablespoons olive oil
⅔ cup thinly sliced shallot
⅓ cup thinly sliced celery
Salt
Cayenne pepper

Cut the stem out of each lettuce leaf. Thinly slice the stems, reserving 1⅓ cups. You should have about 4 cups of tightly packed greens remaining. Bring a pot of salted water to a boil and add the greens and cook until tender, 3 to 4 minutes. Transfer to an ice bath. In a medium sauté pan, heat the olive oil over medium heat. Add the shallot and celery and sweat until tender, 3 to 4 minutes. Add the romaine stems and ⅓ cup water and cover with a parchment paper lid. Cook until tender, about 4 minutes. Remove from the heat and spread in a single layer on a 9 by 13-inch baking sheet lined with parchment paper. Chill in the refrigerator until cold. Transfer the blanched lettuce greens and the chilled stems to a blender and puree until smooth. Strain through a chinois and season with salt and cayenne pepper to taste.

Buttermilk Dressing

½ cup Crème Fraîche (page 499)
½ cup buttermilk
Lime juice
Salt
Cayenne pepper

In a small bowl, combine the crème fraîche and buttermilk, whisking until smooth. Season with lime juice, salt, and cayenne pepper to taste.

To Finish

2 tablespoons cold butter
1 tablespoon canola oil
4 romaine lettuce hearts
½ cup Chicken Stock (page 499)
Baby romaine
Dandelion greens
Olive oil
Salt

In a medium sauté pan over medium heat, warm 1 tablespoon of the butter with the canola oil until foamy. Add the romaine hearts and cook for 1 minute. Flip and cook for another minute. Add the chicken stock and cover with a parchment paper lid. Cook over medium heat until tender, 6 to 7 minutes. Remove the parchment paper, add the remaining 1 tablespoon of butter, and cook until reduced to a glaze. Spoon the lettuce puree onto a plate. Place 1 braised romaine heart in the center of the plate. Aerate the buttermilk dressing with a hand blender and spoon the frothy dressing onto the plate. Toss baby romaine and dandelion greens in olive oil and season with salt to taste. Garnish with the dressed baby romaine and dandelion greens. Repeat with the remaining ingredients, to serve 4.

Lettuce Salad with Button Mushrooms and Smoked Pork

SERVES 4

Smoked Pork Jerky

1 (8-ounce) piece pork loin
1¾ cups salt

Trim any excess fat off of the pork loin. Combine the salt with 1 gallon of water in a large pot and bring to a boil over high heat. Cool the brine over an ice bath. Place the pork in a large nonreactive container and pour in the brine. Cover and refrigerate for 8 to 9 hours. Remove the pork from the brine, cut into 1½-inch cubes, and place on a wire cooling rack. Soak 6 cups of applewood chips in water and preheat the oven to 170°F.

Remove the cooking grate from a charcoal grill and light 8 cups of charcoal in a chimney starter. When the coals are white-hot, arrange them in a pile on one side of the grill bottom. Drain the wood chips and place on top of the hot charcoal. Return the cooking grate to the grill. When the chips begin to smoke, position the roasting rack with the pork on the cool side of the grate (that is, not on top of the coals). Cover the grill and smoke for 30 to 45 minutes. Check frequently and add more wood chips if necessary to maintain heavy smoke. Remove the pork from the grill and place in the oven for 9 to 10 hours, until the pork is shriveled and dry. Remove from the oven and cool in the refrigerator. **Note:** Any leftover smoked pork jerky can be stored in the refrigerator, tightly wrapped, for up to 1 week. It can be shaved over salads, pasta, or pizza.

Sherry Vinaigrette

1 egg
⅓ cup sherry vinegar
1 cup olive oil
Salt

Bring a medium saucepan of salted water to a very low simmer and prepare a small ice bath. Swirl the water gently with a spoon to create a slight vortex. Crack the egg into the water and poach until the white has set but the yolk is still runny, 5 to 6 minutes. Transfer the egg to the ice bath until cold. Once it is cold, place the egg in a blender. Add the sherry vinegar and blend on high speed while gradually streaming in the olive oil. Season with salt to taste. **Note:** Any leftover vinaigrette can be stored in the refrigerator for up to 1 day. Use it to dress salads.

To Finish

1 pound mixed salad greens, such as butter lettuce, red-veined sorrel, green frill mustard, speckled romaine, salad burnet, Lolla Rossa, and purslane
8 ounces sliced (¹⁄₁₆ inch) button mushrooms
Olive oil
Salt

Toss the greens and mushrooms in a small amount of olive oil and season with salt to taste. Arrange the salad on 4 plates. Grate cold smoked pork jerky over the salad with a Microplane grater. Aerate the sherry vinaigrette with a hand blender and spoon the frothy vinaigrette around the salad.

Lobster

Homarus

Brian McGovern and Jordan Elkin were introduced in 2007 and immediately discovered they share a mutual love of lobster. Motivated by this kinship, each quit his job—Brian in documentary film and Jordan in real estate. They enthusiastically began drawing up a business plan for Manhattan's next great eatery: a lobster roll shop. However, the eager young men were halted in their tracks by an inability to find quality purveyors in the city. "We looked at how lobsters were getting into New York, who was touching them, and what their prices were," recalls Brain. Ultimately, they concluded that lobster is more efficiently procured by going directly to Maine's lobstering wharves.

Like lobsters that savagely defend their underwater turf, lobstermen at sea and on land are extremely territorial. "We weren't the first two guys from New York to show up at these places looking to buy lobsters," says Brian. With determination, though, they pushed forward, networking among weary fisherman and fierce loyalists. By 2009, Homarus was fully operational, selling prized New England lobsters to top Manhattan restaurants. A clear indicator of their success was when the son of a prominent Maine fisherman joined the Homarus team.

Owning a lobster company is not glamorous. Two days a week at 3:00 a.m., three delivery trucks arrive in Queens hauling fifty to sixty thousand pounds of live lobsters to a converted warehouse space in Long Island City, Queens. Fresh catches at Homarus are handled delicately. The lobsters are slowly introduced into aquatic holding tanks that are laced with active bacteria to clean the water. Vigorous jostling can cause the lobsters to release more ammonia than the bacteria can handle, killing the entire lot of lobsters, so they are transferred with the utmost care. Unwilling to send empty trucks back to Maine, Homarus fills vehicles with fish scraps to use on the lobster boats. These actions show that Homarus's superior lobsters are the product of a sustainability-minded company. After each order is filled, the Homarus crew loads three vans and personally delivers live lobsters to their 175 clients five days a week. In a span of less than forty-eight hours, the lobsters complete the long trek from the ocean floor to the kitchen counter. Unsurprisingly, the product's high quality attracts a particular clientele. "We have the pickiest customers," says Jordan. But he adds, "These are the clients that we want to work with."

Instead of realizing their original vision of opening a restaurant, Brian and Jordan captured a niche market. They now offer a quality of lobster that they could not initially obtain for themselves.

(We should point out that the fact that Homarus's lobsters come from Maine makes them the only purveyor in this book that sources their product from more than 150 miles from Manhattan. But their gumption and their commitment to bringing the best lobsters to New York in the best way possible earned them a spot.)

Lobster Roll

SERVES 4

Lobster

2 (1½-pound) live lobsters

Bring a large pot of salted water to a boil. Add the live lobsters and cook for 3½ minutes. Transfer to an ice bath. When the lobsters are cool enough to handle, remove the knuckles and claws. Return the knuckles and claws to the boiling water for an additional 3 minutes and return to the ice bath. When cool, cut the lobster meat out of the shells and into large chunks.

Potato Chips

4 russet potatoes
Canola oil
Salt

Peel the potatoes, placing them in a bowl of cold water as you work to prevent oxidation. Using a mandoline, slice the potatoes with the waffle blade, rotating the potato 45 degrees after each slice. Rinse the slices thoroughly under running cold water until the water runs clear. Pour 3 inches of canola oil into a large saucepan and bring the oil to 325°F over medium-high heat. Drain the potatoes, pat dry, and fry the potatoes in small batches until golden, 3 to 4 minutes. Drain on paper towels and season with salt to taste.

Brown Butter Vinaigrette

½ cup butter
¼ cup lemon juice
Salt
Ground black pepper

In a small saucepan over medium heat, melt the butter. Continue warming until the solids toast to a deep caramel color. Remove the browned butter from the heat and whisk in the lemon juice. Season with salt and pepper to taste. Strain through a quadruple layer of cheesecloth, discarding the solids.

To Finish

4 brioche buns
¼ cup butter, at room temperature
Leaves from 1 head of butter lettuce
2 tablespoons Crème Fraîche (page 499)
¼ cup sliced chives
Sea salt
Cracked black pepper

Preheat the broiler. Slice the rolls in half and spread butter on the cut sides. Place on a baking sheet and toast them under the broiler until golden. Toss the lettuce with the crème fraîche and chives. Dress the lobster with the warm brown butter vinaigrette and season with sea salt and pepper to taste. Divide the lettuce among the toasted buns and top with the lobsters. Serve the lobster rolls with the potato chips.

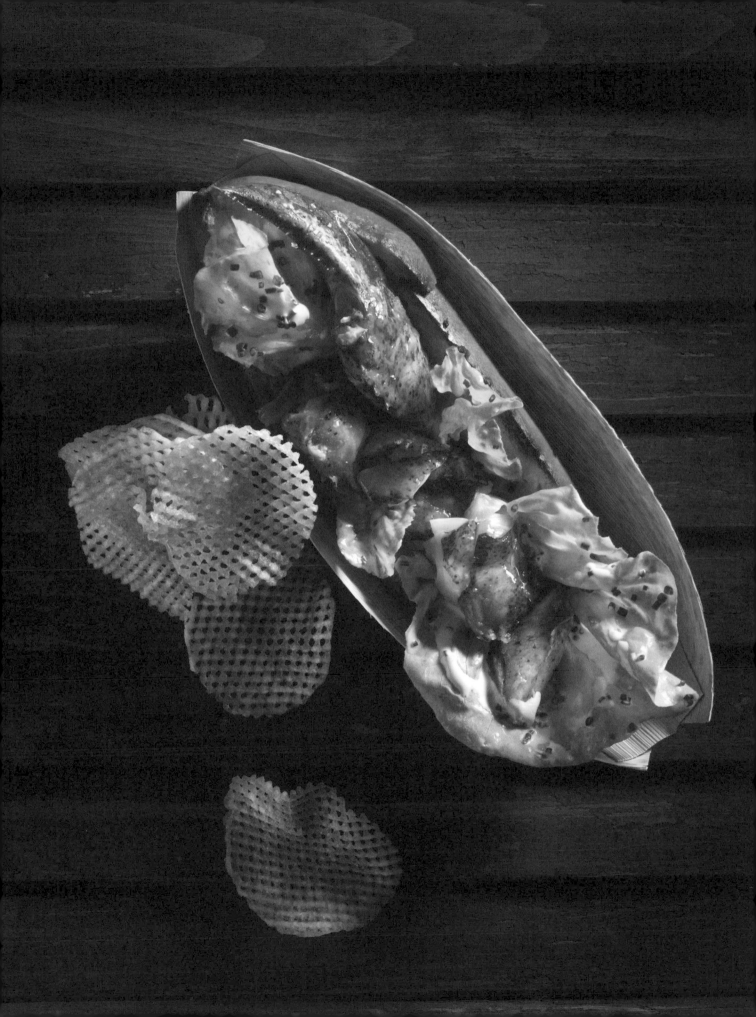

Pan-Roasted Lobster with Potato Chips and Tarragon

SERVES 4

Lobster

2 (1½-pound) live lobsters
1 tablespoon Crème Fraîche (page 499)
1 tablespoon lobster roe, if necessary
Salt

Using the tip of a knife, pierce the head of each lobster and cut the body in half lengthwise. Remove and discard the stomach. Remove and reserve the roe, if present. Remove the legs, claws, and knuckles from the body and refrigerate. In a small mixing bowl, whisk the crème fraîche with 1 tablespoon of the roe and pass through a chinois. Season the flesh side of the lobster bodies with salt and brush with the roe mixture.

Potato Chips

¼ cup salt
2 Yukon Gold potatoes, scrubbed
Canola oil

In a saucepan, bring 2 quarts of water and the salt to a boil. Meanwhile, slice the potatoes paper-thin on a mandoline, putting the slices in a large bowl of cold water as you work to prevent oxidation. Drain the slices, return to the bowl, and pour the boiling water over them. Cool to room temperature. Pour 3 inches of canola oil into a large saucepan and bring the oil to 325°F over medium-high heat. Drain the slices, pat dry, and fry in small batches until crisp, 1½ to 2 minutes. Drain on paper towels and cool to room temperature.

Tarragon Butter

2 cups plus 1 tablespoon loosely packed tarragon leaves
1 pound butter, at room temperature
1 tablespoon sea salt
1 teaspoon lemon juice
Pinch of cayenne pepper

In a large pot of boiling salted water, blanch 2 cups of the tarragon for 10 to 15 seconds. Shock in a bowl of ice water, remove from the water, and transfer to a blender. Blend on high speed with 1 tablespoon of ice water to make a puree, and then strain through a chinois. Using a spatula, combine the tarragon puree with the butter, salt, lemon, and cayenne until fully emulsified. Chop the remaining 1 tablespoon of tarragon and fold into the butter. **Note:** Any leftover butter can be tightly wrapped and frozen for up to 1 month. It is great with fish and shellfish and with roasted potatoes.

To Finish

2 tablespoons butter
1 lemon, cut into wedges
Tarragon sprigs

Bring a large pot of salted water to a boil. Add the knuckles and claws from the lobster to the boiling water and cook for 4 minutes. Remove from the water and when cool enough to handle, remove the meat from the shells. In a large sauté pan, heat the butter over medium heat until it begins to foam. Add the lobster bodies, flesh side down, and sauté for 2 minutes. Flip the lobsters and cook, basting with the butter, for 2½ to 3 more minutes. Add the warm knuckles and claws and tarragon sprigs to the pan and squeeze fresh lemon over the lobster. Add the potato chips to the pan, coating them with the butter. Spoon 1½ to 2 tablespoons of the tarragon butter into the head of each lobster half. Garnish each plate with additional tarragon sprigs and lemon wedges.

Potato Chips

There are few things as consistently comforting as a bag of potato chips. They are available the world over, with almost every country laying claim to a specific flavor or brand. But few people know that they were created in New York in the small town of Saratoga Springs. The story goes that in 1853, a customer at Moon's Lake House, a restaurant on Saratoga Lake, ordered fried potatoes, a house specialty. Those potatoes were typically served in thick slices, much like traditional French fries. The customer, finding the potatoes to be too thick and soggy, sent them back to the kitchen, asking for them to be sliced thinner. The cook obliged, but still, the man was dissatisfied and sent them back twice more, both times dissatisfied with the results. Finally, the cook, George "Speck" Crum, who by this time had lost his patience, sliced them as thinly as possible, while also aggressively salting them to make them inedible. He deep fried them to a crisp and served them to the guest. While he was expecting a reaction of horror, the guest loved them and enthusiastically ordered a second serving. The cook tasted the potatoes himself and to his surprise, discovered that in his anger, he had actually stumbled upon a sensational snack.

Maple Syrup

Upstate Farms

Since the early 1990s, in ardent support of the farm-to-table philosophy, Michael Kokas and Jan Greer have been forging personal relationships in the food world by way of Upstate Farms and their Paisley Farm CSA (see page 309). "We want to interface chefs with our CSA members," they explain, and they accomplish this goal by hosting gatherings that celebrate the seasons' bounty—such as foraged nettles in the spring and roasted pig in the summer. But one of their favorite events happens during the off-season, when they invite guests to help them make maple syrup at their home in Tivoli, New York.

Each year, as winter slowly transitions to spring and the snow melts into the thawing ground in the messy "mud season," farm work slows to a lull. Jan and Michael take advantage of this down time and, in what has now become a yearly tradition, they make maple syrup with their neighbors. "It takes all day and is a lot of work, but we wanted to try it anyway," Jan explains. Between January and March, it is anybody's guess when to tap the trees, because success is contingent on soil temperature. When they first began making maple syrup in 2005, Michael was immediately hooked by the thrill of the gamble. Conditions have to be just right: the temperature has to remain above freezing and below 60°F for a number of consecutive days. If it's too cold, the sap will stay dormant in the maple trees' roots; if the temperature spikes too high, the sap will be contaminated with chlorophyll. Michael and Jan are always pleasantly surprised by the steady number of people that partake in this event, especially given the "on-call" nature of production. But it is only when all of the elements align that the tree-tapping can begin.

Once the sap is collected, it is immediately transferred to a large kettle for cooking in the outdoor shed Jan fondly named "the Sugar Shack." Billows of smoke fill the small hut, perfuming the air with the scent of sweet maple. The sap turns to syrup in a three-chamber evaporator pan. As new sap is added, it pushes the denser syrup through the canals until it reaches the final chamber. Most producers achieve their desired consistency over a fire, but Upstate Farms does it a little differently. "We finish by boiling it on the stove, because if you burn your equipment, it is very costly." Just ask their neighbor why he earned the nickname "crème brûlée." During the final boiling, Michael tests the moisture content with a hydrometer, striving for a measure that surpasses industry standards.

Ultimately, forty gallons of sap yield only one gallon of syrup. Michael explains that the process is long and involved but completely worth it: "There are so many small jobs, but it is actually quite methodical." Due to its uniqueness, Upstate Farms' syrup must be refrigerated to retain its enhanced aroma and flavor. The precious syrup, siphoned from metal drums and bottled to order, truly represents Michael and Jan's relationship to their land and to their customers—a relationship that is at once spontaneous and methodical, and always gratifying and rewarding for everyone involved.

Maple Smoked Sturgeon with Rösti

SERVES 4

Smoked Sturgeon

1 cup salt
½ cup maple sugar
1 (8- to 10-ounce) sturgeon fillet

Mix together the salt and maple sugar in a bowl. Place the sturgeon in a shallow dish and cover with the salt and sugar mixture. Cure for 1 hour in the refrigerator. Rinse the salt from the fish and pat dry with paper towels. Place the fish on a wire rack set in a rimmed baking sheet and allow to dry in the refrigerator overnight.

Soak 2 cups of maple smoking chips in cold water for 10 minutes. Remove the cooking grate from a charcoal grill and light 1 pound of charcoal in a chimney starter. When the coals are white-hot, arrange them in a pile on one side of the grill bottom. Drain the wood chips and place on top of the hot charcoal. Return the cooking grate to the grill. Place the cured sturgeon on a maple plank and, when the chips begin to smoke, set the plank on the cool side of the grate (that is, not on top of the coals). Cover the grill and smoke for 30 to 35 minutes, until the fish is cooked to medium.

Rösti

2 or 3 large russet potatoes
1½ teaspoons salt
½ cup plus 1 teaspoon canola oil
Diced chives
Crème fraîche

Preheat the oven to 400°F. Peel and finely julienne the potatoes on a mandoline or a spiral slicer. You should have about 7 cups. Rinse under cold water, pat dry, and season with the salt. Allow to stand 10 minutes. Drain off any water the potatoes have released and pat dry again. Heat the 1 teaspoon of oil in a medium sauté pan or cast-iron skillet over high heat until it begins to smoke. Reduce the heat to low, pour out the oil, and wipe out the pan with a paper towel. This process of seasoning the pan will keep the potatoes from sticking to it. Return the pan to medium heat and add ¼ cup of the oil. When the oil is very hot and begins to shimmer, pull the pan off the heat and carefully add the potatoes. Return to medium heat. Using a metal or heat-resistant spatula, loosen the potatoes from the sides of the pan and press them down in the center to help form the cake. Add the remaining ¼ cup of oil to the pan, pouring it down the sides of the potatoes. Continue cooking for 7 to 8 minutes over medium heat, rotating the rösti frequently to ensure even browning. Use a spatula to flip the cake. Cook for 7 to 8 more minutes. Remove the rösti from the pan and transfer to a rack. Place the rack on a baking sheet and bake for 8 to 10 minutes to crisp the rösti and drain any excess oil. Remove from the oven and rest on the rack for 5 minutes before serving with the smoked sturgeon and chive-topped crème fraîche.

Sturgeon

In North America, before the nineteenth century, sturgeon was considered to be an undesirable fish, one that destroyed fishermen's nets and whose meat had no value. By the 1800s, though, the sturgeon that populated the American oceans were found to have roe comparable to that of Russian sturgeon. At one point, there was more caviar going to Europe from the United States than from Russia. It was also discovered that smoking sturgeon resulted in a product that was on par with the other types of smoked fish that had long been a part of American immigrant cuisine. But overfishing in the early 1900s all but depleted the American sturgeon population, forcing the American market, which had acquired a taste for both smoked sturgeon and caviar, to import these delicacies—once so plentiful in our own backyard—from overseas.

Maple Sundae

SERVES 4

Spice Cake and Spice Cake Tuiles

⅓ **cup butter, softened**
½ **cup loosely packed dark brown sugar**
⅓ **cup almond oil**
⅓ **cup molasses**
Zest of ½ lemon
1½ **tablespoons ground ginger**
1 **tablespoon ground cinnamon**
1½ **teaspoons salt**
1 **teaspoon ground cloves**
2 **eggs**
1 **tablespoon vanilla extract**
⅓ **cup Crème Fraîche (page 499)**
1½ **cups flour**
¾ **teaspoon baking powder**
¾ **teaspoon baking soda**

Preheat the oven to 325°F. Prepare an 11 by 3-inch terrine mold with nonstick vegetable cooking spray. In the bowl of a stand mixer fitted with the paddle attachment, cream the butter with the brown sugar, oil, molasses, lemon zest, ginger, cinnamon, salt, and cloves. Slowly add the eggs and vanilla, scraping down the sides of the bowl. Add the crème fraîche and mix well. Sift together the flour, baking powder, and baking soda. Add the dry ingredients to the mixture and mix until just combined. Pour the batter into the prepared mold and bake until a tester comes out clean when inserted into the center of the cake, about 45 minutes. Cool slightly and then remove from the mold and cool completely on a rack. Once cooled, cut off the crusts and cut the cake in half crosswise. Crumble half and use the other half for the tuiles.

To make the tuiles, preheat the oven to 200°F. Chill the intact half of the cake in the refrigerator until cold. Slice the cake as thinly as possible and lay the slices on a baking sheet lined with parchment paper. Dry in the oven until crisp, about 30 minutes. Cool at room temperature, and then store in an airtight container. **Note:** Any leftover cake and tuiles can be stored in an airtight container at room temperature for 2 to 3 days. They can be folded into ice cream or blended into a milkshake for a great fall treat.

Spice Streusel

½ **cup flour**
2 **tablespoons maple sugar**
3 **tablespoons plus 2 teaspoons cold butter, diced**
¾ **teaspoon ground cinnamon**
¾ **teaspoon ground ginger**
¼ **teaspoon salt**

Preheat the oven to 325°F. Combine all of the ingredients in a food processor. Process until the dough forms little pebbles. Turn out onto a parchment-lined baking sheet and bake until dry and golden, 15 to 20 minutes.

Maple Whipped Cream

1 **cup cream**
¼ **cup maple sugar**

In a large bowl, using a whisk, whip the cream with the sugar to soft peaks.

Maple Ice Cream

2½ **cups half-and-half**
1 **cup maple syrup**
1½ **teaspoons salt**
6 **egg yolks**
4 **teaspoons cornstarch**

In a medium saucepan over medium heat, warm the half-and-half with the maple syrup and salt. In a medium bowl, whisk together the egg yolks and cornstarch. Slowly pour the hot half-and-half mixture into the egg yolk mixture, whisking constantly. Return the mixture to the saucepan and cook over medium heat to 190°F, stirring constantly. Strain through a chinois, and then chill over an ice bath. Freeze in an ice cream machine. **Note:** Store any leftover ice cream in the freezer for up to 1 month.

To Finish

Maple syrup

Place 4 shallow bowls in the freezer until very cold. Place a large scoop of maple ice cream in each bowl and make a well in the ice cream with the back of a spoon. Mound spice streusel and spice cake crumble next to the ice cream on one side, and then set a few spice cake tuiles in the mound. Spoon a quenelle of maple whipped cream on the other side. Fill the well in the ice cream with maple syrup.

Sundaes

Ice cream sundae legends name various cities around the country as the birthplace of the dessert and the 1890s as the decade of its creation. One such story comes from Ithaca, New York, where a minister reportedly stopped into a pharmacy after church. The fountain clerk put together a bowl of ice cream topped with cherry syrup and a candied cherry for the preacher. The dish was so beautiful and tasted so good that the minister and shopkeeper decided to christen the dish for the day it was created. Linguists believe that the shift from "Sunday" to "sundae" came about because religious leaders felt that the word Sunday was sacred and should not be commercialized.

Milk

Battenkill Valley Creamery

For more than one hundred years, the McEachron family has farmed the Battenkill Valley region in upstate New York. Don McEachron founded Black Creek Dairy in 1982, putting the estate to proper roaming use for his cows. This built on the groundwork established by his father thirty-eight years before. More recently, the Battenkill milk brand was established in February of 2007, after the family did extensive research into the idea of bottling their own milk, and then renovated their space and updated their machinery.

Previously, Don's milk had been sold in bulk and blended with products of inferior quality. "We needed a way to stabilize milk prices," recounts Don's son, Seth. "We could do that by bottling." After Seth obtained a business degree from Skidmore College, returning to the family's hilly Washington County estate was not a given. Don had a stipulation for his son. "My father told me to spend four years away and make sure this is what I wanted to do." Obediently, Seth secured a banking job. However, after only two years, he was back home sketching plans for a creamery.

The business is run with an even divide—Don continues to expertly raise Holstein and Jersey cows, while his son runs the bottling plant of Battenkill. Seth's responsibilities range from business management to hands-on processing. His flawlessly designed facility houses a sustainable operation. To reduce energy consumption, gravity is used to transfer milk from one station to the next. The pasteurization mechanism—which heats milk to 161°F for only 15 seconds—has strategically placed pipes that efficiently raise and lower the temperature of neighboring liquid. Ultrapasteurization is considered a dirty word at Battenkill, and the McEachrons skip this aggressive treatment for their highly regarded cream and half-and-half. "Our shelf life is shorter," admits Seth, "but we do not sacrifice flavor for longevity."

Butterfat content is an indicator of the quality of milk, and Battenkill Valley Creamery's products clearly surpass their competition. Their whole milk rings in at 4 percent butterfat, and their cream and half-and-half are also at the high end of the spectrum, containing 36 percent and 18 percent butterfat, respectively. These numbers indicate minimal manipulation, which guarantees richness and standout results. For the ultimate indulgence, sample Battenkill's custard-thick chocolate milk.

Seth and Don offer a wholesome, artisan product rather than a liquid commodity. Bottling in retro glass jars, Battenkill encourages local residents to either fill up at the creamery or wait at home for the milkman's delivery—a throwback to simpler times.

Curd with Garden Peas and Mint

Fresh Milk Curd

4 cups milk
2 cups cream
Salt
2 tablespoons lemon juice

In a medium saucepan, combine the milk and cream and bring to 183°F over medium heat. Season with salt. Add the lemon juice and allow the temperature to climb to 190° to 195°F. It will take 15 to 20 minutes for curds to develop. Gently stir the mixture with a spatula until the curds separate from the whey. Remove from the heat and carefully drain the curds through a chinois lined with cheesecloth. Continue draining in the refrigerator for 6 to 8 hours or overnight. You will end up with about 2 cups of milk curd. Transfer to a container, cover, and refrigerate. **Note:** Reserve any leftover curd in the refrigerator for up to 1 week.

To Finish

½ cup shelled English peas
½ cup sugar snap peas
½ cup snow peas
2 tablespoons Lemon Vinaigrette (page 500)
Salt
Flowering mint
Pea tendrils
Olive oil
Ground black pepper

Bring a saucepan of salted water to a boil. Blanch the English peas until tender, 2 to 3 minutes, and transfer to an ice bath. Repeat with the sugar snap peas, blanching for 3 to 4 minutes, and then shocking. Rinse the snow peas, trim off the tips, and slice half of them into thin ribbons. Blanch the other half in the boiling water until tender, 1 to 2 minutes, and then shock in the ice bath. Drain the peas and toss all of them in the lemon vinaigrette and season with salt to taste. Spoon fresh curd onto 4 plates. Arrange the dressed peas on and around the curd and garnish with flowering mint and pea tendrils. Finish with olive oil and pepper.

Milk Jam with Brioche au Tête

MAKES ABOUT 2 CUPS MILK JAM AND 16 TO 20 BRIOCHE

Brioche

3 cups bread flour
¼ cup plus 1 teaspoon sugar
2 packed tablespoons fresh yeast
2½ teaspoons salt
5 eggs
3 tablespoons milk
1 cup butter, cut into ½-inch cubes and softened

Place the flour, sugar, yeast, and salt the bowl of a stand mixer fitted with the dough hook. Mix at medium speed. In a separate bowl, whisk together 4 of the eggs and the milk. Gradually add the egg mixture to the dry ingredients. The dough will initially be like a loose batter; as the gluten develops, the dough will bind up and start to pull away from the sides of the bowl. This process will take 15 to 20 minutes. Once the dough pulls away from the sides of the bowl, add the butter, 1 cube at a time, and continue to mix until the dough appears silky, another 1 to 2 minutes. Place the dough in a greased bowl, cover with plastic wrap, and proof for 1 hour at room temperature. Transfer to the refrigerator and proof for an additional hour. Punch down the dough and place a piece of plastic wrap directly on its surface. Refrigerate overnight.

Lightly grease 20 (3-inch) fluted brioche molds. Scale out a 1¾-ounce piece of dough and then scale out a ⅓-ounce piece of dough. Continue doing this until you have used all of the dough. You should have the same number of large pieces as you do small ones. Shape the large pieces into balls. For the small pieces, gently press in the center and roll one side to create an elongated end with a rounded bulb at the opposite end. Using a dowel, make a small hole in the center of each large roll. Drop the elongated end of a small piece into each hole. Place the shaped dough in the greased molds with the rounded bulbs on top and proof at room temperature until doubled in size, about 1½ hours.

Preheat the oven to 325°F. Whisk the remaining egg with a few drops of water and brush the brioche. Bake for 15 minutes until golden.

Milk Jam

4 cups milk
1½ cups sugar
½ teaspoon baking soda
½ teaspoon salt

Combine all of the ingredients in a large saucepan. Bring to a boil while stirring to prevent the mixture from boiling over. Reduce the heat to medium and cook to 225°F, stirring constantly. Once the jam has reached 225°F, transfer the mixture to a blender and blend until smooth. Pour into a bowl or glass jar and serve with the brioche. **Note:** Any leftover milk jam can be refrigerated for up to 1 month and eaten straight from the jar with a spoon. It can also be swirled into ice cream or brownies for a decadent treat.

Nettles

Paisley Farm

At Paisley Farm, Michael Kokas and Jan Greer painstakingly battle weeds to successfully grow crops like eggplant, tomato, and watermelon. Knowing how much care they invest in maintaining these crops, one might wonder why half of their one-hundred-acre Hudson Valley property remains intentionally uncultivated. "Seventeen years ago, I didn't just find a patch of ramps on our property," recalls Michael. "I found ten acres." He trekked the "virgin farmland" in search of other wild vegetation that he knew would appeal to their Upstate Farms CSA (see page 295) subscribers, who had already fallen in love with their produce and maple syrup. In addition to the ramps and fiddlehead ferns—two darlings of spring—it was an abundance of nettles that caught these farmers' eyes.

When Jan first encountered the wild nettles on their property, she recalled her previous career in as an importer of chanterelles and morels from the Pacific Northwest. Her clients had fallen in love with wild mushrooms, and she knew that New Yorkers would be similarly enchanted by wild nettles. She and Michael began distributing them to New York City's best chefs, who became entranced with not only the product itself but also with the idea that they were foraged from just outside of the city.

Nettles flourish alongside rivers in shaded and moist areas where the soil is rich with decaying matter. To reach all his nettle patches, Michael must trek up hills, splash through puddles, and climb over logs. Nettles mature as spring turns to summer, the army-green leaves developing their distinctive nutty, spinachlike flavors. Conditions at this time are prime for harvest, but foragers must tread with care—picking wild nettles is not for the faint of heart.

Nettle plants at harvest time are two to four feet high, their leaves supported by a sturdy ribbed stem. The coarse and papery leaves are covered with thousands of tiny hairs. Chemicals in the hairs unleash a nasty sting, making gloves a requirement when handling the plant. Although nettles are poisonous when eaten raw, the plant's toxins are broken down when heat is applied to them. The plant's versatility and utility have been known since the Bronze Age: the leaves and stems were used medicinally, either steeped as tea or topically applied to relieve joint pain. Today, they are enjoying a culinary renaissance.

Michael and Jan, farmers to the core, are so attuned to their land that they know to allow some of it to grow wild with indigenous vegetation, yielding uncultivated land that rewards foragers with some truly wonderful ingredients.

Nettle Soup with Quail Eggs

SERVES 4

Soup Base

1 tablespoon olive oil
¾ cup diced (¼ inch) carrot
¾ cup diced (¼ inch) onion
2¼ cups diced (¼ inch) Yukon Gold potato
3 cloves garlic, crushed but kept whole
3 sprigs thyme
4 cups Chicken Stock (page 499)
Salt

In a medium saucepan, heat the olive oil over medium-low heat. Add the carrot and onion and sweat until tender, 4 to 5 minutes. Add the potato and cook until the pieces begin to soften, about 3 minutes. Tie the garlic and thyme in cheese-cloth and add to the vegetables. Pour in the stock and simmer for 45 minutes. Remove and discard the garlic and thyme. Transfer to a blender and blend until smooth. Pass the soup base through a chinois and season with salt to taste. **Note:** Any leftover soup base can be refrigerated for 2 to 3 days or frozen for up to 1 month. It is delicious on its own but can also be mixed with spinach or pea puree for a quick and easy soup.

Nettle Puree

8 cups packed nettles
Salt

Bring a large pot of salted water to a boil and blanch the nettles for 45 seconds. Transfer to an ice bath. With gloved hands, squeeze the excess water out of the nettles and transfer to a blender. Add ⅓ cup of ice water and blend until smooth. Pass through a chinois and season with salt to taste.

Garlic Foam

1½ heads garlic
2 tablespoons butter
2 sprigs thyme
Salt
2 cups cream
2 cups skim milk
2½ teaspoons Crème Fraîche (page 499)
Lemon juice

Preheat the oven to 350°F. Wrap the garlic, butter, thyme, and 1 teaspoon of salt in aluminum foil. Roast in the oven until tender, about 40 minutes. Squeeze the roasted garlic out of the skins and combine with the cream and milk in a medium saucepan. Bring the mixture to a simmer, remove from the heat, and add the crème fraîche. Transfer to a blender and puree until smooth. Strain through a chinois. Season with lemon juice and salt to taste. **Note:** Any leftover garlic foam can be stored in the refrigerator for 2 to 3 days. It can then be refrothed with a hand blender and used as a flavorful garnish for any soup.

To Finish

¼ cup Clarified Butter (page 498)
1 cup torn baguette
2 cloves garlic, crushed but kept whole
2 sprigs thyme
8 quail eggs
Salt
Garlic chive flowers
Cracked black pepper

To make the croutons, heat the clarified butter in a small sauté pan over medium-high heat. Add the diced baguette, garlic, and thyme, and sauté until golden brown, 2 to 3 minutes. Place the quail eggs in a small pot of cold water over high heat. Bring to a rolling boil and cook for 20 to 30 seconds, and then transfer the eggs to an ice bath. When cool, peel the eggs and cut in half. Season the eggs with salt to taste. In a saucepan, combine 2½ cups of soup base with 1 cup of nettle puree. Bring to a simmer over medium-high heat, and then divide the soup among 4 bowls. Using a hand blender, froth the garlic foam. Spoon just the foam over the soup and garnish with quail eggs, croutons, garlic chive flowers, and black pepper. Serve immediately, as the soup may begin to oxidize if it sits out for too long.

Nettle Toast with Lardo

SERVES 4

4 cups nettles
2 teaspoons butter
1 teaspoon diced (⅛ inch) shallot
Salt
2 tablespoons olive oil
8 (¼-inch-thick) bias-cut slices of baguette
1 cup ricotta
8 (¹⁄₁₆-inch thick) slices lardo
Pickled Red Pearl Onions (page 501)
Ground black pepper

Wearing gloves, remove the stems from the nettles and discard.

In a medium sauté pan, melt the butter over medium heat. Add the shallot and sweat until tender, 2 to 3 minutes. Add the nettles and sauté until wilted. Season with salt to taste and cool on paper towels.

Heat the oil in a large sauté pan over medium-low heat. Add the baguette slices and cook on one side until golden brown, 4 to 5 minutes. Remove from the pan and pat off excess oil on a paper towel. Top each toasted side of the baguette slices with ricotta and sautéed nettles. Cover with a slice of lardo and garnish with the pickled red pearl onions. Season with salt and pepper to taste.

Onions

S.&S.O. Produce Farms

Mark Rogowski grows a broad range of vegetables on the 450 acres of S. & S. O. Produce Farms: potatoes, artichokes, cabbage, cilantro, and celery root. But his specialty is onions, the crop that is highly favored—and, in many cases, grown exclusively—by farmers of the black dirt, or "muck soil," in this corner of upstate New York.

Mark was raised on a six-hundred-acre onion farm and moved less than a mile away upon marrying Alyson Osczepinski. Alyson's great-grandfather, Ludwig, emigrated from Poland to the United States in 1918, settling in New York. He carried with him a special onion seed unknown to American farmers, an heirloom given to him by an Italian friend back in Europe. Alyson's father and grandfather—two generations of Stanleys—established a solid reputation with this variety, and joined their initials to create S. & S. O. Produce Farms in the 1960s. The Osczepinskis' sweet red onions are what held S. & S. O. up during the 1980s, when many of their neighbors went under in the poor economy.

Thousands of years ago, this land and the acres around it were at the bottom of a lake. Now the land is rife with decaying matter, making it most hospitable to onions. The black dirt envelops the bulbs, creating the appearance of flying saucers suspended in the blackness of outer space. Onions of varying character—from an earthy spiciness to an astounding sweetness—flourish here in the soft and aerated soil that allows unobstructed growth, yielding beautifully rounded bulbs.

His palm full of tiny black seeds, Mark demonstrates how tricky the work of an onion farmer can be in the field: "Every onion species looks the same as a seed." Because of this, growers can easily confuse a seed's destiny—will it sprout an onion or a leek? A chive or a green onion? Therefore, once spring planting begins, constant monitoring is crucial in keeping the crops organized and healthy. Furthermore, onions are sensitive and can suffer casualties due to human error, weather, and bugs. Mark explains, "Even microfractures to the onions are devastating and can ultimately cause a rotten ring to form inside the onion."

With decades of experience under his belt, Mark knows what it takes to overcome these obstacles: painstaking focus and careful planning. Roughly a hundred days after delicate new shoots bud from his bulbs' centers, the top green leaves turn brown and the onions begin to cure in the field. This process allows for safe storage throughout the cold winter weather.

As he collects a handful of onions, Mark shares his motivations. "It is gratifying to see everything come to harvest and have people appreciate it." Standing in the middle of his beloved field, he pledges, "I will never take this land for granted."

Grilled Green Onions with Buttermilk Dressing

SERVES 4

Grilled Green Onions

2 bunches green onions
Olive oil
Salt

Toss the green onions in olive oil and season with salt. Grill the onions over high heat either on an outdoor grill or in a cast-iron grill pan for 3 to 4 minutes on each side until lightly charred.

Lemon Buttermilk Dressing

¾ cup buttermilk
1 tablespoon lemon juice
1 tablespoon olive oil
1 teaspoon salt
1 teaspoon sugar
Zest of ½ lemon

Combine all of the ingredients in a small bowl and whisk to combine. **Note:** Any leftover dressing can be stored in the refrigerator, covered, for up to 1 week and can be used to dress green salads.

To Finish

2 hard-boiled eggs
Salsa Verde (page 89)
Pickled Red Pearl Onions (page 501)

Peel the eggs and remove the white, reserving only the hard-boiled yolk. Arrange one-fourth of the grilled onions on each of 4 plates. Spoon lemon buttermilk dressing and salsa verde onto the plates. Using a Microplane grater, grate egg yolk over each dish. Finish with pickled red pearl onions.

Onion and Blood Sausage Bread Pudding

SERVES 4

Roasted Onions

4 large onions, unpeeled
¾ cup olive oil
¼ cup salt

Preheat the oven to 350°F. Cut 4 large squares of aluminum foil. Place 1 onion in each of the squares. Begin to make a pouch around the onions and evenly distribute the oil and salt among the onions. Seal the pouches and place on a rimmed baking sheet. Bake for 2½ hours. Cool in the foil.

Sautéed Onions

2 tablespoons bacon fat
3 cups diced (¼ inch) onion
2 bay leaves
1 clove garlic, crushed but kept whole
1 tablespoon thyme leaves
1 teaspoon salt
½ cup white wine

In a large straight-sided sauté pan over high heat, heat the bacon fat until just before it begins to smoke. Add the onion, bay leaves, garlic, thyme, and salt. Reduce the heat to medium and cook until the onion is translucent and just beginning to brown. Deglaze with the wine and reduce until dry. Cool to room temperature.

Custard

2 eggs
1 egg yolk
1 cup Crème Fraîche (page 499)
⅓ cup milk
1½ teaspoons salt
½ teaspoon nutmeg
¼ teaspoon ground black pepper

Combine all of the ingredients in a bowl and blend with a hand blender.

Blood Sausage Filling

2 cups diced dried baguette, crusts removed
1 cup diced (¼ inch) blood sausage
Sautéed Onions
Custard

In a bowl, mix together all of the ingredients and let soak for 30 minutes.

To Finish

1 egg
1 teaspoon salt
4 teaspoons butter

Preheat the oven to 350°F. Whisk the egg with the salt and let stand for 5 minutes. Remove the roasted onions from the foil. Using a serrated knife, cut off the tops of the onions. Using a spoon and a paring knife, gently scoop out the insides of the onions, leaving enough of the outside to give support. Be careful to avoid ripping holes in the bottoms. Place the onions in a small baking dish and brush the insides with the egg wash. Bake for 5 minutes to create a seal. Repeat if necessary to ensure that the onions are well sealed. Once the onions are fully sealed, fill them to the top with the blood sausage filling. Place 1 teaspoon of butter on top of each filled onion and cover the dish with aluminum foil. Bake for 30 to 40 minutes or until the filling is just set. Remove the aluminum foil and continue baking until the tops are golden brown, another 15 minutes. Serve warm.

Braised Onion with Bacon

SERVES 4

Braised Onion

4 medium-large Spanish onions
6 tablespoons cold butter
2 cups Chicken Stock (page 499)

Leaving the skins on and the root ends attached, slice a ½-inch thick plank from the center of each onion. In a medium sauté pan, melt 4 tablespoons of the butter over medium-low heat. Add the onion planks and sweat for 3 minutes. Flip and sweat for another 3 minutes. Add the stock and cover with a parchment paper lid. Simmer until the onions are tender, 12 to 14 minutes. Add the remaining 2 tablespoons of butter. Reduce the liquid to a glaze.

Roasted Shallots

1 tablespoon canola oil
2 large shallots, halved lengthwise
1 tablespoon butter
5 sprigs thyme

Preheat the oven to 300°F. In a small sauté pan, heat the oil over medium heat. Add the shallots cut side down and sear for 2 minutes. Flip the shallots over and add the butter and thyme. Baste the shallots with the butter for 2 minutes, flip again so the cut side is facing down, and transfer to the oven. Roast until the shallots are tender, 18 to 20 minutes.

Pork Shortbread

1 cup plus 1 tablespoon bread flour
1 tablespoon plus 1 teaspoon granulated sugar
1 tablespoon packed dark brown sugar
1½ teaspoons salt
3 tablespoons cold bacon fat
1 tablespoon plus 1¼ teaspoons milk

Preheat the oven to 325°F. In a stand mixer fitted with the paddle attachment, combine the flour, sugars, and salt. Mix well, and then add the cold bacon fat. As the dough comes together, slowly stream in the milk and mix until thoroughly incorporated. Roll the dough ⅛ inch thick between 2 sheets of parchment paper. Transfer to a baking sheet and peel off the top layer of parchment paper. Bake in the oven until golden brown, 18 to 20 minutes. Cool to room temperature and break the shortbread into pieces. Transfer to the food processor and pulse until the shortbread resembles coarse sand.

Onion Sauce

1 tablespoon canola oil
½ cup diced (¼ inch) bacon
1 cup diced (¼ inch) onion
⅓ cup diced (¼ inch) celery root
¼ cup diced (¼ inch) carrot
¼ cup diced (¼ inch) celery
2 teaspoons tomato paste
3 tablespoons red wine
6 cups Chicken Stock (page 499)
Sherry vinegar
Salt
2 tablespoons olive oil

In a medium saucepan, heat the oil over medium heat. Add the bacon and cook until the fat has rendered and the bacon begins to caramelize, about 5 minutes. Add the onion, celery root, carrot, and celery and cook until lightly caramelized, about 6 minutes. Add the tomato paste and cook for 1 more minute. Deglaze the pan with the red wine and continue to cook for about 2 minutes. Add the stock and bring to a simmer. Simmer for 30 minutes over medium-low heat. Strain the sauce through a chinois and return to the pan. Raise the heat to high and reduce to 1 cup, skimming frequently. Remove the sauce from the heat and season with sherry vinegar and salt to taste. Top with the olive oil.

To Finish

½ teaspoon canola oil
4 (1 by 5 by ¼-inch) slices bacon
½ cup sherry vinegar
½ cup sugar
Fresh Milk Curd (page 305)
Pickled Shallots (page 501)
Olive oil
Sea salt

In a small sauté pan, heat the canola oil over medium heat. Add the bacon slices and cook until they begin to brown, 1½ to 2 minutes. Flip the bacon over, lower the heat, and cook for 2 more minutes. Combine the sherry vinegar and sugar in a small bowl and add it to the pan. Raise the heat to medium and reduce the liquid to a glaze.

Divide the fresh curd among 4 plates and create a well in the center. Arrange a braised onion plank and a roasted shallot half on each plate and spoon pork shortbread in a mound beside them. Place pickled shallots on top of the braised onion and set a strip of glazed bacon on top of the shallots. Spoon the onion sauce around the curd. Finish by filling the well in the fresh curd with olive oil and season with sea salt to taste.

Oysters

Widow's Hole Oyster Company

When Mike Osinski exits his Greenport, Long Island, home, sweeping views of the Atlantic Ocean paint the skyline for miles. Upon buying this waterfront oasis in 1999, Mike envisioned the estuary providing years of summertime tranquility. He had retired young thanks to a successful start-up, and with an abundance of time and self-admitted boredom, he uncovered a statute from the 1870s indicating that Greenport waterfront properties include ownership 500 feet into the bay. With a zeal for history and a love of New York, Mike put his newfound underwater real estate to good use: "Greenport used to be the oyster capital of New York, so I decided to get an oyster permit myself." In 2001, Widow's Hole Oyster Company sold its first oysters.

The rise of New York City owes a lot to oysters. In the early 1800s, carts peddled them at Fulton Market. As a late-night post-work indulgence, businessmen slurped oysters and drank martinis in saloons on Broad Street. Long Island villages like Greenport were rich in oyster farmers and oyster canneries. The Long Island Rail Road ran no fewer than two trains daily, hauling only oysters into the heart of Manhattan. However, overfarming and pollution brought the industry to a halt.

Oysters relate taste to place like no other ingredient, making them the ideal ambassadors of marine flavor. Mike buys high-quality spats (baby oysters) that are a mere three millimeters long. They go into plastic drums that sit in Widow's Hole, a small inlet of the ocean and the namesake of Mike's company. When ready, the lots are put into cages and placed in the bay, spending eighteen to thirty months there until fully mature.

The Peconic Bay, specifically Greenport Harbor, is sandwiched between Long Island's North Fork and Shelter Island; the water sweeping through these narrows transports a royal feast of plankton for growing oysters to feed on. Mike's ultimate hope is to capitalize on the natural resources of this area and revitalize the oyster farming tradition that has its roots so firmly planted here. In creating a high-quality product, he aims to create a virtuous cycle in Greenport, one that inspires others to do what he's doing. "I want more competition—that is my goal. I'd like to see fifty more companies here in the next five to ten years."

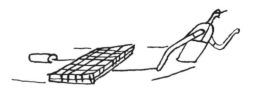

Oyster Pan Roast

SERVES 4

Pan Roast Sauce

1 tablespoon olive oil
5 pounds Quahog clams
½ cup finely diced celery
½ cup finely diced shallot
2 tablespoons brown sugar
1 tablespoon sweet paprika
1 teaspoon ground celery seed
½ teaspoon chopped ginger
½ cup white wine
2 tablespoons Pernod
2 cups tomato juice
1 tablespoon Worcestershire sauce
½ bunch parsley
1½ cups cream
1 tablespoon lemon juice
½ teaspoon salt
⅛ teaspoon cayenne

Heat a large stockpot over high heat. Add the olive oil, and then the clams, stirring constantly. Lower the heat to medium. Add the celery, shallot, brown sugar, paprika, celery seed, and ginger. Sweat for 2 minutes. Add the white wine and Pernod and cook out the alcohol, about 3 minutes. Add the tomato juice, Worcestershire sauce, and parsley and bring to a simmer. Cover and simmer for 15 minutes. Strain through a chinois; you should have about 3½ cups of sauce. Return the sauce to the pot. Simmer over medium-low heat until reduced to 1½ cups. Add the cream and bring to a simmer. Season with the lemon juice, salt, and cayenne.

To Finish

¼ cup Clarified Butter (page 498)
1 cup diced (¼ inch) baguette
2 cloves garlic, crushed but kept whole
2 sprigs thyme
32 fresh oysters, shucked
Paprika
Chervil
Parsley
Tarragon

To make the croutons, heat the clarified butter in a small sauté pan over medium-heat high. Add the diced baguette, garlic, and thyme, and sauté until the bread is golden brown, 2 to 3 minutes. Warm the pan roast sauce over low heat. When the sauce has reached a simmer, remove from the heat and add the shucked oysters. Poach until cooked, 30 seconds to 1 minute, depending on the size of the oysters. Remove the oysters with a slotted spoon and divide them among 4 bowls. Aerate the pan roast sauce with a hand blender until frothy. Spoon about ¼ cup of the sauce into each bowl and sprinkle with paprika. Top with croutons, chervil, parsley, and tarragon.

Dating back to the early 1900s, the Grand Central oyster pan roast is among the oldest dishes still served in New York. Oysters, though, have been part of the New York culinary lexicon for much longer than that. The first native New Yorkers, the Lenape, ate oysters. When the Dutch arrived in the 1600s, they continued eating this bountiful bivalve, going as far as calling Ellis Island "Oyster Island" and Liberty Island "Great Oyster Island." During the late 1700s, oysters were sold from boats or street carts throughout the city before oyster cellars began popping up and serving oysters in as many preparations as imaginable, from raw, to in stews, to baked in pies. When oyster numbers began to dwindle, New Yorkers began farming them; as a result, by the 1850s, oystering was one of New York's biggest and most prosperous industries. Over time, the water surrounding New York became polluted and New York oysters were no longer a viable industry, so much so that when the Grand Central Oyster Bar opened in 1913, it didn't serve New York oysters. To this day, New York oysters are virtually extinct, ironically resulting in this classic New York dish having always been made with oysters from other waters.

Oysters with Fennel and Apples

SERVES 4

Oyster Cream

2½ sheets gelatin
1¼ cups cream
½ tablespoon butter
1 tablespoon minced shallot
5 fresh oysters, shucked (about ¼ cup)
1½ teaspoons Pernod
1½ teaspoons vermouth
1½ teaspoons lime juice
Salt

Bloom the gelatin by placing the sheets in a bowl of ice water for 10 minutes until pliable. In the meantime, in a stand mixer fitted with the whisk attachment, whip 1 cup of the cream to soft peaks. Reserve over an ice bath in the refrigerator.

Heat the butter in a small sauté pan over medium heat and sweat the shallot until soft and translucent, about 2 minutes. Add 4 of the oysters to the pan and sweat for 1 minute. Deglaze the pan with the Pernod and vermouth and reduce for 2 minutes. Add the remaining ¼ cup of cream and the lime juice. Squeeze out the excess moisture from the gelatin and stir it into the oyster and cream mixture until it is melted. Transfer the mixture to a blender, add the remaining oyster, and blend until smooth. Season with salt to taste. Pass the mixture through a chinois and chill over an ice bath, stirring constantly to keep the gelatin from setting.

Remove the whipped cream from the refrigerator. Keeping it over the ice bath, quickly incorporate a third of the oyster mixture into the whipped cream with a rubber spatula. Then fold the whipped cream into the oyster mixture in 2 additions. Make sure they are fully and evenly incorporated to achieve an even texture.

Allow the oyster cream to set over an ice bath in the refrigerator for 3 hours. Just before serving, whisk the cream to achieve a smooth, buttery texture. **Note:** Any leftover cream can be stored, covered, in the refrigerator for 2 days. Serve with crackers and oysters.

Cooking Broth

1 tablespoon canola oil
¼ cup diced celery root
¼ cup diced celery
¼ cup diced leek
¼ cup diced onion
½ cup white wine
1 bay leaf
1 sprig tarragon
1 sprig thyme
4 black peppercorns
Juice of ½ lemon
1 teaspoon salt

In a medium saucepan, heat the canola oil over medium-high heat. Add the celery root, celery, leek, and onion and sweat the vegetables until they are translucent. Deglaze with the white wine and reduce by half. Add 4 cups of water and the remaining ingredients and bring to a simmer. Simmer over low heat for 30 minutes. Strain and reserve for poaching.

Fennel-Apple Sauce

1 tablespoon canola oil
1½ cups finely diced fennel
1 cup peeled and finely diced Granny Smith apple
1½ cups fennel fronds
Salt

Heat the oil in a medium saucepan over medium heat. Add the fennel and apple and sweat for 1 minute. Add 2 cups of water and cover. Simmer over medium-low heat until the fennel and apple are tender, 10 to 12 minutes. Meanwhile, bring a pot of salted water to a boil and blanch the fennel fronds for 15 seconds. Transfer to an ice bath and, once cooled, drain. Squeeze out the excess moisture. Transfer the fennel and apple mixture to a blender and puree with the blanched fennel fronds. Blend on high until smooth. Strain the puree through a chinois. Chill over an ice bath and season with salt to taste. **Note:** Store any leftover sauce in the refrigerator for 2 to 3 days. Serve alongside seafood or over roasted vegetables.

To Finish

16 fresh oysters, shucked, liquor reserved
3 tablespoons Granny Smith apple juice
2 tablespoons olive oil
1 fennel bulb
1 Granny Smith apple
Lemon Vinaigrette (page 500)
Fennel fronds
Onion blossoms

In a small saucepan, warm the cooking broth over low heat. When the broth comes to a simmer, remove from the heat and add the shucked oysters and their liquor. Poach until the oysters are warmed through, 30 seconds to 1 minute, depending on their size. Remove the poached oysters with a slotted spoon and arrange 4 on each of 4 plates.

Measure out ⅓ cup of the fennel-apple sauce, season with the apple juice, and add the olive oil. Cut the fennel into quarters and slice lengthwise 1/16 inch thick on a mandoline. Using a paring knife, trim each slice into a wing shape. Cut the apple into 1½ by ⅛-inch batons. Dress the fennel and apple with lemon vinaigrette and arrange on the oysters. Spread a spoonful of the oyster cream on the plate and finish each plate with the fennel-apple sauce. Garnish with fennel fronds and onion blossoms.

Parsnips

Schoharie Valley Farms

Anyone who has been to Schoharie, New York, knows the Carrot Barn, a fresh food emporium on Route 30 named for the carrots that grow so well in this region. The famous Carrot Barn is part of the lesser-known Schoharie Valley Farms. "The previous owner of the farm supplied Beech-Nut, the baby food company, with carrots," explains Richard Ball, who assumed ownership in 1993. He preserved the name to pay homage to the root crop's local history, to which he is closely tied: he grew up farming nearby with his grandparents. "My mother would have been the fifth generation carrot farmer, but she wanted to be a nurse." When it came time to choose his profession, Richard had no intention of seeking any career path outside of farming. As he puts it, "I had already caught the bug."

Although Richard embraced the tradition of growing carrots, he also wanted to expand his horizons. He knew that with the composition of his land, he could grow much more. "We have one of the best soils in the world from a fertility standpoint," says Richard. With fifteen feet of topsoil, most every plant can thrive there—including parsnips.

Having explored New York's food scene, Richard knew that parsnips were not the most popular vegetable. And furthermore, they take a lot of persistence to cultivate; a common saying among farmers goes, "That's as bad as a one-year-old parsnip seed," referring to the seeds' short shelf life. Plus, the seeds are oddly shaped, demanding extra attention during planting. Despite these drawbacks, Richard says, "Parsnips are really one of my favorite crops." He was convinced that parsnips could not only be grown successfully but could also be enjoyed both at home and at fine restaurants, and eventually he began to see the vegetable pop up at restaurants throughout the greater New York area—as chips, pureed, in risottos, and simply roasted. Richard is partial to the Lancer and Javelin varieties, which are not as broad-shouldered as others; they grow long and can be densely planted in the fields. And Richard knows how to coax the most sugar out of them: "They need prolonged periods of cold exposure to develop the most sweetness. Farmers used to pick them in the spring, but instead, we imitate an extended growing environment in cold houses."

Richard, who found success by expanding the farm's horizons many years ago, constantly aims to introduce new enterprises to the farm. "It keeps things interesting around here," he says. Not surprisingly, both of Richard's daughters, Sarah and Jolyn, contributed to the Carrot Barn's concept upon their return to the farm after college, adding a general store and serving homemade soups and sandwiches. As Sarah says, "This farm is our way of life, and it allows us to be together with our family." Literally, and figuratively, roots do run deep at Schoharie Valley Farms.

Parsnip and Pear Soup

SERVES 4

Almond-Vanilla Oil

¼ cup almond oil
⅛ vanilla bean, split lengthwise and scraped

Place the oil and vanilla bean in a small saucepan. Heat to 190°F. Remove from the heat and cool to room temperature. Cover and set aside to infuse at room temperature for 24 hours.

Parsnip Soup

2 tablespoons butter
¼ cup diced (¼ inch) shallot
2 cups diced (¼ inch) parsnip
½ cup diced (¼ inch) celery root
3 sprigs rosemary
1 cup diced (¼ inch) pear
1 cup white wine
5 cups Chicken Stock (page 499)
½ cup half-and-half
Pear vinegar
Salt

In a medium stockpot, melt the butter over medium-low heat. Add the shallot and sweat for 2 to 3 minutes. Add the parsnip, celery root, and 2 sprigs of the rosemary and continue sweating for 5 to 6 minutes. Add the pear and continue cooking for 4 to 5 minutes. Add the white wine, raise the heat to high, and reduce the liquid by half, to about ½ cup. Add the chicken stock and bring to a boil. Lower the heat and simmer for 45 minutes. Remove the pan from the heat and stir in the half-and-half. Remove the rosemary and transfer the soup to a blender. Blend on high speed until smooth. Place the remaining sprig of rosemary in a chinois and strain the blended soup over it. Season with pear vinegar and salt to taste.

To Finish

Divide the soup among 4 bowls. Top with a drizzle of the almond-vanilla oil.

Parsnip Cake

Parsnip Puree

1½ cups thinly sliced parsnips
Milk

Place the parsnips in a medium straight-sided sauté pan. Cover with milk, and then a parchment paper lid. Bring to a simmer over medium heat. Cook until tender, and then strain, reserving the milk. Puree the parsnips in a blender, using as little of the reserved milk as possible to make it smooth. Set aside to cool.

Cinnamon Glaze

1 cup confectioners' sugar, plus more as needed
¼ cup milk
½ teaspoon ground cinnamon
¼ teaspoon salt

Combine the sugar, milk, cinnamon, and salt in a large bowl and whisk until smooth, adding a little more sugar if necessary to thicken to a drizzling consistency.

Parsnip Cake

1 cup plus 2 tablespoons flour
1 teaspoon baking soda
½ teaspoon ground ginger
¼ teaspoon ground cinnamon
½ cup walnut oil
¼ cup olive oil
½ cup granulated sugar
½ cup loosely packed light brown sugar
2 teaspoons salt
1 egg
1 egg yolk
½ cup Parsnip Puree
1 tablespoon vanilla extract
2 cups grated parsnips (grated on a box grater)
1 cup chopped walnuts, lightly toasted
½ cup dried currants
½ cup golden raisins

Preheat the oven to 325°F. Sift the flour with the baking soda, ginger, and cinnamon. Whisk together the walnut oil, olive oil, granulated sugar, brown sugar, and salt. Add the egg, egg yolk, parsnip puree, and vanilla and whisk to combine. Add the flour mixture and mix until smooth, being careful not to overwork the batter. Fold in the grated parsnips, walnuts, currants, and raisins. Spray an 11 by 3-inch terrine mold with nonstick vegetable cooking spray, and then dust it with flour. Pour the batter into the terrine mold and bake until a cake tester comes out clean, about 45 minutes. Cool for 30 minutes in the pan. Gently turn out the cake onto a cooling rack (it should release easily from the mold), set it upright, and cool to room temperature before spooning the cinnamon glaze over the top.

Pears

Migliorelli Farm

At Migliorelli Farm, an old farming adage still applies: "You plant pears for your heirs." Traditionally, pear trees took as many as twenty years before they produced fruit. Nowadays, because of modern developments in pear farming, they don't take nearly as long, but, with a lifespan of up to two hundred years, they still last for generations. Ken Migliorelli admires the timelessness and composure of his stoic-looking trees. He grew up in the Bronx, where his grandfather, Angelo, ran a fresh vegetable business at the market in Hunts Point. Angelo specialized in broccoli rabe from Lazio, the seeds of which he brought with him when he immigrated to New York in the 1930s. In 1970, at the age of ten, Ken left the Bronx with his father, Rocco, who took up the management of the family dairy farm in the Hudson Valley. In 2002, Ken branched out in his own direction, purchasing orchards in Tivoli, New York, and growing not only pears and apples but also a variety of stone fruits, like peaches, nectarines, plums, and cherries. Today, he is proud of the entire farm, but his preference is clear. He motions toward a hill beyond his apple trees and says, "Pears are my favorite crop."

Ken has a keen awareness of the crops on his one thousand acres of land, almost as though he single-handedly cultivates each fruit and vegetable himself. With such an impressive consciousness, he is able to constantly improve his farming technique, and he is driven to keep evolving. In the pear orchard, he recently noticed inconsistent planting patterns. The land's original pear trees, which were planted in 1989, were widely spaced. Ten years later, more trees were planted between the older trees, increasing the orchard's density. Intrigued, Ken decided to try an innovation of his own: "A few years ago I started pruning differently by leaving more branches on the tree. And we just had our biggest harvest ever!" Now, he waits to see if the next harvest can top the last one.

Ken's expertise in soil studies allows him to successfully grow Bosc, Bartlett, and Seckel pears in Tivoli's dense clay. As harvest nears, he assesses the resulting fruit for optimum ripeness: "We test for pressure, and we use a Brix meter to analyze the sugar." Fruits that ripen fully on the tree are sold at farmers' markets or to restaurants; others are picked slightly green to maximize their cold-storage potential.

Because the Scenic Hudson Land Trust facilitated a conservation easement with Migliorelli Farms, Ken's land is protected from development. Ken, who has been building a relationship with his customers for thirty years, takes comfort in knowing that the integrity of his land will be preserved for generations to come. Gazing past a masonry stone wall toward his poised and stately pear trees, Ken cannot help but dream about the Italian countryside. He has become increasingly nostalgic for his familial roots and recently made plans to spend a season in Italy. Spending time on the land in his ancestral home will, he hopes, allow him to "learn some techniques in Italy and bring the knowledge back to my orchards."

Pear Coffee Cake

MAKES 1 CAKE; SERVES 8

Macerated Pears

3 cups diced (¼ inch) Bosc pears, skin on
½ cup pear brandy
⅓ cup sugar

Mix the pears, brandy, and sugar together in a bowl. Cover and refrigerate overnight. The next day, before making the cake, drain, reserving both the liquid and the pears.

Crumble

4 tablespoons butter
½ cup almond flour
¼ cup plus 1 tablespoon bread flour
3 tablespoons granulated sugar
1 tablespoon light brown sugar
1 teaspoon salt

In a stand mixer fitted with the paddle attachment, beat together all of the ingredients on medium speed until the mixture is crumbly. Refrigerate until ready to use.

Swirl Mixture

2 tablespoons cocoa powder
1 tablespoon sugar
1 teaspoon ground cinnamon
1 teaspoon ground ginger

In a small bowl, mix together all of the ingredients.

Cake

1 cup butter, softened
1¼ cups granulated sugar
⅓ cup light brown sugar
2 teaspoons salt
2 eggs
⅓ cup plus 1 tablespoon Crème Fraîche (page 499)
2 tablespoons vanilla extract
2 cups plus 3 tablespoons flour
2 teaspoons baking powder
½ teaspoon baking soda

Preheat the oven to 325°F. Butter and flour an 11 by 3-inch terrine mold. In the bowl of a stand mixer fitted with the paddle attachment, cream the butter with the granulated sugar, brown sugar, and salt until light and fluffy. Add the eggs one at a time, and then add the crème fraîche, vanilla, and 1 tablespoon of the reserved macerated pear liquid. Into a separate bowl, sift together the flour, baking powder, and baking soda. Lower the mixer speed and add the flour mixture to the batter, mixing until just combined. Finish folding with a spatula to make sure the batter is completely mixed. Fold in the drained macerated pears.

Spoon half the batter into the prepared terrine mold and spread it into an even layer with an offset spatula. Sift half of the swirl mixture over the batter to evenly coat. Spoon the batter into the mold, spread it out, and then sift the remaining swirl mixture on top. Scatter the crumble over the batter and bake for 50 to 60 minutes, until a cake tester comes out clean when inserted into the center of the cake. Cool for 30 minutes in the mold. Gently turn out the cake onto a cooling rack (it should release easily from the mold), set it upright, and cool to room temperature.

Pear Variations with Honey and Ginger

SERVES 4

Pear Sorbet

6 cups peeled, cored, and sliced pear
½ cup sugar
1 teaspoon citric acid
3 tablespoons Crème Fraîche (page 499)
1 tablespoon lemon juice
¼ teaspoon salt

As you cut the pears, transfer them to a bowl of water with lemon to keep them from oxidizing. Once peeled and sliced, drain and combine the pears in a saucepan with the sugar and citric acid. Cook over high heat for a few minutes until the pears are soft, but make sure they do not burn. Transfer to a blender and puree. Strain through a chinois and combine with the crème fraîche, lemon juice, and salt. Chill over an ice bath and then freeze in an ice cream machine. **Note:** Store in the freezer for up to 1 month.

Ginger Spice Crumble

2 tablespoons cold butter
½ cup flour
¼ cup sugar
1 teaspoon ground ginger
½ teaspoon ground cinnamon
¼ teaspoon salt

Preheat the oven to 325°F. Combine all of the ingredients in a food processor, mixing just until the dough forms little pebbles. Place on a baking sheet lined with a silicone baking mat and bake until dry and golden, 15 to 20 minutes.

Pear Puree

2 large Bosc pears
1 tablespoon butter
½ cup white wine
¼ cup dry vermouth

Peel, core, and dice the pears. As you cut them, transfer them to a bowl of water with lemon to keep them from oxidizing. Melt the butter in a medium sauté pan over medium heat. Drain the pears and shake off as much water as possible. Add to the butter and sweat until the pears release their juices, about 5 minutes. In a small bowl, combine the wine and vermouth. Add a small amount of the wine mixture to the pears, cover with a parchment paper lid, and cook until the liquid is absorbed. Continue this process with the remaining liquid, only adding a little at a time. Once all of the liquid has been absorbed and the pears are soft, puree in a blender until smooth. Strain through a chinois.

Burnt Honey Cream

2 sheets gelatin
¼ cup honey
1½ cups half-and-half
4 egg yolks
3 tablespoons sugar
1 teaspoon salt

Bloom the gelatin by placing the sheets in a bowl of ice water for 10 minutes until pliable. Cook the honey in a medium saucepan over high heat until the honey becomes a dark caramel, 4 to 5 minutes. Meanwhile, warm the half-and-half in another saucepan. Pour the warm half-and-half into the honey caramel. Be careful, as the caramel will bubble. Whisk the egg yolks with the sugar until a pale ribbon forms. Pour the hot caramel liquid into the egg yolk and sugar mixture, whisking constantly. Pour back into the pan and cook over medium heat until the mixture coats the back of a spoon and reaches 183°F, stirring constantly with a spoon so as not to aerate it. Remove the gelatin from the ice water and squeeze to remove the excess moisture. Stir into the hot mixture along with the salt. Chill over an ice bath.

Poached Bosc Pear Rings

4 cups white wine
1 cup pear nectar
¾ cup honey
¾ cup sugar
Peel from 3 lemons
2 large Bosc pears
Burnt Honey Cream

To make a poaching liquid, bring the white wine, pear nectar, honey, sugar, and lemon peel to a boil in a large saucepan. Once the sugar is dissolved, remove from the heat. Transfer 2 cups of the liquid to a small saucepan and reduce over medium heat to about 1 cup. Chill over an ice bath. Return the remaining 2 cups of poaching liquid to the heat and bring to a bare simmer. Cut the pears crosswise into ½-inch slices. Place the slices in the poaching liquid and cook until just fork tender, about 10 minutes. Cool in the syrup to room temperature. Once cooled, cut the skin away from the slices using a round cutter. Use a small round cutter to cut out the core. Brush with the cooled reduced syrup. Place the rings on a baking sheet lined with acetate or plastic wrap and fill the centers with the burnt honey cream. Refrigerate until the cream is set.

continued >

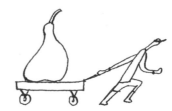

Candied Lemon

2 lemons
4 cups sugar
½ cup glucose syrup

Thinly slice the lemons crosswise and place the slices in a small straight-sided sauté pan. Cover with ice and bring to a bare simmer. Strain and repeat this process until the bitterness is gone from the lemons, 3 or 4 more times. In a saucepan over medium heat, make a syrup with the sugar, glucose syrup, and 1 cup of water. Add the blanched lemon slices and bring to a simmer. Remove from the heat and set the saucepan in a warm place, such as near a warm oven or stove, until the rind turns translucent. Transfer the lemon slices to a container, cover with a little syrup, and refrigerate.

Candied Ginger

2 cups peeled and thinly sliced (¹/₁₆ inch) ginger
4 cups sugar
½ cup glucose syrup

Place the ginger in a saucepan and cover with cold water. Bring to a boil, and then strain. Repeat this process 4 or 5 more times to remove the spiciness from the ginger. In another saucepan over medium heat, make a syrup by combining the sugar, glucose syrup, and 4 cups of water. Drain the ginger and add to the syrup. Cook until the temperature reaches 225°F. Remove from the heat, cool the ginger in the syrup to room temperature, and then refrigerate.

Pear Slices

1 Bosc pear
Lemon juice

Slice pear into thin rounds. Use a round cutter to cut the slices into leaf-like shapes. Store in lemon juice to prevent oxidation.

Pear Parisiennes

½ cup honey
½ cup lemon juice
1 large Bosc pear

Whisk the honey and lemon juice until well combined. Using 20 millimeter (¾-inch) and 25-millimeter (1-inch) Parisian scoops, scoop balls from the pear. Store the balls in the honey lemon syrup.

To Finish

½ cup Crème Fraîche (page 499)
Honey Brittle (page 269)

Using a whisk, whip the crème fraîche to soft peaks. Drain the candied ginger and lemon. Mince very finely and stir together along with some of their syrups so that the mixture is spreadable. Using a small offset spatula, spread 1 teaspoon of minced candied ginger and lemon down the center of each of 4 plates. Place one poached Bosc pear ring in the center of each plate. Dot with pear puree and whipped crème fraîche. Using the back of a small spoon, gently make an indentation in half of the pear puree dots. Arrange a few of the pear parisiennes down the plate, followed by pear slices. Place 1 tablespoon of the ginger spice crumble on top of the poached Bosc pear ring. Finish with 1 teaspoon of honey brittle and a quenelle of pear sorbet.

Peas

Quail Hill Farm

In 1989, Deborah Ann Light made a significant decision that ultimately led to Quail Hill Farm's founding. After being diagnosed with terminal cancer, she had to make plans for her Suffolk County estate. Following her instinct, she decided, "Leave it alone!" By endowing her property to Long Island's Peconic Land Trust, she intended the land to be protected from development. However, the board issued a ruling that made an exception: it allowed for the land to be developed into farmland. The ruling delighted Deborah, and she put her faith in the Land Trust's new agricultural manager, Scott Chaskey. This white-bearded poet-turned-farmer had just relocated to the East End from the cliffs of Mousehole, England, and he would come to play a significant role in turning Deborah's land into thriving, bountiful farmland.

The CSA at Quail Hill aims to help members gain an especially intimate understanding of the agricultural process. Shareholders enjoy rights that extend beyond those offered at other programs. Specifically, they are invited to visit the sprawling, Edenic farm and harvest their own crops. This system lets members control their own mix of produce, in contrast to the conventional CSA model in which the farm determines each allotment. "Members make decisions here—from what we plant, to the themes of food-related events on the farm," says Scott. This autonomy does bring with it a certain amount of danger. Scott smiles as he relates how tension can build on the farm. "I see the horror spread fast when a member pulls an entire basil plant out instead of plucking the top leaves. But these minor risks pale in comparison to the overall benefit."

Encountering pea-plant tendrils dangling in the brisk autumn air puzzles most onlookers. Scott explains, "Peas help fix nitrogen in the soil, so I use a hearty, cool climate Austrian winter pea as a late-season cover crop." The peas that are grown as cover crops don't taste the same as the ones that herald spring's arrival, but they serve to put nutrients back into depleted soil. When the time comes to pick spring peas, Scott says that the advantage of picking-to-order is in the flavor, as sugar content reduces with time spent off of the vine. Quail Hill grows varieties like sugar snap peas that are trellised upward, giving them an intense flavor. The farm also offers plenty of shucking peas, including the heirloom Lincoln and Scott's favorite, the sweet Green Arrow.

Deborah ultimately gave 200 acres of her land to the Peconic Land Trust—and beat the odds after her diagnosis. She finds it incredibly rewarding to see her donation thrive with a purpose beyond preservation. Scott is wholeheartedly devoted to aiding cultivation on the Trust's 10,000 deed-preserved acres, and he is perhaps most proud to provide opportunities for future agriculturalists. He says, "Deborah not only let Quail Hill Farm grow, but now we are able to lease land to other growers just starting out." With over 100 farm apprentices now graduated and 250 CSA families annually participating, Quail Hill Farm is thriving under the Trust's protection.

Pea Soup with Ham Hocks

SERVES 4

Ham Hock Stock

4 ham hocks
3 cups diced (½ inch) onion
2 cups white wine
1½ cups diced (½ inch) carrot
1 cup diced (½ inch) celery
7 sprigs thyme
1 tablespoon black peppercorns
1 bay leaf

Combine all of the ingredients in a large stockpot and add 4 quarts of water. Bring to a simmer and cook over low heat until the ham hocks are tender, about 3½ hours. Strain the liquid through a chinois. Discard the vegetables and pull the meat from the ham hocks. Reserve the ham for garnish.
Note: Any leftover stock can be frozen in ice cube trays for up to 1 month and used in lieu of chicken stock to glaze vegetables and to give a smoky flavor to soups and stews.

Slow-Cooked Eggs

4 eggs

Bring a medium saucepan of water to 145°F. Add the eggs and cook for 35 to 40 minutes, using a digital thermometer to ensure that the temperature remains constant.

Croutons

4 tablespoons butter
1 cup torn country bread
2 cloves garlic, crushed but kept whole
2 sprigs thyme

Melt the butter in a small sauté pan over medium-high heat. Add the bread, garlic, and thyme, and sauté until golden brown, 2 to 3 minutes. Drain on paper towels, discarding the garlic and thyme.

Pea Soup

2 tablespoons butter
1 cup diced (½ inch) onion
1 tablespoon minced garlic
4 cups shelled English peas
4 cups Ham Hock Stock

In a large stockpot, melt the butter over medium heat. Add the onion and sweat for 2 to 3 minutes. Add the garlic and sweat for 1 to 2 minutes. Add the peas and raise the heat to high, stirring frequently to keep the peas from achieving any color. Add the stock and bring to a simmer. Cover with a parchment paper lid and simmer until the peas are tender, 4 to 5 minutes. Transfer to the blender and puree. Strain through a chinois.

To Finish

3 tablespoons cold butter
1½ cups shelled English peas
Salt
Pickled Shallots (page 501)
Garlic chive flowers
Pea tendrils
Olive oil

In a medium sauté pan, melt 2 tablespoons of the butter over medium heat until foamy. Add the peas and sweat for 2 to 3 minutes. Add 1 cup of ham hock stock, bring to a simmer, and cover with a parchment paper lid. Simmer until the peas are tender, 7 to 8 minutes. Remove the parchment paper and add the reserved ham hock meat and the remaining 1 tablespoon of butter. Reduce to a glaze and season with salt to taste. Divide the pea soup among 4 bowls. Crack a slow-cooked egg into each bowl of soup and garnish with the glazed peas and ham. Spoon pickled shallots onto the soup. Add the croutons and garnish with garlic chive flowers and pea tendrils. Finish with olive oil.

Pea Salad with Guanciale

SERVES 4

4½ cups snow peas
2 tablespoons olive oil
½ cup diced (⅛ inch) onion
¼ cup diced (⅛ inch) guanciale
½ cup mint leaves
½ cup shaved Sprout Creek Farm Ouray
   (a raw cow's milk cheese similar to a dry cheddar)
Juice of 1 lemon
Salt
Ground black pepper
Garlic chive blossoms

Rinse the snow peas and trim off the tips from both ends. Slice lengthwise into thin ribbons. In a medium sauté pan, heat the oil over low heat. Add the onion and sweat for 2 minutes. Add the guanciale and continue to sweat for an additional minute. Remove the pan from the heat. Add the peas, mint, cheese, and lemon juice. Season with salt and pepper to taste. Divide the salad among 4 bowls and garnish with garlic chive blossoms.

Plums

Red Jacket Orchards

Joe Nicholson, second-generation owner and CEO of Red Jacket Orchards, is playfully dubbed "Mr. Plum." He wows market-goers with tree-ripened stone fruit—cherries, apricots, peaches—but most notably he grows stellar plums. "The world does a terrible job with plums, and this is a tremendous opportunity," he says.

Joe's family raised poultry on Long Island until they were forced off their land in 1958, when the government approved construction of the Wantagh–Oyster Bay Parkway, which would run right through their farm. Seeking a new livelihood, Joe's father bought Red Jacket Fruit Farm—ninety acres of apple, nectarine, cherry, and plum trees—and eventually changed the name to the homier sounding Red Jacket Orchards. The family took a chance with unconventional marketing techniques in order to avoid sending their fruit to the cannery. "We created a ten-by-ten-foot stand at the end of the road," remembers Joe. His family focused on their customers' preferences, creating the most direct and customized service the neighborhood had ever known. Soon enough, Red Jacket Orchards became a household name for local residents, extending its reputation to Manhattan in the late 1990s.

Joe's particular bias for plums is evident as he makes his rounds through the thirty-five-acre orchard. He marvels at the fruit's beauty, from rounded Japanese varieties to smaller egg-shaped European breeds. "Most people harvest them green and don't allow for ripening," he explains. "They pick them for size and uniformity . . . it is a very flawed system." The plums that leave Red Jacket Orchards are picked at the peak of flavor, in accordance with the company's Tree-Ripened initiative. In addition to enjoying adequate time on the tree, Joe's stone fruits benefit from an enormous temperature variation of 25°F between day and night. These circumstances guarantee showstopping results. July's golden sugar plums and crimson Satsumas gush with sweetness, enhanced with a burst of acidity from their delicate skin. Victory and heirloom yellow egg plums are picked late in the season, giving them a balanced richness and toothsome bite. The specialty greengage plums from France are deceptive, as they are still green when perfectly ripened and abundant in sugar. Joe transports his harvest with care—his plums' only blemishes are brilliant sunspots that hint at the lusciousness within.

Plum trees often bloom triumphantly while snow is still on the ground. Even after an arctic winter, the tree perseveres for another year. Their unwavering, resilient character mirrors Joe's persistence—he's never abandoned his mission to spotlight this often-underappreciated fruit. Joe is honest about what it means to farm: "I've been in this business for thirty-eight years, and I'm just starting to know what I'm doing."

Pickled Plums

MAKES 16 PLUMS

16 Italian plums
3 tablespoons juniper berries
3 tablespoons pink peppercorns
1½ tablespoons black peppercorns
1 tablespoon allspice berries
1½ teaspoons cloves
1½ cinnamon sticks
3 star anise
6½ cups red wine
3 cups red wine vinegar
1½ cups port
1½ cups sugar
3 tablespoons salt
¼ teaspoon ground nutmeg
3 tablespoons Earl Grey tea leaves

Pierce each plum with a cake tester or the tip of a paring knife and place in a glass bowl. In a small saucepan over medium heat, toast the juniper berries, pink peppercorns, black peppercorns, allspice berries, cloves, cinnamon, and star anise until fragrant, about 1 minute. Remove the spices from the heat and transfer to a small stockpot. Add the red wine, red wine vinegar, port, sugar, salt, nutmeg, and 3 cups of water. Bring the mixture to a simmer and reduce by half to about 6 cups. Remove the pickling liquid from the heat and add the tea leaves. Cover the stockpot and let steep for 5 minutes. Strain the liquid through a chinois and pour it while still hot over the plums. Allow the plums to cool to room temperature. Cover and refrigerate for 2 weeks before serving. **Note:** These plums can be used as a condiment with roasted pork or venison. Store them in the refrigerator, covered, for 1 to 2 months, depending on the ripeness of the fruit.

Variations of Plums with Ricotta

SERVES 4

Oven-Roasted Apricots

4 small apricots, not too ripe
½ cup sugar
1 bunch tarragon

Preheat the oven to 325°F. Halve the apricots and toss in the sugar. Line a rimmed baking sheet with the tarragon and lay the apricots, cut side down, on the tarragon. Roast in the oven for 10 to 12 minutes until they begin to soften. Pour about ½ cup of hot water into the baking sheet and roast for a few more minutes to steam. Remove from the oven, cool to room temperature, and transfer to a parchment paper–lined baking sheet. Refrigerate, and, once cool enough to handle, peel off the skins. Keep covered in the refrigerator.

Apricot Tuile and Crumble

1½ cups diced (½ inch) ripe apricots
1 egg
1 egg yolk
¾ cup sugar
¼ teaspoon citric acid

Preheat the oven to 170°F. (If your oven temperature doesn't go down to 170°F, set it to the lowest temperature and leave the oven door ajar, monitoring the inside temperature with a thermometer and adjusting the temperature and oven door as necessary to reach 170°F.) Puree the apricots in a blender until smooth. Pass through a chinois. You should have about 1 cup of puree. Whip the egg, egg yolk, and sugar in the bowl of a stand mixer fitted with the whisk attachment at high speed until the mixture forms a ribbon. Fold in the apricot puree and citric acid. Spray a sheet of acetate or a silicone baking mat with nonstick vegetable cooking spray and wipe to remove any excess. Spread the batter ⅛ inch thick on the acetate and dehydrate in the oven until crisp, about 3 hours. Allow to cool to room temperature. To make the apricot crumble, grind half of the tuile in a food processor until it resembles coarse sand. Store in an airtight container.

Oat Streusel

1 cup old-fashioned rolled oats
¾ cup flour
½ cup plus 1 tablespoon light brown sugar
⅓ cup plus 1 tablespoon cold butter
¼ teaspoon ground cinnamon
1 teaspoon salt

Preheat the oven to 325°F. In the bowl of a stand mixer fitted with the paddle attachment, mix all of the ingredients until crumbly. Spread out on a rimmed baking sheet and bake, stirring often, until evenly golden brown, about 20 minutes. Cool to room temperature, and then grind in a food processor. **Note:** Any leftover streusel can be stored in an airtight container at room temperature for up to 1 week.

Plum Sorbet

8 cups (about 3½ pounds) pitted and diced black plums
1 cup sugar
1 teaspoon citric acid

Toss the plums with the sugar and citric acid. Puree in a blender and strain through a chinois. Chill over an ice bath. Freeze in an ice cream machine. **Note:** Store in the freezer for up to 1 month.

Tarragon Ricotta and Tarragon Plums

½ cup sugar
1½ tablespoons roughly chopped tarragon
2 cups ricotta
4 plums of several varieties

In a small saucepan over medium heat, combine the sugar with ½ cup of water. Warm until the sugar is completely dissolved. Pour over the tarragon and let cool to room temperature. Strain, discarding the tarragon. Puree the ricotta in a food processor, thinning out slightly to a spreadable consistency using a few tablespoons of the tarragon syrup. Cut the plums into various shapes and sizes. Toss with the remaining tarragon syrup.

To Finish

Apricot Puree (page 498)
Tarragon leaves
Ricotta Ice Cream (page 501)

Using a small offset spatula, spread about 2 teaspoons of the apricot puree across the surface of each of 4 plates. Using the same motion, spread about 2 teaspoons of the tarragon ricotta almost perpendicular to the apricot puree. Spoon about 1 tablespoon of oat streusel at the base of the apricot puree, and about 1 tablespoon of apricot crumble at the base of the tarragon ricotta. Place two of the oven-roasted apricots, cut side down, in the center of the plate. Arrange tarragon plums next to the oven-roasted apricots and on either end of the plate. Garnish with a few tarragon leaves. Place a quenelle of plum sorbet on the apricot crumble and a quenelle of the ricotta ice cream on the oat streusel. Finish with a piece of apricot tuile on top of the ricotta ice cream.

Upside-Down Plum Cake

Red Syrup

¼ cup sugar
3 tablespoons red fruit juice, such as pomegranate
or cranberry
1 tablespoon glucose syrup
⅛ teaspoon citric acid, plus more to taste

In a small saucepan over medium-high heat, bring all of the ingredients to a boil. Once the sugar has dissolved, remove from the heat. Add more citric acid to taste.

Almond Cake

8 to 10 medium Italian plums, halved and pitted
Red Syrup
2 tablespoons almond paste
5 teaspoons light brown sugar
1 tablespoon salt
3 tablespoons butter, softened
¼ cup buttermilk
2 tablespoons olive oil
1 teaspoon vanilla extract
¼ cup almond flour
2 eggs
¼ cup granulated sugar
⅓ cup flour
¼ teaspoon baking soda

Preheat the oven to 325°F. Spray the sides of an 8-inch cake pan with nonstick vegetable cooking spray. Cut each plum half into 4 wedges and arrange the plums in a pinwheel pattern in the bottom of the pan. Make sure that they are tightly packed but still laying flat. Pour the red syrup over the plums.

In the bowl of a stand mixer fitted with the paddle attachment, mix the almond paste, light brown sugar, and salt on medium-low speed until the almond paste is just broken up. Add the butter and cream and mix until the mixture is light and fluffy. Slowly stream in the buttermilk, oil, and vanilla. Fold in the almond flour. In a clean bowl, whisk the eggs with the sugar until fully ribboned. Sift together the flour and baking soda. Fold the egg mixture and the flour mixture into the almond mixture, alternating additions. Pour the batter over the plums and bake until the cake is golden brown and firm to the touch, about 45 minutes. Cool completely to room temperature before turning out the cake onto a serving plate.

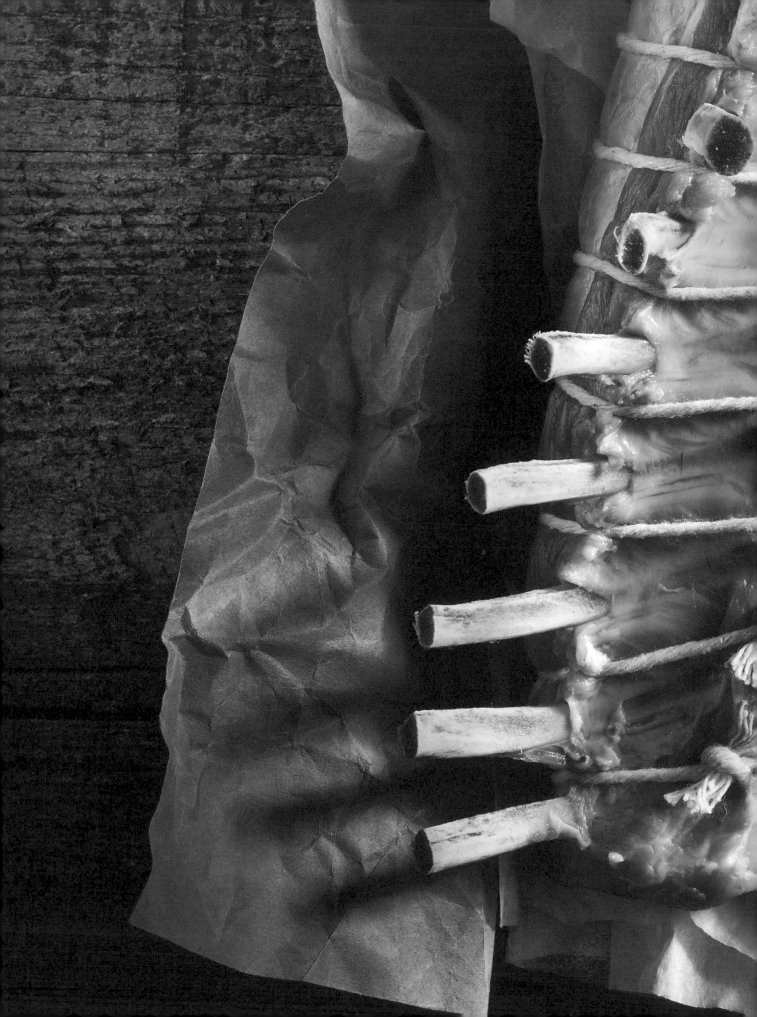

Pork

Four Story Hill Farm

In 1992, Steve and Sylvia Pryzant decided to launch a farming venture that revolved around their customers' specific needs. They wanted to share their hard work with chefs who truly respected their labor. "We could not compete with large farms, nor did we want to," Sylvia says. Committed to their target market, they began by working with veal before broadening their scope to heritage breeds of poultry. Now they focus closely on ever-popular English Berkshire suckling pigs.

The pair met in the 1970s in Israel, where Steve, a native New Yorker, was working with dairy cows on a kibbutz farm and French-born Sylvia was studying at Tel Aviv University. After falling in love, they moved to a *moshav* farm collective where they learned about farming and agriculture. When the couple relocated to New York City, they each secured employment: Steve in food services at a nursing home and Sylvia as a secretary for a nonprofit. But they felt unfulfilled and longed for the agricultural lifestyle they had come to love in Israel. Taking hold of their destiny, they left the big city for Honesdale, Pennsylvania—a mere 110 miles from Manhattan.

Citing their operation as "a real mom-and-pop farm," Steve and Sylvia manage every aspect of their farm together. Full-grown hogs eat organically, feasting on local apples and acorns. Newborn Berkshire pigs feed only on their mother's milk until they reach eighteen to twenty pounds. The suckling pigs are slaughtered on site in accordance with USDA guidelines. This part of the process still rattles Steve, but he accepts the necessity: "There is nobody within 146 miles that does this." Sylvia chooses not to watch, but she is proud of their work. "It is very rare to have an all-encompassing farm with a slaughterhouse. This is a true step in providing a farm-to-table product."

Most days of the week, Steve rises at 6:00 a.m. for the slaughter (depending on the number of orders he has), and then takes a short nap before driving the deliveries to Manhattan. The Four Story Hill van arrives to kitchens around the city carrying the freshest meat. Their suckling pig is regarded as some of the best—full-flavored, moist, and downright mouthwatering.

Baby Pork Rack with Apricots

SERVES 4

Onion Petals

1 Spanish onion
8 sprigs thyme
2 tablespoons butter
Salt

Preheat the oven to 350°F. Place the onion on a piece of aluminum foil. Top with the thyme, butter, and 1 tablespoon of salt. Bring the corners of the foil together and create a package. Line a small baking dish with a 1-inch bed of salt. Place the onion package on top and roast until tender, 2½ to 3 hours. Allow the onion to cool. Cut into quarters and separate the petals.

Roasted Apricots

1 bunch lemon thyme
5 bay leaves
4 apricots
Salt
¼ cup confectioners' sugar

Preheat the oven to 350°F. Line a 9 by 13-inch rimmed baking sheet with the lemon thyme and bay leaves. Peel the apricots, cut them in half, remove the pits, and season with salt. Place the apricot halves, cut side down, on the bed of thyme and bay leaves. Sprinkle the sugar over the apricots and roast in the oven for 7 minutes until softened. Flip the apricots over and pour ½ cup of hot water into the baking sheet. Return to the oven and roast for 7 more minutes.

Apricot Sauce

2 tablespoons sugar
1 cup diced (⅛ inch) apricot
1 teaspoon white balsamic vinegar, plus more to taste
1 tablespoon canola oil
4 ounces pork trim, diced (¼ inch)
¼ cup thinly sliced shallots
½ cup white wine
2 cups Chicken Jus (page 498)
1 cup Chicken Stock (page 499)
7 sprigs thyme
Salt

Melt the sugar in a small sauté pan over medium-high heat. When the sugar has caramelized to a dark amber color, add the apricots and toss to combine. Cook for 2 minutes, and then add the vinegar. Simmer for 6 to 7 minutes until thickened. Remove from the heat. In a large straight-sided pan, heat the canola oil over high heat. Add the pork trim and sear until evenly browned, 4 to 5 minutes. Lower the heat to medium-low and add the shallots. Sweat until the shallots are tender, 1 to 2 minutes. Deglaze the pan with the white wine, raise the heat, and reduce until almost dry, about 3 minutes. Add the apricot mixture, chicken jus, chicken stock, and thyme and bring to a simmer. Simmer over medium-low heat for 30 minutes. Strain the sauce through a chinois and return to the pan. Reduce over medium heat to about 1½ cups. Season with white balsamic vinegar and salt to taste.

To Finish

2 tablespoons canola oil
1 (1-pound) baby pork rack, frenched
Salt
5 tablespoons cold butter
4 sprigs thyme
2 cloves garlic, crushed but kept whole
8 green onions
¼ cup Chicken Stock (page 499)
Pickled Mustard Seeds (page 500)
Sea salt
Baby mizuna

Preheat the oven to 300°F. Heat the oil in a medium cast-iron skillet over high heat. Truss the rack with butcher's twine and season liberally with salt. Add the rack to the skillet, fat side down, and sear for 1 to 1½ minutes. Flip and sear for another 1 to 1½ minutes. Flip one more time, lower the heat, and add 2 tablespoons of the butter, the thyme, and the garlic. Baste for 1 to 2 minutes. Transfer the pork to a wire rack set in a rimmed baking sheet and place in the oven. Roast for 5 minutes, turn the pork, and baste. Roast for another 5 minutes, turn, and baste. Roast for 3 to 5 more minutes, until the internal temperature registers 135° to 140°F. Allow the rack to rest for 10 to 12 minutes before carving.

Bring a saucepan of salted water to a boil. Add the green onions and blanch until tender, 2½ to 3 minutes. Transfer to an ice bath, and when cool, drain. Place the onion petals and blanched green onions in a small sauté pan with 2 tablespoons of the butter. Add the chicken stock and simmer for 1 to 2 minutes. Add the remaining 1 tablespoon of butter and reduce to glaze. Spoon apricot sauce onto a plate, along with 2 roasted apricot halves. Arrange 2 glazed green onions and onion petals on the plate and spoon pickled mustard seeds around. Season the pork chops with sea salt and place on the plate. Garnish with baby mizuna leaves. Repeat with the remaining ingredients, to serve 4.

White Pork Sausage

MAKES 12 TO 15 SAUSAGES, TO SERVE 6 TO 8

Four-Spice Mix

¼ cup black peppercorns
2 cinnamon sticks
2 whole nutmeg
1 tablespoon whole cloves

Combine all spices in a spice grinder and grind to a fine powder. **Note:** Store leftovers in an airtight container at room temperature and use to season pork, beef, and game.

White Pork Sausage

18 ounces boneless skinless chicken breast, diced (¾ inch) and chilled
18 ounces boneless pork shoulder, diced (¾ inch) and chilled
¼ cup salt
½ teaspoon pink curing salt
1 tablespoon ground white pepper
1 teaspoon Four-Spice Mix
4 cups cream
2 tablespoons beaten egg
16 egg egg whites
15 feet of hog casings
2 tablespoons canola oil

Chill a meat grinder and all of its parts in the refrigerator for 2 hours. Pass the chicken and pork through the cold meat grinder fitted with the medium die. Then, grind again through the small die. You should have about 6 cups of ground meat.

In a bowl, combine the ground meat with the salt, curing salt, white pepper, and four-spice mix. Cover and refrigerate for 1 hour. Combine the cream, beaten egg, and egg whites in a large bowl. Transfer half of the meat mixture to a food processor. With the processor running, slowly pour in half of the egg and cream mixture to emulsify. Transfer to a mixing bowl and repeat with the remaining meat and egg mixture. Cover and chill the forcemeat in the refrigerator until ready to make the sausages.

Rinse the hog casings well under cold running water. Transfer the forcemeat to a sausage stuffer and pipe into the casings. Twist off and tie the sausages with butcher's twine, creating 5-inch links.

Heat a large pot of salted water to 170°F and poach the sausages until their internal temperature reaches 155°F, 25 to 30 minutes. Remove from the water and cool to room temperature. Score the sausages with a paring knife and separate the links. Heat the canola oil in a large pan over high heat and sear the sausages until browned, 1 to 2 minutes on each side. Serve with Potato Puree (page 501) and roasted apples and shallots.

Bacon Marmalade

MAKES 1 QUART

3 tablespoons canola oil
3 cups diced (⅜ inch) bacon (about 1¼ pounds)
1½ cups diced (¼ inch) onion
⅓ cup diced (¼ inch) carrot
⅓ cup diced (¼ inch) celery
2¼ cups apple cider
⅓ cup sherry vinegar
1 tablespoon maple syrup
1½ teaspoons molasses
5 teaspoons whole-grain mustard
5 teaspoons Pickled Mustard Seeds (page 500)
1 tablespoon thyme leaves

In a medium sauté pan, heat the oil over high heat. Add the bacon and brown, stirring frequently, for 2 to 3 minutes. Lower the heat and add the onion, carrot, and celery and sweat, stirring frequently until the vegetables are tender, 6 to 7 minutes. Add the cider and vinegar and raise the heat to high. Reduce the liquid until thickened, 7 to 8 minutes. Add the maple syrup and molasses, stirring over medium heat until a glaze forms on the bacon. Remove the marmalade from the heat and stir in the mustard and pickled mustard seeds. Fold in the thyme leaves. **Note:** Store in a jar in the refrigerator for up to 2 weeks. Bacon marmalade is ideal on sandwiches or simply spread on hot toast; as a condiment for pork, roasted or seared fish, or scallops; or with fresh peas, carrots, cabbage, or brussels sprouts.

Potatoes

Balsam Farms

Potato fields used to cover the coast of Long Island from Nassau to Montauk. But over the years, farmers slowly ceased to cultivate this crop because of its small financial returns. But Alex Balsam and Ian Calder-Piedmonte, both Cornell graduates, always save a spot for potatoes on their Bridgehampton farm because of their confidence in the quality of their product. Ian explains that the secret to growing excellent potatoes is in the soil: "The more conventional potato growers here are capable of producing more per acre than even Maine or Idaho." He says of the loam's fantastic structure, "It drains well, holds nutrients, and is not too heavy."

Despite his young age, Alex has already been farming for a long time. When he was only twelve years old, he contacted Scott Chaskey (see page 353) of the Peconic Land Trust to rent a quarter of an acre of land, just to keep himself busy. This jumpstarted his career in independent farming, and, in 2003, still in his early twenties, he was ready to invest all of his energy in the agricultural lifestyle. He worked alone for a year until his friend Ian joined him. Alex is pleased with their progress: "We've come a long way," he says.

While the yields are spectacular—averaging roughly fifty thousand pounds per acre—there are marked challenges in potato farming. Alex and Ian combat the dreaded Colorado beetle, one of the potato farmer's fiercest enemies. "They're horrible," says Ian with a pained look on his face. "They can devour the crop." Because Alex and Ian are dedicated to an organic philosophy, they have worked particularly hard over the past few years to battle the beetles without using pesticides, including "a bug vacuum that goes over the rows, sucks up the bugs, and chops them to pieces." Potato farmers are also challenged by the high rate at which their crop sucks essential nutrients from the soil. At Balsam Farms, Alex and Ian use cover crops to replenish the soil and provide an optimal environment for their fingerlings, Yukon Golds, and Kennebecs. While potatoes are easily stored year-round, Ian prefers to eat them straight from the ground at the end of July. "Most people don't think about potatoes as seasonal crops, but when they are fresh and the skin has not firmed up, there is nothing like them."

Balsam Farms has successfully carved its own special niche in Long Island's agricultural scene by embracing the crop that once predominated in that area. Alex and Ian's roadside farm stand operation, harkening back to the early days of the farm-to-table movement, sits on a small side road that is frequented only by motorists trying to avoid traffic on other thruways. "We have become a little bit of a destination. We are even seeing repeat customers," says Ian. They also deliver seven days a week to chefs throughout Long Island, providing them with the finest specimens of a humble ingredient that once helped establish Long Island as one of New York's farming havens.

Duck Fat French Fries

SERVES 4

3 russet or other starchy potatoes
10 cups rendered duck fat (about 5 pounds)
6 cloves garlic, crushed but kept whole
10 sprigs thyme
Sea salt

Wash the potatoes and, leaving the skins on, cut them length-wise into chunky fries about ¾ inch thick. Place the cut fries in water while you work to avoid oxidation. In a large stockpot, heat the duck fat to 300°F over medium-high heat. Thoroughly rinse the potatoes of any starch, drain well, and pat dry. Cook the fries in the duck fat until tender but not golden, 3 to 4 min-utes. Remove the fries from the duck fat and drain on paper towels. Reserve the fat for the second round of frying. Place the fries on a baking sheet lined with parchment paper and freeze until solid, about 2 hours. Once the fries are frozen, heat the duck fat to 375°F over medium-high heat. Lower the frozen fries into the fat and fry until crispy and golden brown, 5 to 6 minutes. Drain on a cooling rack. Rub the inside of a mixing bowl with the garlic cloves. Toss the fries in the bowl with the garlic cloves and thyme. Season with salt to taste.

Potatoes Baked in Puff Pastry

SERVES 4

2 (11 by 16-inch) sheets frozen all-butter puff pastry dough
6 sprigs thyme
2 cloves garlic, crushed but kept whole
1 bay leaf
1 tablespoon black peppercorns
1 teaspoon red chile flakes
1¾ pounds fingerling potatoes, peeled
Salt
½ cup olive oil
2 eggs
3 tablespoons finely chopped marjoram
2 tablespoons finely chopped thyme
1 tablespoon finely chopped rosemary

Partially thaw the puff pastry dough in the refrigerator or at room temperature. Preheat the oven to 400°F. To make a sachet, tie the thyme, garlic, bay leaf, peppercorns, and chile flakes in a piece of cheesecloth. Place the potatoes in a saucepan and cover with cold water. Season the water with salt and add the sachet. Bring to a simmer and cook until the potatoes are tender, about 35 minutes. Drain off the water, discard the sachet, and allow the potatoes to rest for 5 minutes, letting the moisture steam off. Mash the potatoes with a fork and stir in the olive oil. Beat one of the eggs and stir it in. Mix in the marjoram, thyme, and rosemary, and season with salt to taste. Cut a 13¾ by 4⅜-inch rectangle from each of the sheets of puff pastry. To make the top of the pastry case, place one of the pastry rectangles on a parchment paper–lined baking sheet. Beat the remaining egg and brush the puff pastry with it. Place a wire rack directly on top of the dough to allow it to rise only about ¾ inch as it bakes and bake in the oven for 12 to 15 minutes until puffed and golden brown.

Lower the oven temperature to 350°F. To make the base, place the second pastry rectangle between 2 sheets of parchment paper. Place on a baking sheet and top with a second baking sheet to keep the pastry from rising too much as it bakes. Bake until light golden brown, about 30 minutes.

Lower the oven temperature to 325°F. Place a 13¾ by 4⅜-inch straight-sided tart mold around the baked pastry base on the baking sheet. Fill the mold with the potato mixture and bake in the oven until the potatoes are set, about 30 minutes. Brush the bottom of the top pastry case with egg wash and place on the potatoes. Bake in the oven until set, 12 to 15 minutes. Cool for a few minutes at room temperature and then gently remove the mold. Slice and serve warm alongside a simply dressed green salad.

Potato and Bacon Bread

MAKES 1 LOAF

½ pound fingerling potatoes, plus 3 additional potatoes
Salt
½ cup diced (¼-inch) bacon
2⅔ cups flour
1 packed teaspoon fresh yeast
1½ teaspoons chopped thyme
¼ teaspoon coarsely ground black pepper

Place the ½ pound of potatoes in a saucepan and cover with cold water. Season the water with salt. Bring to a simmer and cook until the potatoes are tender, about 35 minutes. While the potatoes are cooking, render the bacon in a small sauté pan over medium heat. Drain the potatoes, allow to cool, and then peel and dice into ½-inch pieces. You should have about ⅔ cup of diced cooked potatoes. Drain the bacon and set aside.

Combine the flour, 1 teaspoon of salt, the yeast, and 1⅓ cups of water in the bowl of a stand mixer fitted with the dough hook. Mix for 3 minutes on the lowest speed, and then for 3 more minutes on the next lowest speed. Check the dough for elasticity; you should be able to stretch the dough to make a translucent "windowpane." If it does not make a windowpane, continue mixing. Once the dough is elastic enough, add the diced potatoes, bacon, thyme, and pepper, and mix on the lowest speed until well incorporated. Lightly oil a clean bowl, transfer the dough to it, and cover with plastic wrap. Rest for 2 hours in a warm place, such as near a warm oven or stove. Turn the dough out onto a floured surface and push out any bubbles. Loosely shape into a ball with the seam side down, cover with a kitchen towel, and let rest for 10 to 15 minutes.

Place a pizza stone on the bottom shelf of the oven and preheat the oven to 450°F. Thinly slice the remaining 3 potatoes on a mandoline. Store in cold water until ready to use. Shape the dough into a round loaf. Place on a well-oiled flat surface and cover with a kitchen towel. Rest at room temperature for 45 minutes to 1 hour until doubled in size. When the dough is ready, place it on a floured surface and flatten it out, gently stretching the dough into a rounded triangle about ½ inch thick and with a point facing away from you. Using a bench knife or paring knife, make a cut down the center of the triangle all the way through the thickness of the dough but do not cut the dough into 2 separate pieces. Cut slits along either side of the center cut. Gently widen the slits with your fingers after you've made the cuts. Transfer the shaped dough to a well-floured board. Pat the potato slices dry on paper towels and completely cover the top of the loaf with the sliced potatoes. Slide the dough onto the pizza stone and bake for about 20 minutes or until golden brown. Cool on a wire rack.

Radishes

Red Tail Farm

After spending years studying plants at Cornell University, Brent Welch and Teresa Vanek began to feel that their careers had become too academic. They decided to take a more hands-on approach to their learning, and looked to their ancestral roots for inspiration. "My granddad was a farmer, and Teresa's grandmother was a beekeeper," says Brent. After an inspirational trip to Bolivia, it became evident that farming was their calling, and they reestablished the direction of their future. "We worked alongside subsistence farmers, and we learned to develop sustainable ecosystems. This experience complimented our interest in people, plants, and working outdoors," Brent says of their time at Cornell. These days, their Red Tail Farm allows them to implement their intellectual knowledge of plants, their shared personal narratives, and their passion for camaraderie and the land they've come to call home.

Guided by the principles of subsistence farming, Brent and Teresa began their farming venture by strengthening their soil with cover crops. Then they planted an apple orchard, blueberry fields, and vegetables, among them a long-time favorite: radishes. The couple now cultivates five acres of their land on their own and leases thirty-five acres to an organic grain farmer; one-fifth of their property, or ten acres, is preserved as a hardwood forest. They find themselves invigorated by the range of wild plants and animals on their land. Following in the footsteps of Teresa's grandmother, they also tend an apiary for plant pollination. Chickens freely roam the property, and rodent patrol is assumed by two beloved red-tailed hawks—the namesakes of the farm.

Red Tail's uncommonly sweet and spicy radishes epitomize Brent and Teresa's exacting standards and their profound agricultural knowledge. The radishes, which thrive in the cooler weather that comes just before and after the prime of summer, grow in silty loam soil that offers excellent drainage and allows the farmers to plant early in the season. Bicolored French breakfast radishes are grown in naturally heated hoop houses and require careful attention because they can "get pithy pretty quickly," according to Teresa. If timed just so, they are ready at the same time as the first spring vegetables. In August, two more radish varieties are planted and are ready for harvest before winter's brutal chill: watermelon radishes and daikon. Brilliant, red-centered watermelon radishes, with their sweetness and crunch, have gained popularity in the last few years; daikons, Brent says, "are especially delicious just after harvest when they are still sweet." While daikon radishes are most commonly pickled or slow-cooked in stews, Brent and Teresa favor a very simple preparation: "We love to cut them like carrot sticks, drizzle them with lime juice, and season them with sea salt and cayenne."

It is this penchant for beautiful simplicity that is at the heart of what Brent and Teresa have built at Red Tail, a farm that is intricately woven with ancestral heritage, a learned craft, and a desire to farm sustainably—a farm that turns up, in the simplest of terms, extraordinary produce.

Radishes with Buttermilk

SERVES 4

Buttermilk Panna Cotta

3 sheets gelatin
2 cups buttermilk
Salt
Cayenne pepper

Bloom the gelatin by placing it in a bowl of ice water until pliable, about 10 minutes. Season the buttermilk with salt and cayenne pepper to taste. When the gelatin has softened, squeeze to remove excess moisture, and transfer to a small saucepan with the buttermilk. Warm until the gelatin is just melted and remove from the heat. Line an 18 by 13-inch plastic tray with plastic wrap. Spray the plastic wrap with nonstick vegetable cooking spray and wipe away the excess with a paper towel. Pour the buttermilk mixture into the prepared tray and refrigerate for 3 hours, until set.

To Finish

10 Easter egg radishes
2 baby radishes
1 English cucumber
1 tablespoon Lemon Vinaigrette (page 500)
Thinly sliced chives
Cucumber Relish (page 204)
Pickled Radishes (page 56)
Dill fronds
Nasturtium flowers
Nasturtium leaves
Cucumber Dressing (page 205)
Sea salt
2 teaspoons olive oil

Using a mandoline, thinly slice the Easter egg radishes crosswise and the baby radishes lengthwise to make rounds and heart shapes. Peel the cucumber and thinly slice lengthwise using the mandoline. Dress the sliced radishes and cucumber in the lemon vinaigrette. Using a paring knife, cut the panna cotta and the plastic wrap liner into quarters. Using a 4-inch round cutter, cut out a round of 1 panna cotta quarter and clean the excess away from the outside of the cutter. Remove the cutter, and using a large spatula slid beneath the plastic wrap, carefully flip the panna cotta onto the center of a plate. Peel away the plastic and sprinkle chives over the panna cotta. Arrange the sliced radishes on top. Spoon cucumber relish on top of the radishes. Place pickled radishes and shaved cucumber on the plate. Garnish with dill, nasturtium flowers, and nasturtium leaves. Spoon cucumber vinaigrette around the plate and season with sea salt to taste. Finish with ½ teaspoon olive oil. Repeat with the remaining ingredients, to serve 4.

Thinly Sliced Radishes

SERVES 4

¼ cup Crème Fraîche (page 499)
¼ cup buttermilk
Lime juice
Salt
Cayenne pepper
2 black radishes
2 watermelon radishes
1 tablespoon Lemon Vinaigrette (page 500)
4 small Easter egg radishes
4 breakfast radishes
4 tablespoons trout roe
8 baby radishes with greens attached
Dill fronds
Sliced chives
Fennel flowers

In a small bowl, combine the crème fraîche and buttermilk, whisking until smooth. Season with lime juice, salt, and cayenne pepper to taste. Thinly slice the black radishes and watermelon radishes on a mandoline. Toss with lemon vinaigrette. Thinly slice the Easter egg radishes and breakfast radishes on a mandoline. Divide the different types of shaved radishes among 4 plates, placing them in small piles. Spoon the buttermilk dressing over the watermelon radishes. Top the piles of radish with small spoonfuls of trout roe. Place 2 baby radishes in the center of each plate. Garnish with dill, chives, and fennel flowers.

Ricotta

Salvatore Bklyn

In 2006, Betsy Devine and Rachel Mark took a trip to Italy and returned to New York from their blissful holiday with more than just the requisite snapshots and fond memories. In the town of San Gimignano, the couple befriended Salvatore, the gregarious proprietor of Enoteca Gustavo. Betsy says about him, "Salvatore is one of those restaurant owners that is everywhere." In addition to providing them with some memorable meals, he graciously helped them plan the rest of their holiday itinerary. But what struck the women most about Salvatore, even more than his generous hospitality, was his homemade ricotta: dense and sweet like nothing they had ever tasted before. The seeds of their professional future had been planted.

After searching in vain for New York's equivalent to Salvatore's ricotta, Betsy and Rachel were left with no alternative but to recreate the cheese themselves. They began experimenting with cheese-making at home in Brooklyn. Betsy was the chef de cuisine at Lunetta, and it was her guests there who acted as the first taste-testers—and who begged for quarts of the ricotta to take home. Rachel, who was working in the wine world, liked the idea of starting a new company: "I believe that personality has an enormous influence over the finished product. I love me some quirky producers. Betsy is one of them!" The name of their new business, Salvatore Bklyn, came easily—it paid homage both to their trip to Italy and to their home in New York. In 2008, they launched the company and immediately enjoyed a distinct market advantage among other vendors at the Brooklyn Flea: "There weren't a lot of businesses out there like ours, and we wanted to see if we could fly. We were lucky."

Salvatore Bklyn's ricotta does not adhere strictly to Salvatore's original recipe; rather, "He inspired us to take something simple and wonderful and reinvent it as a serious cheese to savor," says Rachel. "First, we choose to start with whole milk instead of whey, which is blasphemous in Italy!" The milk is from Hudson Valley Fresh, produced where Betsy grew up. The milk is slowly heated to around 190°F in a thirty-five-gallon steam-jacketed kettle. Then salt is added for flavor and lemon juice to induce coagulation. The curds form gradually, and Betsy gently agitates them by swaying a paddle back and forth. She then lifts them carefully into draining pans: "We scoop everything by hand to keep the curds large and moist." The fresh cheese sits for twelve hours in cheesecloth-lined pans; this is longer than the standard draining time, and the result is a dense and distinguished ricotta.

Salvatore, their original source of inspiration, says, "We do make ricotta differently here in Italy," but he is excited for the couple and proud of their success, and looks forward to samples from his Brooklyn namesake. Although burrata and mozzarella are on Salvatore Bklyn's radar, for now, Betsy and Rachel are very happy "doing one thing well."

Ricotta Gnocchi with Summer Squash and Mint

SERVES 4

Gnocchi

3 cups ricotta
1 egg
1½ cups grated Parmesan
½ cup flour
½ teaspoon salt
6 cups semolina flour

Line a colander with a quadruple layer of cheesecloth and place the ricotta in the cheesecloth; cover the ricotta with cheesecloth. Set the colander in a large bowl and set another bowl on top of the ricotta. Weigh down the bowl with a heavy can and let the ricotta drain overnight in the refrigerator.

In a food processor, combine 2¾ cups of the pressed ricotta with the egg and blend until smooth. Transfer to a bowl and fold in the Parmesan, flour, and salt. Transfer the mixture to a pastry bag and pipe tablespoon-sized balls onto a baking sheet lined with parchment paper. Refrigerate for 2 hours until firm. Cover the bottom of a large casserole dish with 2 cups of the semolina flour. Roll each ball between your hands and transfer to the semolina. When all of the gnocchi have been rolled, cover with the remaining 4 cups of semolina flour and refrigerate for 24 hours. It is important that the gnocchi are completely covered so that the semolina absorbs any moisture from the ricotta and a shell forms. **Note:** Gnocchi may be frozen for up to 1 week. Defrost slightly at room temperature before cooking.

Zucchini Puree

5 large zucchini
¼ cup canola oil
¼ cup loosely packed mint leaves
¼ cup olive oil
Salt
Cayenne pepper

Trim the ends of the zucchini and cut lengthwise into quarters. Scoop out the seeds and discard. Slice the zucchini ¹⁄₁₆-inch thick on a mandoline to yield about 8 cups of sliced zucchini. In a large saucepan, heat the canola oil over high heat. When the oil is very hot, add the zucchini and cook, stirring constantly, until softened and translucent, 5 to 6 minutes. Add the mint and wilt, about 30 seconds. Transfer to a bowl and chill over an ice bath or in the refrigerator to maintain the green color. Once the zucchini is completely cooled, transfer to the blender and puree. While the blender is running, stream in the olive oil. Strain through a chinois and season with salt and pepper to taste.

To Finish

2 large zucchini
2 assorted summer squash
5 tablespoons cold butter
12 baby zucchini with blooms
6 patty pan squash, halved
¼ cup Chicken Stock (page 499)
Flowering mint
Mint leaves
Squash blossoms
Sea salt

Bring a large pot of salted water to a boil. Cut 2 center planks lengthwise from each zucchini. Shave the summer squash as thinly as possible on a mandoline. Place the zucchini planks and 2 tablespoons of the butter in a large sauté pan and cover with a parchment paper lid. Sweat the zucchini over medium-low heat for 3 to 4 minutes. Add the baby zucchini and patty pan squash and continue sweating for another 3 minutes. Add the stock and bring to a simmer. Uncover, and remove from the heat. Add 1 tablespoon of the butter, swirling the pan to glaze the vegetables. Remove the gnocchi from the semolina using a slotted spoon and gently shake to remove any excess semolina. The gnocchi should have a sturdy shell on the outside but still be supple to the touch. Drop the gnocchi into the boiling water and simmer until they are hot in the center, about 2 minutes. Remove from the pot with a spider strainer and transfer to a large sauté pan with 2 tablespoons of the pasta water. Add the remaining 2 tablespoons of butter to the pan and reduce to glaze over medium heat. Spoon zucchini puree onto each of 4 plates. Place a large zucchini plank on top of the puree and arrange the gnocchi, baby zucchini, and the patty pan squash around the plate. Add the summer squash shavings and garnish with flowering mint, mint leaves, and squash blossoms. Season with salt to taste.

Ricotta Cheesecake

SERVES 4

Cheesecake

3 egg yolks
1 egg
1 cup ricotta
½ cup Crème Fraîche (page 499)
½ cup sugar
1 teaspoon vanilla extract
Zest of ½ lemon
½ teaspoon salt

Preheat the oven to 275°F. Puree all of the ingredients in a blender and strain through a chinois. Evenly divide the mixture among 4 half-pint mason jars and put on the lids. Place in a large roasting pan and fill the roasting pan halfway with hot water. Bake until the cheesecakes are just set, about 1 hour. Cool to room temperature.

Graham Crumble

¾ cup half-white flour (a stone-milled whole wheat flour that has been sifted from most of its bran)
4 tablespoons butter
2 tablespoons light brown sugar
1 tablespoon honey
1½ teaspoons granulated sugar
½ teaspoon salt

Preheat the oven to 325°F. Combine all of the ingredients in the bowl of a stand mixer fitted with the paddle attachment. Beat on medium speed just until the mixture forms little pebbles. Transfer to a baking sheet and bake until dry and golden, 15 to 20 minutes.

Glazed Blueberries

¼ cup sugar
3 tablespoons red wine
2 tablespoons lemon juice
Zest of ½ lemon
1½ cups wild blueberries
1 tablespoon butter

Bring the sugar, wine, lemon juice, and lemon zest to a boil in a small straight-sided sauté pan over medium-high heat. When the mixture is slightly reduced and the bubbles become larger, after 3 to 4 minutes, add the blueberries and the butter. Stir gently to combine. Cook for 1 minute or just until the blueberries are glazed. Remove from the heat before the blueberries burst.

Lemon Foam

4 sheets gelatin
2 cups skim milk
¼ cup sugar
Zest of 1 lemon

Bloom the gelatin by placing the sheets in a bowl of ice water for 10 minute until pliable. In a small saucepan over medium heat, combine the milk and sugar, stirring until the sugar dissolves. Squeeze the gelatin to remove excess moisture and stir into the milk to dissolve. Pour over the lemon zest and steep for 30 minutes. Strain and let cool slightly.

To Finish

Lightly warm the lemon foam mixture. Top the cheesecakes with the glazed blueberries and a few pieces of graham crumble. Froth the lemon foam with a hand blender and scoop the foam on top.

Salsify

John D. Madura Farms

Even after nearly two decades of farming in Pine Island, New York, John D. Madura continues to learn more about his craft. For some time, John grew only onions, the same crop that all of his neighbors were growing. After all, he was farming in America's onion capital, the black dirt region straddling New York and New Jersey. But about fifteen years ago, John decided to diversify his portfolio, and he began to cultivate the little-known vegetable called salsify. "I looked around and saw that we had to do something new to satisfy our customers—so we diversified our vegetables."

For some time, John was following tradition and harvesting his salsify at the time of year just before the farm's soil froze. However, a few years ago, he decided to experiment: "I left the salsify in the ground through the winter and picked the crop the following spring." The root was heartier than he thought it would be: "I didn't know it would survive the cold." John continues to harvest the majority of his salsify in the fall, but knowing that the cold winter ground mimics a natural cellaring process gives him a flexibility he never knew he had.

Of John's three hundred acres, a quarter of an acre is devoted to this niche root vegetable. After the winter months, when the ground begins to thaw, it is planted at the same time as other root crops. "We plant when the ground is cold—it helps germination," he says. The soft black dirt is rich in nutrients and promotes complete development in ninety to a hundred days, leading to large fall harvests that fill the John D. Madura stands at ten produce markets around New York State.

Even food-savvy New Yorkers are, for the most part, unfamiliar with salsify. But for those in the know, John's salsify inspires nostalgia: "A few years ago, a ninety-year-old woman from Maine contacted me about my salsify. She hadn't seen the vegetable in forty years!" After reading an article praising his work, she contacted John. He was flattered by her excitement—so much so that he shipped up a box for her to enjoy.

These days, salsify is a fall specialty present at New York's Greenmarkets, one that plays well with the rest of the season's hearty bounty. And although many praise it for its distinctive taste and texture, the biggest compliment of all is from John's children: "They eat the vegetable because it's good. If they knew salsify was healthy, they probably wouldn't want it."

Salsify Salad with Mangalitsa Ham and Bulgur

Bulgur Chips

½ cup bulgur wheat

Preheat the oven to 200°F. In a medium saucepan, cover the bulgur with 8 cups of water and cook over medium heat until very tender, about 45 minutes. Drain the bulgur and transfer to a rimless baking sheet lined with a silicone baking mat. Cover the bulgur with plastic wrap and roll as thin as possible with a rolling pin. Remove the plastic wrap and dehydrate the bulgur in the oven until dry, 2 to 2½ hours.

Poached Salsify

8 cups Chicken Stock (page 499)
10 sprigs thyme
3 strips lemon peel
2 cloves garlic, crushed but kept whole
Salt
12 stalks salsify, peeled and trimmed into 4-inch pieces

In a medium saucepan, combine the stock, thyme, lemon peel, and garlic. Season with salt and bring to a simmer over high heat. Lower the heat to medium-low, add the salsify, and simmer until tender, 20 to 25 minutes. Cool the salsify to room temperature in the poaching liquid.

Salsify Jus

1 tablespoon butter
2 cups peeled and sliced (⅛ inch) salsify
1 tablespoon tomato paste
1 tablespoon red wine vinegar, plus more to taste
4 cups Chicken Stock (page 499)
Salt
Olive oil

In a medium saucepan over medium heat, melt the butter. Add the salsify and cook until caramelized, 6 to 7 minutes. Add the tomato paste and continue cooking, stirring frequently, for 1 to 2 minutes. Deglaze the pan with the vinegar. Add the stock and raise the heat to high. Bring to a simmer, and then lower the heat and reduce the liquid to 1½ cups, frequently skimming any impurities that rise to the top. Strain the liquid through a chinois. Discard the solids and return the liquid to a small saucepan. Continue reducing until only about ¼ cup of liquid remains. Remove from the heat and strain through a chinois. Season the jus with salt and vinegar to taste and top with olive oil.

Bulgur Salad

1 cup bulgur wheat
Canola oil
2 tablespoons sliced chives
1 tablespoon finely diced shallot
2 tablespoons Lemon Vinaigrette (page 500)
Bulgur Chips
Salt

Preheat the oven to 200°F. Place the bulgur in a bowl. Bring 2 cups of salted water to a boil and pour over the bulgur. Cover the bowl with plastic wrap and let steep until cooled to room temperature and the bulgur has absorbed all the water, about 20 minutes. Spread one-third of the bulgur in a single layer on a parchment paper–lined baking sheet. Dry the bulgur in the heated oven for 15 minutes. Pour 3 inches of canola oil into a large saucepan and bring the oil to 350°F over medium-high heat. Fry the dried bulgur until crispy, 20 to 30 seconds. Remove from the oil and pat dry on paper towels. In a medium bowl, combine the remaining cooked bulgur and the crispy bulgur. Add the chives and shallot and toss with the lemon vinaigrette. Season with salt to taste. Bring the temperature of the oil up to 400°F. Break the bulgur chips into shards and fry in batches until puffed, 1 to 2 seconds. Remove with a slotted spoon to paper towels and season immediately with salt to taste.

To Finish

2 eggs
12 slices Mangalitsa ham
Chervil
Tarragon

Place the eggs in a small saucepan and cover with cold water. Place over high heat and as soon as the water begins to boil, remove from the heat and cover. Allow the eggs to stand for 7 minutes, and then immediately transfer to a bowl of ice water. Place 3 pieces of poached salsify on each of 4 plates and spoon bulgur salad at one end of each piece of salsify. Peel and break up the eggs and place a piece on each pile of bulgur salad. Top the salsify with bulgur chips and the slices of ham. Spoon the salsify jus on the plate and garnish with chervil and tarragon. Serve any leftover bulgur with the salsify jus family-style.

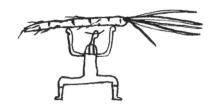

Caramelized Salsify with Apples

SERVES 4

Apple Sauce

2 tablespoons sugar
2 cups peeled, cored, and diced (⅛ inch) Gala apple
1 teaspoon Apple Vinegar (page 25), plus more to taste
1 tablespoon canola oil
¼ cup thinly sliced shallot
½ cup white wine
7 sprigs thyme
2 cups Chicken Jus (page 498)
1 cup Chicken Stock (page 499)
Salt

In a small sauté pan, heat the sugar over medium-high heat. When the sugar has caramelized to a dark amber color, add the apples, toss to combine, and stew for 2 minutes. Add the 1 teaspoon of vinegar and simmer for 6 to 7 minutes. Remove from the heat. In a large saucepan, heat the oil over medium-low heat. Add the shallot and sweat until tender, 1 to 2 minutes. Deglaze the pan with the white wine, raise the heat, and reduce until almost dry, about 3 minutes. Add the apple mixture, thyme, chicken jus, and chicken stock and simmer over medium-low heat for 30 minutes. Strain the sauce through a chinois and return to the pan. Reduce over medium heat to about 1 cup. Season with apple vinegar and salt to taste.

Roasted Garlic Cloves

½ cup butter
8 sprigs thyme
4 large cloves garlic, unpeeled

Preheat the oven to 375°F. In a small baking dish, combine the butter, thyme, and garlic. Roast until the garlic is tender, 25 to 30 minutes.

Apple Chip Topping

1 cup sugar
1 red apple
1 tablespoon sliced chives
1 tablespoon finely chopped parsley
Sea salt

Preheat the oven to 200°F. In a small saucepan, bring the sugar and 1 cup of water to a boil. Remove from the heat and allow to cool. Thinly slice the apple on a mandoline. Dip the apple slices in the syrup and place on a 13 by 18-inch baking sheet lined with a silicone baking mat. Bake in the oven until dry and light golden, 18 to 20 minutes. Immediately remove the apple chips from the pan and allow to cool to room temperature. When the apple chips are cool and crisp, crumble them. Just before serving, combine 1 cup of crumbled apple chips with the chives and parsley and season with sea salt to taste.

To Finish

2 apples
2 pears
6 tablespoons canola oil
8 stalks salsify, peeled and cut into varying lengths
6 tablespoons butter
6 cloves garlic, crushed but kept whole
12 sprigs thyme
¼ cup Chicken Stock (page 499)
1 teaspoon lemon juice
Salt
Olive oil

Slice 1 apple into wedges and the other lengthwise into ¼-inch planks. Slice the pears lengthwise into ¼-inch planks. In a medium sauté pan, heat 2 tablespoons of the oil over high heat and add the salsify. Sear for 1 to 2 minutes on each side, rolling to ensure even caramelization. Lower the heat, pour off the excess oil, and add 2 tablespoons of the butter, 2 garlic cloves, and 3 thyme sprigs. Baste the salsify for 2 to 3 minutes and remove from the heat. Pour out the excess butter, add the chicken stock, and simmer until tender, 3 to 4 minutes. Transfer the salsify to a plate. Repeat the caramelization process with the apple wedges and planks and then with the pears, omitting the stock and cooking the fruit until just tender. Finish the seared salsify, apples, and pears with the lemon juice and season with salt to taste. Spoon apple sauce onto 4 plates and top with olive oil. Arrange the caramelized apples, pears, and salsify on the plates. Add 1 roasted garlic clove to each plate and top with apple chip topping.

Scallops

Captain Anthony Joseph, Stirs One

Captaining a ship takes courage and tenacity—traits that Anthony Joseph acquired at a young age. Growing up near Sheepshead Bay, Brooklyn, he chose to observe the action at the local docks while other eight-year-olds engaged in more typical play. "I always had an interest in the water and fish, and I got attached to the boats," he says. Captain Tony is a soft-spoken man, but he has no trouble coping with the brash personalities of his crew members—who in turn have much to say about him, his work ethic, and his reputation: "Tony's a captain and a half . . . I'll only fish with him," says one. "This job is difficult, dangerous, and it's not for everybody," Tony says about his rigorous profession.

With twenty years of experience under his belt, Tony captains a seventy-five-foot fishing boat called *Stirs One* out of Point Lookout. Atlantic scallops are his specialty. Tony is part of a fishing collective that sells its catch through Jones Inlet Seafood, a fish market and distributor managed by Bruce Larson. Privately owned boats in the collective work autonomously while Bruce assumes landside duties like packaging and selling the daily catch. Success hinges on both parties' ability to collaborate, and there is a palpable sense of camaraderie between the fishermen and their distributor.

Each day, Tony and his four-man crew head out into the Atlantic. When they reach the fishing ground, they release nets off the boat's stern. The boat drags the net, weighted by a ground cable, along the ocean floor and the net scoops up scallops as it goes. When the net is raised, the scallops are dropped on the center deck. Some are shucked immediately and others are left in their distinct, orange-tinted shells. All are iced in the ship's lower chamber for transport back to the dock.

Scalloping off the shores of New York is strictly regulated. "The laws drastically reduce the number of boats fishing for scallops, but they also reduce my catches," says Tony. He now nets about 2,600 pounds annually—a fraction of what he used to harvest. Limits on quantity make Tony more attentive to the quality of his catch, which fluctuates by season and time of day; for example, "In the summer, scallops spawn, and the meat is thicker." Nighttime trolling is best, he explains, because sunlight causes the scallops to burrow into the sand and out of the net's reach. But day or night, winter or summer, the whole crew agrees that nothing beats a fresh scallop raw on the half shell: "The best you can eat is off the deck of the boat—sweet like butter!"

Raw Scallops with Apple, Celery, and Lettuce

SERVES 4

Celery Oil

4 cups green celery leaves
2 cups grapeseed oil

Puree the celery leaves and oil in a blender on high speed.
Transfer the mixture to a medium saucepan and cook over
medium heat, whisking vigorously, until the oil reaches 220°F.
Chill over an ice bath, and then strain through a coffee filter.
Note: Any leftover celery oil can be refrigerated for up to
1 week and mixed with lemon juice to dress fish and shellfish
or a raw celery salad.

Apple Vinaigrette

1 cup fresh Granny Smith apple juice (from about 6 apples)
1 tablespoon Apple Vinegar (page 25)
1 egg yolk
1 cup grapeseed oil
Salt

Combine the apple juice, vinegar, and egg yolk in a blender on
high speed. While the blender is running, slowly stream in the
oil. Season with salt to taste.

To Finish

3 stalks celery
1 Granny Smith apple, cored
2 heads butter lettuce
4 sea scallops
Sea salt
Salad burnet
Yellow celery leaves
Ground black pepper

Peel 2 of the celery stalks and blanch them in a pot of boiling
salted water until tender, 3 to 4 minutes. Transfer to an ice
bath, and, when cool, cut on the bias into 2-inch pieces. Shave
the remaining celery stalk and the apple on a mandoline.
Lightly dress the butter lettuce, the shaved celery, and the
shaved apple with apple vinaigrette. Slice the scallops lengthwise into ⅛-inch sections and arrange on 4 plates. Season
with salt and dress with apple vinaigrette. Arrange the dressed
butter lettuce on the plates and position the dressed shaved
apple among the lettuce. Add the blanched celery batons to
the plates and garnish with salad burnet, celery leaves, and the
dressed celery shavings. Finish with celery oil and pepper.

Seared Scallops

SERVES 4

Roasted Yellow Baby Beets

8 yellow baby beets
1 cup olive oil
⅓ cup red wine vinegar
1 tablespoon sugar
Salt

Preheat the oven to 400°F. Rinse the beets thoroughly and place in a small baking dish. In a small bowl, combine the oil, vinegar, sugar, and 1 cup of water. Season the mixture with salt and pour it over the beets. Cover the dish with aluminum foil and place in the oven. Roast until the beets are tender, 40 to 50 minutes. Allow the beets to cool to room temperature and then peel. Reserve the cooking liquid for the warm beet vinaigrette.

Carrot Puree

3 tablespoons cold butter
4 cups peeled and diced (¼ inch) carrot
2 cups carrot juice (from about 8 carrots)
Salt
Cayenne pepper

Heat 2 tablespoons of the butter over medium heat in a large sauté pan. Add the carrots and sweat for 4 to 5 minutes. Add the carrot juice and bring to a simmer. Cover with a parchment paper lid and simmer until the carrots are tender, 15 to 20 minutes. Remove the parchment paper, raise the heat to high, and reduce the liquid to ½ cup. Transfer to a blender and puree. While the blender is running, add the remaining 1 tablespoon of butter. Strain through a chinois and season with salt and cayenne to taste. **Note:** Any leftover carrot puree can be refrigerated for 2 to 3 days.

Butter-Braised Baby Carrots

3 tablespoons cold butter
8 baby yellow carrots, peeled
¼ cup Chicken Stock (page 499)
Salt

In a medium sauté pan, heat 2 tablespoons of the butter over medium heat. When the butter is foamy, add the carrots and sweat for 3 to 4 minutes. Add the stock, bring to a simmer, and cover with a parchment paper lid. Cook until tender, 8 to 10 minutes. Uncover, add the remaining tablespoon of butter, and reduce to a glaze. Season with salt to taste.

Warm Beet Vinaigrette

Cooking liquid reserved from making
**   Roasted Yellow Baby Beets**
½ cup Brown Butter (page 498)
1 teaspoon caper juice

Pour the reserved beet cooking liquid into a tall narrow container and let it stand so that the oil separates to the top. Remove the separated oil with a spoon and discard. You should be left with about 1 cup of liquid. Transfer the liquid to a small saucepan and reduce to ½ cup. Add the brown butter and stir in the caper juice until completely combined.

To Finish

1 tablespoon canola oil
4 scallops
2 tablespoons butter
5 sprigs thyme
2 cloves garlic, crushed but kept whole
1 baby yellow beet, shaved
1 baby yellow carrot, shaved
Cape gooseberries
Yellow raspberries
Yellow cherry tomatoes
Lemon Vinaigrette (page 500)
Capers
Yellow nasturtium flowers

In a medium sauté pan, heat the oil over high heat. Add the scallops and sear until caramelized, 1 to 2 minutes. Add the butter, thyme, and garlic and baste the scallops for 1 minute. Remove the pan from the heat and let stand for 2 minutes. Spoon carrot puree onto each of 4 plates. Place a scallop, seared side up, on each plate and arrange the butter-braised baby carrots on the plate. Toss the shaved beet, shaved carrot, roasted yellow baby beets, gooseberries, raspberries, and cherry tomatoes in lemon vinaigrette and divide among the plates. Garnish with capers and nasturtium flowers. Spoon warm beet vinaigrette around the dish to finish.

Sheep's Milk

Old Chatham Sheepherding Company

In picturesque Old Chatham, New York, sheep roam on sprawling pastures enclosed by picket fences, and impressively restored red barns complete the land's well-manicured aesthetic. When Tom and Nancy Clark created Old Chatham Sheepherding Company in 1993, they settled on six hundred Hudson Valley acres that were previously home to the Shaker community. Although Shakers are known for their expertise as wood craftsmen, the Clarks set out in a different artisan direction: sheep dairying. "Somebody from Cornell University told us that this land is great for raising sheep," says Tom. That somebody seemed to know their stuff—Old Chatham now stamps their elegant green label on a wide array of sheep's milk products, from crumbly Ewe's Blue cheese, to all shapes and sizes of bloomy-rinded Camembert, to their addictively delicious yogurt.

The quality of sheep's milk depends, naturally enough, on the composition of the ewe's diet. At Old Chatham, a herd of one thousand East Friesian purebred and crossbred ewes grazes at pasture on clover and alfalfa. And, to ensure a stock of healthy food for the sheep year round, the farmers wrap the same grasses wet to ferment into silage. Travis Burrows, the farm manager, explains that "by feeding them protein-rich grasses, we keep our animals healthy." He says that when in top physical condition, "sheep breed naturally when the daylight is short and give birth from February through April." However, Old Chatham maintains an unusual schedule, only breeding the herd from May to August. They do this so their ewes will give birth in the fall and lactate in the winter, guaranteeing sufficient milk production during the off-season. Old Chatham then collaborates with other local lamb dairies to acquire fresh milk during summer months.

Fresh sheep's milk is a delight for yogurt makers because of its rich fat content—nearly 5 percent higher than cow's milk. No gums or stabilizers are needed to thicken the final product, and the milk naturally self-homogenizes for even fat distribution. The yogurt-making process begins by bringing the milk to a temperature between 175° and 185°F to denature the proteins. Fermentation then ensues, at 105°F, with the introduction of two bacterial cultures. These bacteria work together, transforming lactose into lactic acid and coagulating the proteins, and giving sheep's milk yogurt its telltale sour tang. Finally, Old Chatham enriches their yogurt with a probiotic mixture. By the time the process is complete, the yogurt is alive with one billion active cells per gram.

Apple Salad with Ewe's Blue Cheese

SERVES 4

Red Wine–Apple Puree

2 cups port
2 cups red wine
¼ cup grapeseed oil
5 Granny Smith apples, peeled, cored, and diced (¼ inch)
Juice of 1 lime
Salt

Combine the port and red wine in a medium saucepan and reduce over medium-high heat to ½ cup. In a large pot, heat 3 tablespoons of the oil over high heat. Add the apples to the pot and stir to prevent them from developing any color. Continue stirring for 3 minutes and then add ½ cup of water. Cover with a parchment paper lid. Lower the heat to medium and continue cooking until the apples are tender, about 5 minutes. Remove the parchment paper and cook, stirring, until most of the excess moisture has evaporated. Transfer the apples to a blender and blend on high speed. While the blender is running, slowly stream in the remaining 1 tablespoon of oil and the reduced red wine and port mixture. Once the puree is smooth, chill over an ice bath. When cold, season with the lime juice and salt to taste. **Note:** Any leftover puree can be stored in the refrigerator, covered, for 3 days. Serve with cheese and crackers.

Vinegar-Poached Apple Rings

¼ cup apple cider vinegar
2 Granny Smith apples

In a small saucepan, bring the vinegar and 3 cups of water to a simmer. Cut two ½-inch-thick slices crosswise from the mid section of each apple. Punch the apple rounds with a 3½-inch round cutter, removing the skin. Cook the apple rounds in the simmering liquid until tender, about 4 minutes. Remove the apples and allow to cool on a cutting board. Punch the cores out of the apple rounds with a 1¾-inch round cutter.

Pickled Apples

1 Granny Smith apple
1 Red Delicious apple
1½ cups White Balsamic Pickling Liquid (page 501)

Using a 10-millimeter (⅜-inch) Parisian scoop, scoop at least 12 spheres from the Granny Smith apple. Using a 25-millimeter (1-inch) Parisian scoop, scoop at least 4 spheres from both the Granny Smith apple and the Red Delicious apple. Place all of the spheres in a bowl. Bring the pickling liquid to a boil in a saucepan over medium heat and pour over the apples, making sure they are fully submerged in the liquid. Allow the apples to cool to room temperature.

To Finish

Old Chatham Sheepherding Company Ewe's Blue Cheese
1 red endive
1 yellow endive
White Balsamic Vinaigrette (page 501)
Candied Walnuts (page 487)
Celery leaves

Spread red wine–apple puree on each of 4 plates. Cut ½-inch-thick slices of the cheese and punch with a 1¾-inch round cutter. Nestle the cheese rounds into the poached apple rings and place one on each plate. Add a few pickled apple spheres to each plate. Trim the individual leaves of the red and yellow endives into spears, toss with white balsamic vinaigrette, and arrange on the plates. Garnish with the candied walnuts and celery leaves.

Sheep's Milk Yogurt with Granola

SERVES 4

2¾ cups old-fashioned rolled oats
1 cup slivered almonds
1 cup unsweetened coconut chips
⅓ cup shelled pumpkin seeds
Sea salt
½ cup loosely packed light brown sugar
⅓ cup cold-pressed sunflower oil
⅓ cup maple syrup
¾ cup golden raisins
Sheep's milk yogurt
Fresh fruit

Preheat the oven to 300°F. In a large mixing bowl, toss the oats, almonds, coconut, pumpkin seeds, and salt to taste. In a small saucepan over medium heat, heat the sugar, sunflower oil, and maple syrup until the sugar is dissolved. Fold the sugar mixture into the oat mixture, evenly coating all of the dry ingredients. Spread out onto a rimmed baking sheet and bake in the oven, stirring every 5 minutes, until dry and lightly golden, 15 to 18 minutes. Remove from the oven and fold in the raisins. Allow to cool before serving with yogurt and fruit.
Note: Leftover granola can be stored in an airtight container at room temperature for up to 1 week.

Summer Squash

Norwich Meadows Farm

Zaid Kurdieh of Norwich Meadows Farm believes that it is flavor above all else that distinguishes his squash from the rest. "If you buy produce from the store, it tastes bland," he says. Poor growing conditions and inadequate ripening time account for the mediocre quality found in American supermarkets. But Zaid can do wonders with ordinary squash: "If I grow that same variety, it has flavor!" The son of Palestinian citrus farmers, Zaid has fond memories of his mother stuffing squash with lamb, pine nuts, and spices, frying them in olive oil, and dressing them in yogurt sauce. Since 1998, he and his wife, Haifa, have been growing squash of uncommon personality and character in Norwich, New York.

Zaid and Haifa are committed to organic farming, which means that their crops are susceptible to types of disease and bug infestation that are much less prevalent with conventionally grown produce. As a result, Norwich Meadows vegetables enjoy an unprecedented level of pampering, especially with the farm's soil enrichment program in which the earth is fortified with beneficial micronutrients. Zaid knows that "plants' basic needs are nitrogen, phosphorous, and potassium," but he prefers to go above and beyond and add some lesser-known elements. "Just like humans, plants also need trace elements—which are responsible for flavor."

New York's summer heat creates an ideal environment for squash. A number of varieties thrive on the farm, including slender zucchinis, patty pans, eight-balls, and Zaid's favorite, the Middle Eastern. After ten to fourteen days developing in a greenhouse, the squash plants are moved to the field, and they are ready for harvesting approximately forty days later. Zaid eats squash every day—bitter zucchini, sweet yellow squash, or nutty Middle Eastern, as the mood takes him. Regardless of the variety, he is partial to one classic preparation. He removes the core, which he considers to be the vegetable's "tender jewel," and fries it. "Simple does it best."

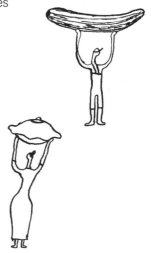

Crookneck Squash with Chèvre

SERVES 4

Fresh Tomato Jam

3 heirloom tomatoes
Olive oil
Salt
½ bunch thyme plus 1 tablespoon picked thyme leaves
1 teaspoon sugar
½ teaspoon sherry vinegar

Preheat the oven to 400°F. Cut the tomatoes in half and remove the seeds. Coat with olive oil and season with salt. Line a 13 by 18-inch rimmed baking sheet with the thyme sprigs and place the tomatoes cut side down on the thyme. Roast in the oven for 10 minutes. Remove and allow to cool to room temperature. Peel the tomatoes and remove the cores. Chop the flesh and transfer to a food processor. Pulse just until the tomatoes are broken up. Season with 1 teaspoon of salt and hang in a quadruple layer of cheesecloth over a bowl for 2 hours. Discard the liquid. Remove the tomatoes from the cheesecloth and combine with 2 tablespoons of olive oil, the thyme leaves, sugar, and vinegar. Season with salt to taste.

Summer Squash

4 crookneck squash
3 tablespoons butter
8 patty pan squash, halved
4 baby zucchini, halved
¼ cup Chicken Stock (page 499)
Salt

Cut 2 center planks lengthwise from each crookneck squash. Place the planks in a large sauté pan with 2 tablespoons of the butter and cover with a parchment paper lid. Sweat over medium-low heat for 3 to 4 minutes. Add the patty pan squash and the baby zucchini, cut side down, and continue sweating for another 3 minutes. Add the stock and bring to a simmer. Remove the parchment paper and remove the pan from the heat. Add the remaining tablespoon of butter, swirling the pan to glaze the vegetables. Season with salt to taste.

To Finish

3½ ounces chèvre
Flowering mint
Mint leaves
Squash blossoms
Cracked black pepper
Olive oil

Divide the summer squash evenly among 4 plates. Spoon chèvre and fresh tomato jam onto the plates. Garnish with flowering mint, mint leaves, and squash blossoms. Finish with cracked black pepper and olive oil.

Mashed Zucchini with Mint

SERVES 4

Sautéed Zucchini

8 large zucchini
¼ cup olive oil
2 cloves garlic, crushed but kept whole

Slice the top and bottom ends off of the zucchini. Cut down the length of the zucchini so the seeds remain separate from the skin and flesh. Rotate the zucchini, and do the same on the remaining three sides. You will be left with four strips of flesh and skin and a rectangle of just seeds; discard the seeds.

Heat a large straight-sided pan over medium-high heat and add the olive oil. Add the garlic and cook until golden, 2 to 3 minutes. Add the zucchini to the pan, raise the heat to high, and cook, stirring frequently to prevent the zucchini from taking on any color. Cover with a parchment paper lid. Turn down the heat to medium-low and continue cooking until the zucchini is tender, 7 to 8 minutes.

To Finish

20 mint leaves
10 squash blossoms
Salt

Stack 5 mint leaves at a time on top of one another and slice into ribbons. Trim off and discard the bottoms of the squash blossoms and slice the blossoms into ribbons as you did the mint. Mash the cooked sautéed zucchini in a serving bowl with a fork. Fold in the mint and squash blossoms and season with salt to taste.

Sunchokes

Muddy River Farm

After twenty-five years in the construction business, John Schmidt wanted a "less stressful job" and decided to return home to Orange County. With his wife, Kathy, he purchased and began cultivating twelve acres of land; the yield of this land initiated a connection with the Bronx Greenmarket. Now with seventy-five acres (including the land that John was raised on) and an expanded market base, Muddy River Farm—named for the murky appearance of the Wallkill River, which was caused by carp thrashing in its silt—devotes a small parcel to growing sunchokes. But this wasn't always the case.

At the Bronx Greenmarket, John learned how to tailor his farming to the preferences of customers of different ethnicities. He incorporated certain crops into his repertoire based on his customers' suggestions, even if he wasn't yet familiar with the product. One day at the market, an Eastern European customer asked if he had any sunchokes. Sunchokes, also called Jerusalem artichokes, had always been treated like weeds at Muddy River Farm. Their vivid yellow flowers grew faster than the neighboring crops, and John and Kathy did whatever they could to eliminate the tubers. Suddenly, this "weed" that had been growing rampantly on their farm was in demand. Everybody benefited, as the plant's vigor made it a delight for John to grow. "If you want to produce something that is organic and sustainable, sunchoke is your crop," he says.

Shaved portions of mature sunchokes are planted in October to hibernate underground through the winter before sprouting in the spring. John tells us how easy the vegetable is to maintain: "You don't have a big weed, bug, or fungus problem. It's like the people's idea of farming—plant the seed and watch it grow." The following autumn, most of the sunchokes are harvested and brought to market, but some remain in the ground to become an early spring specialty for the next year. Regardless of the season, John consistently sells every last one of his sunchokes.

John and Kathy are always open to cultivating new crops, and they have decided to start experimenting with new planting techniques as well. They are considering planting crops on higher ground, for example, to avoid the flooding that can plague their fertile land. "There is now room for experimentation, like finding out what sunchokes will taste like from mineral soil," says John. As long as the Schmidts continue producing some of the most fantastic crops in the state, their customers won't protest a bit of experimentation. After all, it's what made Muddy River Farm the thriving success it is today.

Roasted Sunchokes with Rambler

Roasted Sunchokes

2 pounds sunchokes
6 sprigs thyme
4 tablespoons butter
Salt
1 tablespoon canola oil

Preheat the oven to 350°F. Thoroughly scrub the sunchokes. Bring a large pot of salted water to a boil. Blanch the sunchokes for 5 minutes. Transfer to an ice bath, and, once cool, drain. Pat dry with paper towels. Divide the sunchokes between 2 large pieces of aluminum foil. Top each pile of sunchokes with 3 sprigs of thyme and 2 tablespoons of butter. Season with salt. Bring the corners of the foil together to create a package and place the packages on a baking sheet. Roast in the oven until very tender, about 1¾ to 2 hours, depending on the sunchokes' size. Remove the sunchokes from the foil and allow them to cool to room temperature. When cooled, slice the sunchokes into ¾- to 1-inch pieces. Heat the oil in a medium sauté pan over medium-low heat. Sear the sunchokes until golden brown, 2 to 3 minutes per side.

Dehydrated Grapes

1½ cups seedless red grapes
2 cups sugar

Preheat the oven to 200°F. Pierce the grapes with a cake tester or the tip of a paring knife. Combine the sugar with 2 cups of water in a medium saucepan and bring to a boil. When the sugar has dissolved, lower the heat and add the grapes. Simmer the grapes for 5 minutes. Remove the grapes from the syrup and drain. Spread the grapes on a 9 by 13-inch rimmed baking sheet lined with parchment paper. Dehydrate in the oven until shriveled and about two-thirds of their original size, 1½ to 1¾ hours.

Toasted Hazelnuts

1½ cups peeled hazelnuts
1 tablespoon olive oil
Salt

Preheat the oven to 350°F. Toss the hazelnuts in the olive oil and season with salt. Place on a rimmed baking sheet lined with parchment paper. Toast in the oven until golden brown, 9 to 10 minutes. Allow the nuts to cool and then coarsely chop.

Verjus Vinaigrette

5 tablespoons white verjus
¼ cup olive oil
Salt

In a small mixing bowl, whisk together the verjus and olive oil. Season with salt to taste.

To Finish

1½ cups seedless green grapes
**1 cup crumbled Tonjes Rambler cheese (a raw
 cow's milk cheese similar to aged cheddar)**
Salt
Watercress

Place the warm roasted sunchokes in a mixing bowl. Add the dehydrated grapes, toasted hazelnuts, green grapes, and crumbled cheese to the bowl and toss with the verjus vinaigrette. Season with salt to taste. Divide among 4 bowls and garnish with watercress.

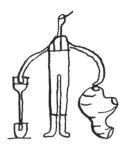

Sunchoke Soup with Hazelnuts

SERVES 4

Sunchoke Velouté

1½ pounds sunchokes
4 tablespoons butter
8 sprigs thyme
1 cup cream
Lime juice
Salt
Cayenne pepper

Peel the sunchokes, slice them about ¼ inch thick, and place them in water immediately to keep them from oxidizing. You should have about 6 cups of sliced sunchokes. In a large pot over medium heat, melt the butter until it begins to foam. Reduce the heat to low, drain the sunchokes, and add them to the pot. Sweat for 5 minutes without browning. Add 6 cups of water and the thyme and simmer until the sunchokes are tender, about 30 minutes. Remove and discard the thyme. In a blender, puree the sunchokes, their cooking liquid, and the cream until smooth. Strain through a chinois and season with lime juice, salt, and cayenne to taste.

Hazelnut Foam

2 teaspoons canola oil
2 cups hazelnuts, skinned
½ cup thinly sliced shallot
½ cup white wine
1 cup cream
1 teaspoon hazelnut oil
Lime juice
Salt

Heat the oil in a large saucepan over high heat, add the hazelnuts, and reduce the heat to medium. Toast the hazelnuts until deep brown, 6 to 7 minutes, tossing frequently to prevent the nuts from burning. Reduce the heat to low, add the shallot, and sweat until soft and translucent, about 5 minutes. Add the wine, raise the heat to high, and reduce the wine until 2 tablespoons remain. Add 2 cups of water and the cream and bring to a simmer. Remove from the heat and add the hazelnut oil. Transfer to a blender and pulse to break the hazelnuts, but do not puree them. Return the mixture to the pot, cover, and steep for 1 hour. Strain through a chinois. Season with lime juice and salt to taste.

Hazelnut Tuiles

15 large hazelnuts, skinned
⅔ cup sugar
2 tablespoons softened butter
2 teaspoons 100 percent hazelnut paste
3 tablespoons flour
Simple Syrup (page 22)
½ teaspoon fleur de sel

Slice the hazelnuts as thinly as possible on a mandoline. Combine the sugar and 3 tablespoons of water in a mixing bowl set over a pot of simmering water. Incorporate the butter and hazelnut paste until just melted. Whisk in the flour. Cool to room temperature.

Preheat the oven to 325°F. Line a 13 by 18-inch baking sheet with a silicone baking mat. Evenly spread ½ cup of the tuile batter onto the mat so that it is a little less than ⅛ inch thick. Bake until deep golden brown, 10 to 15 minutes. Let cool for 2 minutes at room temperature, and then cut into ¾ by 6-inch rectangles. Gently brush the tuiles with simple syrup. Place sliced hazelnuts on the tuiles and sprinkle with fleur de sel. Warm the tuiles in the oven to make them pliable, about 1 minute. Form the tuiles over a cooling rack with straight wires or use pencils to create a wavy shape. Work quickly because as the tuiles cool, they become brittle. Cool to room temperature.

To Finish

Divide the sunchoke velouté among 4 bowls. Aerate the hazelnut foam with a hand blender, and then spoon the foam onto the soup. Garnish each bowl with a hazelnut tuile.

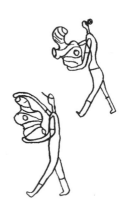

Swiss Chard

Bodhitree Farm

Bodhitree Farm sits incongruously among a tangle of commodity farms in Burlington County, New Jersey. Paying tribute to enlightenment, purity, and excellence, owner Nevia No named the property after the fig tree under which Buddha is said to have achieved enlightenment. Although she does not expect customers to have a religious experience from her squash, nor gain revelation from her radishes, she does aspire to encourage people to eat healthy foods. And along the way, they will certainly experience a kind of nutritious nirvana from her extraordinary produce, particularly her incomparable Swiss chard.

In 2009, after selling other farmers' produce for ten years, Nevia redirected her professional routine. "I had to transition from the farmers' market to being a farmer." She built seven green houses from the ground up and has since expanded across 135 total acres of land. Despite such dramatic growth, very little of her operation is mechanized. Nevia still insists that plants be seeded by hand, and then harvested gently, one plant at a time. Bodhitree employees continually maintain a personal relationship with each plant.

A holistic approach to farming works wonders for Nevia's beloved Swiss chard. Vibrant red, yellow, and golden stalks thrive in soil fed with her nutrient-rich compost. She plants chard once a month, making sure to not overwhelm her plots. Once the stalks are picked, they are individually cleaned in cold water. This not only makes them pristine and ready to eat but also reduces their field heat, which keeps them sturdy and vibrant and prevents them from wilting. From planting to picking to cleaning, Nevia raises vegetables with the utmost care. "I want to grow with good intentions," she says.

Because Nevia spent many years working with farms and farmers, selling their produce and becoming familiar with different ways of approaching agriculture, she gained an appreciation for innovative methods farming. She recognizes the value of experimentation and, as such, her farming techniques continue to evolve. For instance, she and her farmhands operate a greenhouse owned by Rutgers University. A nearby landfill generates methane gas, which is then used to power the greenhouse. In the spirit of education, she invites agriculture students to take part in farming internships. The program has proven to be mutually beneficial, as one group of interns guided the staff at Bodhitree to a discovery in mold prevention: mayonnaise! Brushing the leaves with mayonnaise in the field makes them less susceptible to excessive water absorption.

At any time, Bodhitree is growing upward of forty different plants, creating a diversity that mirrors Nevia's interests outside of the field. She studied drama at the Peabody Institute, plays the piano, and throws beautiful ceramic teapots. She happily extends an invitation to visit her working farm, replete with beautiful stone barns and horses that roam the land. But there's more to take in than just the picturesque scenery—Nevia's dynamic yet grounded approach to farming and the peaceful yet vibrant setting instill in visitors an invigorating sense of balance and well-being.

Swiss Chard Gratin

SERVES 4

Mornay Sauce

1½ teaspoons butter
1½ teaspoons flour
3 cups milk
¼ onion, peeled
2 whole cloves
1 bay leaf
½ cup grated Consider Bardwell Farms Rupert
  (an aged raw cow's milk cheese made in the
  style of Gruyère)
Ground nutmeg
Salt
Ground white pepper

In a small saucepan over medium heat, melt the butter. Add the flour and stir, cooking until the mixture is lightly golden, 4 to 5 minutes. Add the milk, whisking to combine. Bring the mixture to a boil and reduce to a simmer. To make an *oignon piqué*, use the cloves to pierce the onion and the bay leaf, tacking them together. Add the *oignon piqué* to the sauce and simmer for 30 minutes. Remove the saucepan from the heat, remove the onion from the sauce, and whisk in the cheese. Strain through a chinois and season with nutmeg, salt, and pepper to taste. **Note:** Any leftover sauce can be stored in the refrigerator, covered, for up to 5 days. Toss with warm pasta.

Swiss Chard Ragout

15 to 20 leaves white-stemmed Swiss chard
¾ cup diced (¼ inch) onion
2 tablespoons butter
¼ cup Chicken Stock (page 499)
1 cup diced (⅛ inch) ham
Ground nutmeg
Salt
Ground white pepper

Clean the chard, separating the leaves from the stems. Dice the stems to ¼-inch pieces. In a medium sauté pan, melt the butter over medium-low heat. Sweat the chard stems and onion until wilted, 2 to 3 minutes. Add the stock, bring to a simmer, cover with a parchment paper lid, and sweat until tender, 4 to 5 minutes. Remove the parchment paper, add the chard leaves, and wilt over medium heat, stirring frequently. Add the ham, remove from the pan from the heat, and season with nutmeg, salt, and pepper to taste.

To Finish

¼ cup grated Consider Bardwell Farms Rupert

Preheat the oven to 400°F. Pour 1½ cups of the mornay sauce into a shallow 1-quart gratin dish. Spoon the Swiss chard ragout into the dish and drizzle about 1 more cup of mornay sauce over the top. Top the gratin with the cheese and place in the oven. Bake for 10 minutes, and then broil until lightly browned, 30 to 45 seconds.

Swiss Chard Roulade with Bacon and Sherry

SERVES 4

Bacon-Wrapped Chard Roulade

24 rainbow Swiss chard leaves
Ground nutmeg
Salt
Ground black pepper
20 (⅛ inch thick) slices bacon

Wash the Swiss chard, cut the stems from the leaves, and reserve the stems. Bring a large pot of salted water to a boil and blanch the leaves until tender, 2½ to 3 minutes. Transfer the leaves to an ice bath, squeeze out the excess water, and reserve 4 leaves for frying. Stack 10 of the blanched chard leaves on a piece of plastic wrap. Season with nutmeg, salt, and pepper. Roll lengthwise into a cylinder that is 1 inch in diameter, being sure to keep the chard as tight and compact as possible. Poke small holes in the plastic wrap with a pin or a cake tester and twist both ends tightly to compress the chard into a dense roulade. Repeat with the remaining 10 blanched leaves so that you have 2 roulades. Lay out 10 slices of the bacon on a sheet of plastic wrap slightly overlapping each other. Repeat with the remaining 10 slices. Remove the chard roulades from the plastic wrap and roll each in bacon. Trim the bacon so that it only overlaps slightly at the seam. Chill in the refrigerator while preparing the rest of the recipe.

Chard Sauce

1 teaspoon canola oil
16 Swiss chard stems, reserved from making Bacon-Wrapped Chard Roulade, sliced (¼ inch)
1 tablespoon sliced (¼ inch) shallot
1 tablespoon tomato paste
2 cups Chicken Stock (page 499)
Sherry vinegar
Salt

Heat the canola oil in a small saucepan over medium-high heat. Add the chard stems and shallot and cook until golden brown, about 4 minutes. Add the tomato paste, stirring frequently. Add the stock and reduce over medium heat until thick enough to coat the back of a spoon, about 30 minutes. Strain the sauce through a chinois and season with vinegar and salt to taste.

Grilled Chard Stems

8 Swiss chard stems, reserved from Bacon-Wrapped Chard Roulade
½ cup Chicken Stock (page 499)
Salt

In a small saucepan, cover the chard stems with the stock, bring to a simmer over medium-low heat, and cook until tender, 7 to 8 minutes. While the stems are cooking, heat a cast-iron grill pan over high heat. When the stems are tender, drain, pat them dry, cut them in half crosswise, and place in the hot grill pan. Sear each piece to create grill marks, about 20 seconds. Season with salt to taste.

To Finish

Canola oil
Salt
2 tablespoons Chicken Stock (page 499)
8 Swiss chard leaves
2 tablespoons butter
¼ cup Chicken Jus (page 498)
¼ cup sherry vinegar
¼ cup sugar
Ground black pepper
16 baby Swiss chard leaves
1 raw Swiss chard stem
Sherry Vinaigrette (page 243)

Pour 3 inches of canola oil into a large saucepan and bring the oil to 300°F over medium-high heat. Fry the 4 reserved blanched Swiss chard leaves in the oil for 5 seconds, flip and fry for another 5 seconds. Remove, drain on paper towels, and season with salt to taste. In a small sauté pan over medium-high heat, warm the chicken stock. Add the 8 Swiss chard leaves and sauté until wilted, about 15 seconds. Add the butter, swirling to glaze. Remove and drain on paper towels. In a small saucepan, combine the chicken jus, sherry vinegar, sugar, and 2 tablespoons of water and reduce to a glaze over high heat, 8 to 10 minutes. In a medium sauté pan, heat 1 teaspoon of canola oil over medium-low heat. Place the roulades in the pan, seam-side down. Cook, turning often, until the bacon is browned and the fat is rendered, 8 to 10 minutes. Remove the roulades from the pan, strain the rendered bacon fat through a chinois, and add the fat to the chard sauce. Return the roulades to the pan and add the glaze to coat. Slice each roulade in half, season with pepper, and place one half on each of 4 plates. Arrange the grilled chard stems on the plates. Place 4 baby chard leaves, a fried chard leaf, and 2 glazed chard leaves on each plate. Thinly slice the raw chard stem lengthwise on a mandoline, dress with sherry vinaigrette, and place slices on each plate. Spoon the chard sauce onto the plate to finish.

Tomatoes

Eckerton Hill Farm

Tim Stark got his start with heirloom tomatoes long before they were a ubiquitous summer offering. His dead-end career as a writer had him thinking about what he could do to support himself, and, eventually, he turned his attention to tomatoes. "I had been keeping a garden near where I grew up in Lenhartsville, Pennsylvania, and in 1996, I decided to take it more seriously and expand it to two acres," he says. Tim put the writing on hold and turned his Brooklyn apartment into a greenhouse. He used fluorescent lights to incubate roughly three thousand seeds that he then transferred to the fields in Pennsylvania. All of the stars aligned that first season. "We got just enough rain for tomatoes, and the Union Square farmers' market gave us the nod. Everything just worked in my favor."

Newcomers wanting a stand at the Greenmarket typically have to wait patiently to be accepted, but Tim's crop—already boasting sixty heirloom tomato offerings at the time—was impressive enough to grant him instant access and bypass the wait. Although he admits he grew heirlooms because they "looked cool," flavor was never far from his mind. "A commercial hybrid is grown to be red, spherical, and easy to pick," explains Tim. But as an heirloom grower, he has traded this "perfection" for quality of flavor. Back in the day, Tim says, people would save the most flavorful seeds of the season and replant them each year. It was never about uniformity or storage potential; it always came down to flavor. Now, chefs race to the market to get boxes filled with a medley of Tim's tomatoes in the most dazzling array of shapes, colors, and sizes.

Every season, Tim's patience is tested as he transfers lot after lot of tomatoes from greenhouse to field. "My thirty thousand plants are finicky and hard on the nerves." If planted by April, Cherokee Purples jet-set the early summer season with their sweet and acidic flavor profile. The pretty and pink Radiator Charlie's Mortgage Lifters quickly follow. Then, Brandywines cool the palate during the heat of midsummer. Finally, bicolored Hillbillies offer a brilliant season finale. Now growing over one hundred varieties, Tim has a tomato for every palate, and the demand for them is telling. "The phone rings off the hook from a few weeks before the tomatoes come in until they peter out in early October," he says.

Tim credits his success to an "inability to farm the right way." Although he recently bought a fifty-eight-acre farm with a better irrigation system, he is reluctant to use it. "In the early years, we never really had enough water. But our tomatoes were more intensely flavored." Conventionally, it is thought that tomatoes grow best in sandy, nutrient-poor soils. However, Tim's tomato farm sits on a heavy clay plot, which he diligently pumps with beneficial minerals and compost every year: "That flavor gets trapped into the tomato instead of washing down through the lighter sand." Consequentially, when you bite into one of Tim's tomatoes, it bursts with flavor—it tastes like it was salted from within. All Tim can do is smile with pride.

Ketchup

MAKES 1 QUART

8 large red beefsteak tomatoes
¾ cup canola oil
½ cup diced (¼ inch) onion
2 cloves garlic, diced (¼ inch)
1 cup brown sugar
1 cup cider vinegar
2½ tablespoons distilled vinegar
3 tablespoons salt

Preheat the oven to 450°F. Core and quarter the tomatoes and toss with 2 tablespoons of the canola oil. Place the tomatoes on a rimmed baking sheet lined with parchment paper. Roast in the oven until tender, about 15 minutes. Pass the tomatoes through a food mill. This should yield about 5 cups of puree. In a large, straight-sided pot, heat 2 tablespoons of the canola oil over medium-low heat. Add the onion and garlic and sweat until tender, about 5 minutes. Add the tomato puree, brown sugar, and vinegar. Raise the heat to high, stirring frequently to avoid burning, and reduce the mixture to 3½ cups. Transfer to a blender and blend on high while streaming in the remaining canola oil. Pass through a chinois and season with the distilled vinegar and salt. Transfer to a glass jar, cover, and keep in the refrigerator for up to 1 week.

Many would be surprised to know that none of the early ketchup recipes contained any tomato. And although its origins are murky, it was the British who first came across it in Southeast Asia and brought it to Europe and later to the United States. The original ketchup was probably closer to a fish sauce containing anchovies and spices. In fact, a seventeenth-century Chinese concoction made with pickled fish and spices was known as *ke-chiap*. It was only when the British versions (which were made with other ingredients like mushrooms and walnuts) came to New York that ketchup began to be made with tomatoes, an ingredient native to the Americas. As its popularity began to escalate, companies began to bottle it and sell it (Heinz introduced its ketchup in 1876), relieving Americans of the burden of having to make this labor-intensive condiment at home.

Warm Bread Salad with Tomatoes

SERVES 4

½ **cup olive oil**
6 **cloves garlic, crushed but kept whole**
4 **cups torn baguette**
1 **cup diced (½ inch) red onion**
4 **cups diced (½ inch) heirloom tomatoes**
3 **tablespoons red wine vinegar**
1 **bunch fresh basil**
1 **tablespoon capers**
Salt
Ground black pepper
Small basil leaves

In a large sauté pan, heat the olive oil over medium-high heat. Add the garlic and cook until fragrant, 1 to 2 minutes. Add the torn baguette to the pan and sauté until golden brown, 4 to 5 minutes. Lower the heat to medium-low, add the red onion and sauté for 1 minute, and then add 2 cups of the tomatoes. Add the vinegar and remove from the heat. Add the basil, capers, and the remaining tomatoes and toss to combine. Season with salt and pepper to taste and garnish with small basil leaves.

Tomato Soda

SERVES 4

Soda Base

18 large ripe heirloom tomatoes
3 stalks diced (½ inch) celery
6 tablespoons freshly grated horseradish
4½ tablespoons salt
Basil leaves from 2 large bunches
Leaves of 9 sprigs lemon thyme
1½ jalapeño chiles, stemmed and seeded

Bring a large pot of water to a boil. Core the tomatoes and, using a paring knife, score the bottoms with an X. Blanch in the boiling water for 10 to 15 seconds, and then transfer to an ice bath. Once they are cool, peel the tomatoes and cut them into quarters. Puree the tomatoes with the remaining ingredients in a blender. Line a colander with a quadruple layer of cheesecloth. Transfer the puree to the cheesecloth and hang in the refrigerator overnight, draining the liquid into a large bowl. Discard the contents of the cheesecloth. You should have 3 to 4 cups of soda base. **Note:** Any leftover soda base can be frozen and then scraped to make a summery granité or served over ice with a splash of soda water to make another refreshing beverage.

To Finish

¼ cup Simple Syrup (page 22)
¼ cup lemon juice
Ice
Basil sprigs

Combine 3 cups of the soda base with the simple syrup. Add the lemon juice and stir to combine. Transfer to a seltzer bottle and charge with a CO_2 cartridge. Fill 4 glasses with ice and dispense the soda over it into the glasses. Garnish with basil sprigs.

Soda Fountains

Before the ubiquitous bottled and canned sodas of today, there were soda fountains. This definitively American creation came about after the invention of manmade carbonated water in the late eighteenth century. Because carbonated mineral waters were thought to be medicinal, soda fountains were put in the hands of pharmacists and, with the lack of government regulation prior to the Pure Food and Drug Act of 1906, sodas were used as a way to deliver not only flavorings but also medication. It was not uncommon for flavored sodas to be laced with alcohol or even cocaine, heroin, or morphine, as these were all used medicinally. But with increased regulations and awareness, soda fountains became places where families (and not just those in need of a "medicinal" pick-me-up) could spend time together. Soda fountains quickly became an integral part of nearly every American's life—so much so that by 1919, there were an estimated 126,000 shops in the United States. Today, very few remain, though their culinary legacy—malted milk shakes, egg creams, strawberry sodas, root beer floats—have withstood the test of time.

Yellow Bloody Mary

SERVES 4

6 or 7 large yellow heirloom tomatoes
Salt
¼ cup lemon juice
3 tablespoons freshly grated horseradish
3 teaspoons Frank's RedHot sauce
1 teaspoon Worcestershire sauce
1 teaspoon celery seeds
1 teaspoon mustard seeds
½ teaspoon coriander seeds
½ teaspoon white peppercorns
Ice
8 ounces vodka
Dill fronds
Cherry tomatoes
Pickled wax beans
Pickled pearl onions

With a paring knife, lightly score the bottom of each tomato with an X. Bring a pot of water to a boil and blanch the tomatoes for 10 to 15 seconds. Transfer to an ice bath and, once cool, peel the skins. Cut each tomato in half and separate the seeds from the flesh. Cut the flesh into large pieces and season the seeds and flesh with salt. Wrap seeds and flesh separately in a quadruple layer of cheesecloth and suspend both bundles over a large bowl until all of the tomato water is collected, about 2 hours. Discard the seeds. Transfer the flesh and the collected tomato water to a blender and puree. You should have about 6 cups of liquid. Add the lemon juice, horseradish, hot sauce, Worcestershire sauce, and spices and blend until smooth. Fill four 14-ounce glasses with ice. Add 2 ounces of vodka to each and top with the Bloody Mary mixture. Stir to combine and garnish with the dill, cherry tomatoes, and pickled vegetables.

The Bloody Mary

The Bloody Mary is said to be the invention of two different people. In 1926, Fernand Petiot, a bartender at Harry's New York Bar in Paris (formerly known as the New York Bar), mixed equal parts of vodka and tomato juice and named it after either Queen Mary I of England or the Bucket of Blood Club in Chicago. Just one year later, famed actor George Jessel laid claim to its invention at his Palm Beach home after his friend, Mary, spilled the drink on her shirt. She called herself Bloody Mary, and the name for the drink stuck. In 1934, Petiot modified his original recipe while bartending at the King Cole Bar at the St. Regis Hotel in New York. When a patron requested a spicier version, he added cayenne, black pepper, Worcestershire sauce, lemon juice, and Tabasco sauce, resulting in the Bloody Mary as we know it today.

Trout

Beaverkill Trout Hatchery

Strolling through her two-hundred-acre property in the Catskills, Sherry Shaver traces the footsteps made by her great-grandfather, Fred D. Shaver, who bought the land in 1963. He moved there and started a dairy farm that lasted only four years before a trout-farming hobby turned into a passion and, eventually, a vocation. Sherry lovingly describes the estate as "one of the last untouched places on earth." While stunning forest views surround her property, it is the waterways that have carried the family's heritage for so many years. The rivers adjacent to the hatchery are renowned for trout fishing themselves and they are the water source for Sherry's twenty-four horseshoe-shaped dirt ponds. In the fall, she introduces eggs into hatch-outs, or nurseries. The fish are born in the spring, and at one year old, they are transferred to the ponds where they spend the remainder of their time. Spring weather permitting, roughly one thousand trout in each pond are ready to be fished beginning in late March or April.

When it is time to harvest, Sherry and her team suit up in waterproof overalls and enter a pond. First, they concentrate the trout in one area using a large net; a tremor in the water signals the fishes' activity below. The fishermen plunge small rounded nets into the bustling swarm of trout. Standing in the pond, Sherry shouts over the thrashing fish, "It's still fishing, whether it be with a pole or a net!" With the netted catch in tow, the fishermen retrieve their simplest but most often-used tool: a ruler affixed to a floating wooden box. Sherry and her crew inspect and size each fish down to the half-inch, calling out the trouts' length so the team can keep count for each client's order. Some of Sherry's trout are gutted and cleaned; however, the vast majority are transported live for release into private lakes and rivers for more conventional line or fly fishing. Beaverkill's superior trout—brooks, rainbows, goldens, and browns—affirm Sherry's dedication and exacting standards.

Heiress to the Shaver trout tradition, Sherry adds her own legacy as the first to make smoked trout using applewood from the property. A tremendous contributor to trout fishing in New York State, Sherry speaks with extreme pride about the work she does. Just ask her about her lifestyle, and she will look you in the eye and simply say, "I live in one of the best places in the world."

Brook trout was named the official New York State fish in 1975. Found in the clear streams, brooks, and lakes that are scattered throughout the state, trout have been a part of the New York diet since the late 1800s when trout eggs were brought to New York from Germany. As the fish began to populate the waterways, fly fishermen enjoyed the challenge of catching them as much as New Yorkers enjoyed eating them.

Smoked Trout with Almonds and Asparagus

SERVES 4

Smoked Trout

1 tablespoon coriander seeds
2 teaspoons mustard seeds
2 teaspoons ground black pepper
1 teaspoon fennel seeds
1 cup salt
⅓ cup sugar
**2 whole (1½ to 2-pound) trout, filleted,
    skin on, pinbones removed**
¼ cup chopped chervil
¼ cup chopped dill
¼ cup chopped tarragon
¼ cup chopped thyme
½ bay leaf, chopped

Grind the coriander, mustard seeds, pepper, and fennel seeds in a spice grinder. Combine the spices with the salt and sugar and season the trout generously with the mixture. Combine the chervil, dill, tarragon, thyme, and bay leaf and sprinkle the herbs evenly over the top of the fish. Refrigerate for 8 hours to cure, and then rinse thoroughly under cold running water. Refrigerate the fish overnight uncovered to allow it to develop a pellicle (a thin film of protein that facilitates smoking).

Soak 2 cups of applewood chips in cold water for 10 minutes. Remove the cooking grate from a charcoal grill and light 1 to 2 pounds of charcoal in a chimney starter. When the coals are white-hot, arrange them in a pile on one side of the grill bottom. Drain the wood chips and place on top of the hot charcoal. Return the cooking grate to the grill. Place the cured trout in a pan set over a pan of ice. When the chips begin to smoke, position the pan of trout over ice on the cool side of the grate (that is, not on top of the coals). Cover the grill and smoke until the fish is just cooked through, 5 to 10 minutes.

Toasted Almonds

½ cup slivered almonds
1 teaspoon olive oil
Salt

Preheat the oven to 375°F. Toss the almonds in the oil and place on a rimmed baking sheet lined with parchment paper. Toast in the oven until golden brown, 4 to 5 minutes. Season with salt to taste and cool to room temperature.

Trout Roe Vinaigrette

2 tablespoons trout roe
1½ tablespoons Lemon Vinaigrette (page 500)
1 tablespoon diced (¼ inch) lemon segments
2 teaspoons sliced chives
Salt

Combine the trout roe, vinaigrette, lemon segments, and chives in a small bowl. Season with salt to taste.

To Finish

20 pencil asparagus
½ cup Crème Fraîche (page 499)
4 teaspoons lime juice
1 teaspoon salt
Bread Crisps (page 498)
4 large asparagus
Chervil
Dill sprigs
Tarragon
Lemon oil
Sea salt

Trim away the bottom woody ends of the asparagus. Peel the asparagus from the base to the tip. Bring a pot of salted water to a boil and blanch the asparagus until tender, 1 to 2 minutes. Immediately transfer to an ice bath. Once cool, drain. In a mixing bowl, combine the crème fraîche, lime juice, and salt and whip until firm peaks form.

Place 1 fillet of smoked trout on the center of each of 4 plates. Arrange 5 pencil asparagus around the trout. Spoon the crème fraîche at one end of the trout and place bread crisps at both ends. Remove the woody ends of the 4 large asparagus and thinly shave on a mandoline. Top the trout with asparagus shavings and arrange toasted almonds around the plates. Garnish with chervil, dill, and tarragon. Spoon the trout roe vinaigrette around the plates and finish with lemon oil and sea salt to taste.

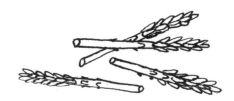

Cucumber Salad with Smoked Trout

SERVES 4

Cucumber Ribbons

6 English cucumbers
1 cup Crème Fraîche (page 499)
8 teaspoons lime juice
Salt
Cayenne pepper

Peel the cucumbers and slice lengthwise on a mandoline into ¼ by ¹⁄₁₆-inch strips. In a small bowl, whisk the crème fraîche to loosen its consistency. Add the lime juice and continue whisking. Season the mixture with salt and cayenne pepper to taste. Toss the cucumbers with two-thirds of the crème fraîche dressing and reserve the remainder to finish the plate.

To Finish

Smoked Trout (page 466)
8 cucamelons, halved
8 flowering cucumbers
Dill sprigs
Flowering dill sprigs

Place the dressed cucumber ribbons on the center of each of 4 plates. Break a trout fillet into 3 sections and place on top of the cucumber. Arrange cucamelon halves around the trout. Add flowering cucumbers and garnish with dill sprigs and flowering dill. Aerate the reserved crème fraîche dressing with a hand blender to create a foam and spoon the foam around the plates.

Blue Trout

SERVES 4

Cooking Broth

8 cups white wine
1 cup diced (½ inch) onion
½ cup diced (½ inch) celery
½ cup sliced (½ inch) carrot
1 bunch parsley
10 black peppercorns
1 bay leaf
Salt

In a large stockpot, combine all of the ingredients and cover with 4 quarts of water. Bring to a boil, lower the heat, and simmer for 45 minutes. Cool to 165°F.

To Finish

6 cups distilled vinegar
2 (1½ to 2-pound) live trout

Pour the vinegar into a shallow dish. Grasp a live trout securely behind the head with a kitchen towel, being careful not to damage the layer of slime that is on the skin. Kill the trout by hitting it once firmly on the head with a blunt object, such as a rolling pin. With a sharp pair of scissors, gut the fish and remove the gills. Repeat with the other trout. Continuing to be careful to preserve the outer layer of slime on the skin, sever the spine by clipping it with the scissors where it meets the head. Immediately transfer the trout to the vinegar bath and flip it over. When the skin has taken on a shiny blue color, transfer the trout to the pot of cooking broth set over low heat and poach the fish, maintaining the temperature at 165°F until cooked through, 13 to 15 minutes. Remove from the broth, fillet, and serve.

Venison

Millbrook Venison Products

At Millbrook Venison Products, Ed Schoonmaker raises the most sought-after venison, but he recognizes that deer will always be wild by nature. Ed explains how important it is to be aware of this—and particularly of the males' activity levels throughout the seasons: "A nerve behind the buck's eye tells him that the days are getting shorter; and once they go into rut, the stags are full of hormones, making them very dangerous."

Ed's venison story began in the mid-1980s when he and his partner Sandy Eberhard decided to leave behind their Charolais cattle and focus their attention on raising venison instead. "I used to hunt all over the place and was interested in deer," he says. As rookies, they began by learning certain basics, which, even now are just as important as the lessons learned from years of experience: "You need to be respectful of the deer, or you will get hurt." Once Ed and Sandy had established a solid foundation and game-raising philosophy, it was time to condition the animals to thrive on Ed's feed. Deer are browsers and foragers—they naturally seek out pine needles, tree bark, flower buds, and, most of all, a farmer's unprotected crops. However, it is possible to train them to feed on other forms of sustenance. With his assistance, the animals gradually go from being foragers to being grazers, their stomach acids slowly adapting to a menu of alfalfa, clover hay, corn, turnips, and the highly favored pumpkins. "Alfalfa is rich in protein," says Ed, "but the deer will only eat the leaves and buds. So I take the best grasses, grind them up, and then sprinkle them on the other feeds."

A healthy diet nourishes a doe population that is capable of birthing strong fawns. The fawns on the forty-five acres are born in May and June to the one hundred females and spend the next seven months consuming mother's milk. Young does join the herd early, while young stags spend the next eighteen to twenty-four months on Millbrook's feeding program. "We harvest to order on premise, about seventy to eighty every week." Since Ed and Sandy's deer are less stressed, their meat is blemish-free.

The size of venison cuts varies depending on the species of deer. Asian Sika deer are relatively small compared to New Zealand Fallow deer and native American elk. Millbrook Venison offers the full range, allowing for a diversity of preparations, flavors, and textures. "Chefs say my venison is mellow and not offensively gamey," says Ed. Now in his sixties and a true venison veteran, Ed's line of work keeps him young and free-spirited. He is not planning to slow down anytime soon. "It's just rewarding to put a quality product out there."

Smoked Venison Tenderloin

Smoked Venison Tenderloin

1 (1-pound) venison tenderloin, split lengthwise
1 cup salt
2 tablespoons ground juniper berries

Trim each half of the tenderloin into 2 long cylinders. Combine 10 cups of water with the salt and juniper berries in a stockpot and bring to a boil over high heat. Chill in an ice bath, transfer the venison to the brine, and refrigerate for 4 hours. Remove the meat from the brine and pat dry with paper towels. Place on a cooling rack set in a rimmed baking sheet and refrigerate uncovered for about 12 hours to allow the venison to develop a pellicle, or thin film of protein.

Soak 2 cups of applewood chips in cold water for 10 minutes. Remove the cooking grate from a charcoal grill and light 1 pound of charcoal in a chimney starter. When the coals are white-hot, arrange them in a pile on one side of the grill bottom. Drain the wood chips and place on top of the hot charcoal. Return the cooking grate to the grill. Place the venison in a pan set over a pan of ice. When the chips begin to smoke, position the pan of venison over ice on the cool side of the grate (that is, not on top of the coals). Cover the grill and smoke for 10 minutes, then rotate and smoke for 10 to 15 minutes more. Remove the venison from the grill, wrap with plastic wrap, and chill in the refrigerator. When cool, roll tightly in plastic wrap and freeze.

Pickled Chanterelle Mushrooms

3 cups White Balsamic Pickling Liquid (page 501)
1 cup chanterelle mushrooms

In a saucepan, bring the pickling liquid to a boil. Clean the mushrooms, place in a bowl, and pour the pickling liquid over them. Allow to cool in the liquid to room temperature.

Juniper Salt

2 tablespoons juniper berries
⅓ cup salt

In a small sauté pan over medium heat, toast the juniper berries until fragrant. Grind in a spice grinder to a powder. Combine the powder with the salt. **Note:** Store leftover juniper salt in an airtight container at room temperature for up to 2 weeks.

To Finish

Pickled Plums (page 362)
½ cup Brown Butter (page 498)
Salt
Baby kale
Ground black pepper

Slice the frozen venison tenderloin into ⅟₁₆- to ⅛-inch-thick slices on a deli slicer or with a very sharp knife. Arrange the rounds on a plate. Quarter the pickled plums and arrange on the plate along with the pickled chanterelle mushrooms. Combine ¼ cup of the plum pickling liquid with the brown butter and season with salt to taste. Spoon sauce over the venison and garnish with kale. Season with juniper salt and pepper to taste.

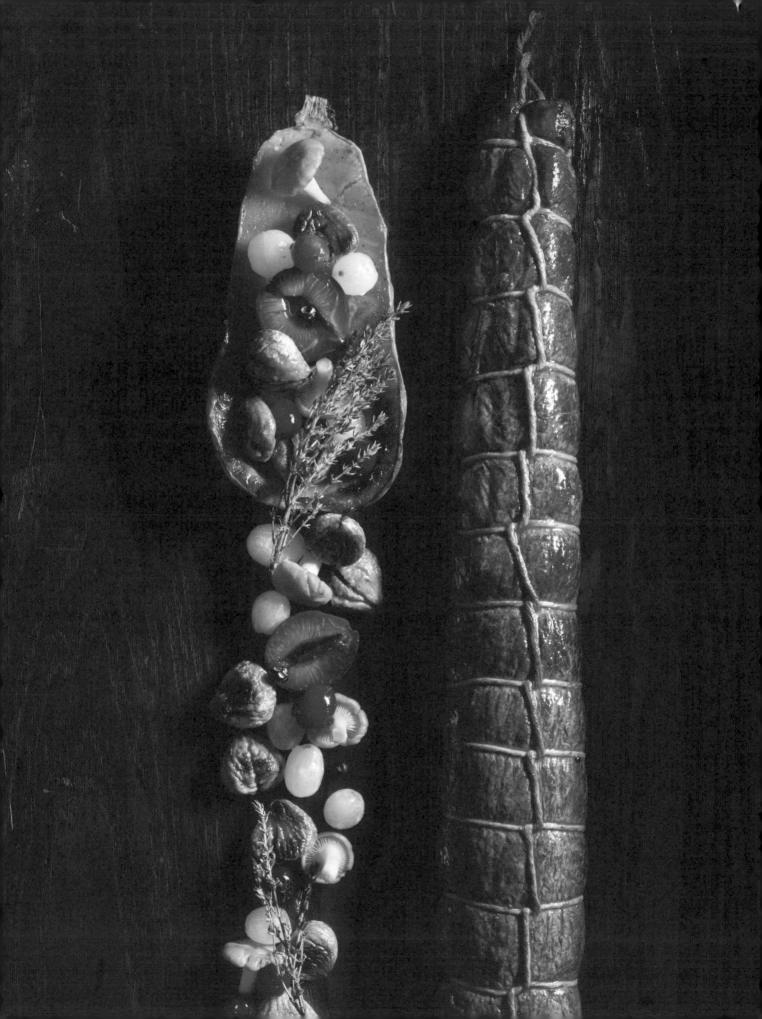

Whole Roasted Venison Loin with Fall Vegetables

SERVES 4

Whole Roasted Venison Loin

1 (2½-pound) venison loin, cleaned
Juniper Salt (page 478)
2 tablespoons canola oil
2 tablespoons butter
5 sprigs thyme
2 cloves garlic, crushed but kept whole

Preheat the oven to 300°F. If you do not have pans large enough to sear and roast the whole venison loin, slice it in half crosswise and roast in 2 pieces. Truss the loin with butcher's twine and season liberally with juniper salt. In a large sauté pan, heat the canola oil over high heat. When the pan is very hot, add the trussed venison loin and sear for 1 minute, and then turn and sear another 45 seconds. Repeat until the entire loin has been seared. Lower the heat to medium and add the butter, thyme, and garlic. Baste the loin with the butter for 1 minute, rolling it around to coat evenly. Transfer the loin to a wire rack set in an 18 by 26-inch rimmed baking sheet and place in the oven. Roast for 10 minutes. Baste with the butter and turn. Roast for an additional 10 minutes, until the internal temperature reaches 130° to 135°F. Remove from the oven and allow to rest for 10 to 15 minutes before slicing.

Game Sauce

20 juniper berries
6 allspice berries
1 teaspoon black peppercorns
1 whole clove
1 cup red wine
¾ cup Concord grapes
4 sprigs thyme
1 bay leaf
1½ cups Chicken Jus (page 498)
1½ cups Chicken Stock (page 499)
3 tablespoons pig's blood
1 tablespoon cornstarch
1 teaspoon Dijon mustard
¼ ounce chopped 72 percent chocolate (about 1 tablespoon)
1 teaspoon red wine vinegar
Salt

In a medium saucepan, toast the juniper, allspice, peppercorns, and clove over medium heat until fragrant. Add the red wine and reduce until the pan is almost dry. Add the grapes, thyme, and bay leaf and crush them into the spices. Add the chicken jus and chicken stock, bring to a simmer, and reduce until the sauce is thick enough to coat the back of a spoon, 30 to 45 minutes. Strain through a chinois. In a small bowl, combine the pig's blood, cornstarch, and mustard, and whisk the mixture into the sauce. Simmer over low heat to thicken slightly, 4 to 5 minutes. Stir in the chocolate until melted and season with the vinegar and salt to taste. Strain through a chinois.

Roasted Butternut Squash

1 medium butternut squash
2 tablespoons olive oil
Salt
Ground black pepper

Preheat the oven to 350°F. Line a 13 by 18-inch baking sheet with parchment paper. Cut the butternut squash in half lengthwise and scoop out the seeds. Coat each side with the olive oil and season with salt and pepper. Lay cut side down on the baking sheet and roast in the oven until tender and browned, about 45 minutes.

To Finish

Serve the loin with the game sauce and roasted butternut squash. **Note:** This venison also goes well with chanterelles, chestnuts, and grapes.

Walnuts

Gillie Brook Farm

"You can't be a farmer unless you somehow appreciate the view you're stuck with," reasons Robert Nogash as he prunes dormant Concord and Catawaba grape vines in the crisp winter air. He and his wife, Roseanne, make their way through vineyards planted by her father as the sun glints off nearby Keuka Lake. After attempting to revive his grape juice company, Robert and Roseanne decided to hold onto this land but also to start their own venture.

The Nogashes have always known that agriculture was their calling. In 1984, the pair purchased ninety acres in Camillus, New York, and started Gillie Brook Farm. But it took time to find a routine that made sense. "Our home was built in 1836, and it had no heat or hot water. I remember waking up with snow on the floor because our front door was so loose," recalls Robert. Bouts of frustration aside, they learned to appreciate the quirks of their new home and also the agricultural yield of their land.

Ask Robert about his favorite crop and immediately he will tell you it is garlic. However, he cannot help but gush about the sixty-year-old black walnut trees growing on the property's back hillside. When the couple first purchased the land, Robert didn't know that the trees were of any significance: "I didn't realize there was such an interest in this nut." He was finally convinced when a representative from the Northeast Organic Farming Association (NOFA) came to review the farm. "We were getting our property certified organic, and he suggested that we include the trees."

North American black walnuts grow happily in the well-draining mineral-rich soil at Gillie Brook. "They don't like getting their feet wet," jokes Rob. In the beginning of October, after the green walnut fruits fall from the trees, they are collected and the flesh is torn away to access the nuts in their shells. The nuts contain a natural black dye (juglone) which has powerful staining abilities and also acts as a natural herbicide: "Other than grasses, most plants will not grow around the trees."

Unlike their blond English cousins, black walnuts are tough and durable, even after they are well dehydrated during the curing process. A hammer is the only tool that can successfully crack their stubborn shells. But they are well worth the effort—the meat is distinctive with a flavor that is "much stronger, richer, and smokier than other nut varieties," according to Robert.

Often in farming, the greatest joy comes from the unexpected, and black walnuts were certainly unexpected for Robert and Rosanne, who have made a life for themselves turning life's surprises into successes and embracing a style of farming that values both tradition and openness to the serendipitous.

Walnut Tart with Caramel and Sea Salt

MAKES TWO 8-INCH TARTS; EACH SERVES 8

Tart Shells

1 cup butter, at room temperature
½ cup sugar
1 egg
Zest of 1 orange
½ vanilla bean, split lengthwise and scraped
¼ teaspoon salt
3 cups flour

In a stand mixer fitted with the paddle attachment, cream together the butter and sugar on medium speed. Once the butter and sugar are light and fluffy, add the egg and continue mixing until thoroughly combined. Add the orange zest, vanilla bean seeds, and salt. Incorporate the flour, 1 cup at a time, and mix until the dough comes together. Divide into 2 equal portions and roll out the portions between 2 sheets of parchment paper to ⅛-inch-thick rounds. Refrigerate for 30 minutes. Remove the parchment paper from one round of dough and lay it in an 8-inch removable-bottom tart pan. Mold the dough into the pan, gently pressing it into the sides with your fingers. Make sure that the dough is of even thickness throughout to ensure even baking. With a paring knife, trim away excess dough. Repeat with the second dough round and another 8-inch tart pan. Chill in the refrigerator for at least 30 minutes before baking. Preheat the oven to 350°F. Place the dough-lined tart pans on baking sheets and bake until golden brown, about 15 minutes. Remove from the oven and cool to room temperature. **Note:** The unbaked dough-lined tart pans may be tightly wrapped and frozen for up to 1 month.

Walnut Frangipane Tarts

2½ cups toasted walnuts
⅔ cup sugar
2 teaspoons salt
⅔ cup butter, softened
10 tablespoons flour
4 eggs
2 tablespoons bourbon
Tart Shells

Preheat the oven to 325°F. Grind the walnuts, sugar, and salt in a food processor until fine but not pureed. Add the butter, followed by the flour, eggs, and bourbon. Process until just combined. Divide evenly between the 2 prebaked tart shells. Bake until the frangipane is cooked and a cake tester comes out clean, about 10 minutes. Cool to room temperature.

Caramel Walnuts

1⅓ cups sugar
⅔ cup cream
¼ cup butter
2 teaspoons salt
3½ cups toasted walnuts
Sea salt

Heat the sugar in a medium heavy-bottomed saucepan over high heat. As the sugar begins to melt, stir vigorously with a wooden spoon. As soon as the sugar begins to bubble, stop stirring. Once all of the sugar crystals have melted and the caramel is dark amber in color, add the cream, butter, and salt. Stir until the butter has melted. Remove from the heat and add the toasted walnuts. Top the tarts with the caramel walnuts and finish with sea salt.

Candied Walnuts

MAKES 1 POUND

3 cups granulated sugar
1 pound walnut halves
Canola oil
2 cups confectioners' sugar
Salt
Cayenne pepper

In a medium saucepan over medium heat, combine the sugar with 3 cups of water. When the sugar has dissolved, add the walnuts and reduce the heat to medium-low. Simmer until the walnuts are tender, 45 to 50 minutes. Drain the walnuts well. Pour 3 inches of canola oil into a large saucepan and bring the oil to 375°F over medium-high heat. Whisk the confectioners' sugar in a medium bowl with 3 tablespoons of water to create a slurry. In small batches, toss the walnuts in the slurry to coat and transfer with a slotted spoon to the oil. Fry until golden brown, 2½ to 3 minutes. Remove the walnuts with a spider strainer and transfer to a baking sheet lined with parchment paper. When the nuts are cool enough to handle but still soft, separate them from each other. Season with salt and cayenne pepper to taste. Serve alongside artisanal cheeses.

Made in New York: Copper, Salt, and Stoneware

Coming from some of our favorite artisans in the state, the products in the pages that follow are used throughout this entire book.

Copper Cookware
Hammersmith and Brooklyn Copper Cookware

Mac Kohler's collection of antique cookware is a sight to behold. A lover of all things copper, he is drawn to copper pots' handcrafted beauty, durability, and, most of all, their utility in cooking. One evening at his stove, he says, "I looked around and noticed that I did not have a single piece of American-made cookware." He possessed a rich stock of French copper pots, and he was familiar with the output of Romania, Spain, and Portugal; he knew, for example, that metalworkers in Romania have been crafting copper cookware for seventy-five hundred years, and that their hammering technique improves the metal's ability to rapidly heat up and cool down. Mac was optimistic that he could track down the remains of an American copper cookware industry in Brooklyn, where the last known American copper pots were crafted more than a generation ago.

In 2008, Mac discovered a saucepan at Brooklyn Kitchen, a specialty shop in the Williamsburg neighborhood of Brooklyn, and traced it back to metal fabricator Jeff Herkes. In 1986, Jeff had purchased the original presses and custom tooling of Bruno Waldrow. Having emigrated from Germany to America in the 1930s, Waldrow came to be a respected leader in the field of metal working. "Bruno was ninety-six years old and still working, but I convinced him to sell," explains Jeff, showing us a pair of hundred-year-old metalworking tongs.

In his early professional years, Jeff did metal fabrication for architectural projects and joined an existing metalworking company. It was then that he first began working with the city of New York, which contracted him for large city initiatives, from staircase railings to trash cans. Recently, his firm helped with the transformation of Manhattan's High Line, a public park situated on an elevated freight rail line that had been out of use for years. He worked on the restoration of the railway tracks and made all of the new metal fittings for the park. Jeff eventually incorporated a subsection of the business, calling it Hammersmith. He sought out smaller-scale projects under this identity—for example, replacing the worn-out linings in vintage Waldrow pots and pans.

Meanwhile, Mac Kohler was piecing together the foundation for his own company, Brooklyn Copper Cookware. He was "noodling with the idea of bringing in copper from Romania" when he serendipitously found what he needed in his own backyard, at Hammersmith. Jeff's factory proved to be historically rich, housing lathes dating back to 1930 and numerous chucks (specialized clamps) that could mold many types of saucepans, sauté pans, casseroles, stockpots, and gratins. Jeff and Mac decided to collaborate: Hammersmith would make the pots and Brooklyn Copper Cookware would sell them.

Since 2010, the two men have been busy making extraordinary copper cookware. An original Waldrow lathe, outfitted with a spinning chuck, rotates while copper is pressed and formed around it. Inspired by the French model, Jeff and Mac use thick (2.5-millimeter) copper to optimize thermal throughput and heat diffusion ("We have always loved copper because a little bit of heat can get the pan uniformly hot, but when you turn it off, it cools quickly."). Then, over an open flame, a thin layer of tin is painted on the interior. Tin creates a strong bond with copper, with which it shares many properties; however, unlike copper, it will not react with acidic foods.

Hammersmith has rejuvenated a lost art in the United States. Jeff believes the quality of the raw material determines the ultimate integrity of the craftsmanship: "It is impossible to make a pot badly because the copper is first-class."

Sea Salt
Amagansett Sea Salt Co.

The name *Amagansett* is derived from the Montaukett Indian word meaning "place of good water." While most locals enjoy sweeping views of this good water, it is the distinctive *taste* of the salty sea that Steven Judelson and his wife, Natalie, have always been attracted to. Early in 2010, they started bottling the essence of the Atlantic, reasoning that, as they put it, "with the bounty of fruits and vegetables that are grown in Long Island, why would you reach for fleur de sel from France when you can locally harvest salt?"

This locally minded couple started dating when they met at Tufts University; Natalie would accompany Steven on his family trips to Amagansett each summer. After graduating from college, they both attended law school at Boston College and, as young lawyers, their trips to Amagansett became a cherished part of their lives. "Sometimes the city only seemed livable knowing that I could take the Hampton Jitney and be in Southampton in two hours," recalls Steven. They began experimenting with sea salt production on a small scale, basing their model on flats they had seen while traveling in Brazil and St. Barts. It started as a hobby, and at first they were only able to make one ounce of homemade salt every six months.

Steven and Natalie evolved their techniques through trial and error. Boiling the water, for example, sped up the process, but they refused to expend extra energy for the convenience of getting to the finish line faster. And besides, the resulting product wasn't so tasty. It took a few years, but the Judelsons perfected their technique and their equipment. Now, every Sunday, Steven collects one hundred gallons of ocean water from Atlantic Avenue Beach, ten gallons at a time, with handheld buckets, and deposits it into plastic drums. Then the water is allowed to settle before Steven decants it of any impurities. Next, a series of solar evaporators dehydrates the water (in the summer, the warm weather does this work). Every gallon of water yields roughly a cup of salt. In five days, the one hundred gallons of water yield fifteen pounds of salt crystals—an astonishingly low 3 percent of the water's volume. This process may seem painstakingly slow, but it's the only way to end up with high-quality salt. Extremely warm weather, which speeds up the process, results in an unusable product. "I remember when we had a series of 90-degree days, and we had salt in half the time—it looked the same but tasted terrible!" recalls Steven.

When they had finally refined their process, the Judelsons reached out to the local agricultural and culinary communities. "We positioned our retail outlets at farmers' markets with other local vendors," explains Steven. In December 2011, they moved to land owned by the Peconic Land Trust. Their salt processing facility is now located on fields reserved for agricultural cultivation. This move is certainly in line with the Judelsons' dream to convert commercial salt consumers into lovers of the unique salt that abounds in their own backyard. Amagansett Sea Salt Co.'s hand-harvested grains maintain the integrity of the Atlantic—robust and intense. As Steven says, "just a few crystals can have the ability to transform flavor."

Stoneware
Jono Pandolfi

In a metropolis made of concrete, Jono Pandolfi has made a life for himself with clay, translating his aesthetic into functional art. Consider throwing a plate. With a forceful smack, a mound of clay lands in the middle of the pottery wheel. Jono forms the spinning clay, applying downward pressure with one hand while framing the exterior with his other hand. Rounded surfaces and gently sloping rims emerge with beauty and precision. However, this master potter prefers his finished pieces to exude a handmade quality. He purposely leaves uneven circumferences and preserves irregular textures in the surface, accentuating the uniqueness of each piece. He appreciates the character that slight imperfections create—an evolution in style from his earlier work: "I used to make everything really smooth and slick."

After obtaining a degree in studio art from Skidmore College in 1999, this New York native was unsure of what direction to take, but he was certain of one thing: "I've always been into functional ceramics." This term refers to tabletop wares—plates, bowls, and vases—and it is a way of differentiating his work from that of art potters. In order to make his stoneware widely marketable, Jono needed to develop his proficiency in product design. With this goal in mind, he moved to Manhattan in 2004, and two years later had a dinnerware collection, called Kona, at Crate and Barrel. Still seeking a more robust portfolio, Jono secured work as a designer for two major firms. "Every project I do now is pretty collaborative," he explains. "I see people react to how samples are glazed, formed, and textured. Then you combine those factors to give the product just the right appeal."

Overlooking some of his own artistic proclivities and prioritizing customers' requests were new challenges for Jono. Nevertheless, he has adjusted well, and major brands now actively pursue him as a designer. For Jono, the design process ultimately comes down to working with the material. "Each design has its own recipe. In the end, ceramics is a negotiation between you and the clay. You can't force it." He always starts with choice ceramic mixes, from which he creates silky porcelain and earth-toned shades of stoneware. Those are his canvases, whether he is working on a commissioned project or simply allowing his creativity to determine the course.

Once a piece is thrown, trimmed on the wheel, and dried for a day, Jono tests the pottery by touching it to his cheek. When the piece is just warm to the touch, it is completely dry. He bisque-fires each unglazed piece at 1,800°F. After they cool, custom glazes are applied, and the work is refired at 2,200°F. This process renders durable and completely vitreous final products.

In support of domestic craftsmanship, Jono now works closely with a quality-minded factory in Ohio to produce and distribute his work on a larger scale. Inspired by domestically made goods, he is excited to contribute to the national movement. Now, with more time for design and business development, his future evolves each day. "There is no singular direction for me. That's why I'm into clay—infinite possibilities."

Basic Recipes

Apricot Puree

MAKES 1/2 CUP

¼ cup sliced dried apricots
3 tablespoons orange juice
1 cup pitted and diced fresh apricots
2 tablespoons sugar
1 tablespoon glucose syrup
1 teaspoon lemon juice
½ teaspoon salt
Zest of ¼ lemon

Combine the dried apricots and orange juice in a small saucepan and bring to just under a boil. Transfer to a bowl, cover with plastic wrap, and allow to rehydrate for 20 minutes at room temperature. In another saucepan, combine the fresh apricots and sugar, cover, and cook over medium-high heat until softened but still slightly firm. Uncover and stir in the glucose. Continue to cook until the liquid is absorbed. Stir in the lemon juice, salt, and lemon zest. Puree the mixture with the rehydrated dried apricot mixture in a blender and pass through a chinois. Cool over an ice bath. Store, covered, in the refrigerator for up to 1 week.

Beef Broth

MAKES 2 CUPS

2 pounds diced beef
½ onion, root attached
8 cups Chicken Stock (page 499)
1 cup diced (½ inch) carrot
1 cup diced (½ inch) celery
1 cup diced (½ inch) leek
1 bay leaf
½ bunch parsley
½ teaspoon black peppercorns
1½ tablespoons cornstarch
2 cups loosely packed lovage
Salt

In a medium stockpot, cover the beef with cold water and bring to a boil. Drain and reserve the beef, and then rinse under cold water. In a medium sauté pan over high heat, cook the onion until blackened, 7 to 8 minutes. Place the blanched beef, blackened onion, stock, carrots, celery, and leeks in a stockpot. Make a sachet by tying the bay leaf, parsley, and peppercorns in cheesecloth with butcher's twine, and add to the stockpot. Bring to a simmer over medium heat and cook for 1½ hours, skimming frequently. Strain the stock through a chinois, reserving only the liquid, and cool over an ice bath. Skim the fat from the surface, return the stock to a medium saucepan, and reduce to 2 cups over medium heat. Prepare a slurry by whisking the cornstarch into ¼ cup of cold water. Whisk the slurry into the reduced stock and simmer for 3 to 4 minutes until the stock is thickened and the starchy flavor has cooked out. Steep the lovage in the stock and season with salt to taste. Store in an airtight container in the refrigerator for up to 1 week.

Bread Crisps

MAKES ABOUT 12

¼ loaf country bread
Olive oil
Salt

Wrap the bread in plastic wrap and place in the freezer until frozen firm, at least 3 hours. Once frozen, preheat the oven to 200°F. Slice the bread on a rotating deli slicer or with a sharp knife to 1/16 inch thick. Brush the bread slices with olive oil and season with salt. Place on a parchment paper–lined rimmed baking sheet and toast in the oven until crispy, 35 to 40 minutes. Cool to room temperature and then store in an airtight container at room temperature for up to 24 hours.

Brown Butter

MAKES 1 1/2 CUPS

1 pound butter
5 sprigs thyme
2 cloves garlic, crushed but kept whole

Place the butter in a medium saucepan over medium heat. Simmer for about 40 minutes, until the butter is clear and a light caramel color. Continue to simmer the butter, whisking vigorously, until the color is walnut brown. Place the thyme and garlic in a chinois lined with cheesecloth. Strain the brown butter over the thyme and garlic. Cool to room temperature and then store in an airtight container in the refrigerator for up to 2 weeks.

Clarified Butter

MAKES 1 3/4 CUPS

1 pound butter

Place the butter in a medium saucepan over medium heat. Simmer for about 30 minutes, until the butter is clear. Strain through a quadruple layer of cheesecloth to remove milk solids. Cool to room temperature and then store in an airtight container in the refrigerator for up to 3 weeks.

Chicken Jus

MAKES 4 CUPS

10 pounds chicken wings
¼ cup canola oil
4 cups sliced onion
2 cups diced carrot
2 cups diced celery
2 cups diced leek
2 cups diced celery root
½ cup tomato paste
4 cups red wine

10 sprigs thyme
2 bay leaves
25 black peppercorns
5 pounds chicken feet
30 pounds ice cubes

Preheat the oven to 375°F. Spread the chicken wings in a single layer on 2 large rimmed baking sheets and roast in the oven until golden brown, 1¼ to 1½ hours, turning every 30 minutes. Heat the oil in a 20-quart stockpot over high heat. Sauté the onion, carrot, celery, leek, and celery root until they caramelize, 10 to 15 minutes. Add the tomato paste and sauté until caramelized, 5 to 7 minutes. Add the red wine and reduce to a syrup consistency.

Make a sachet by tying the thyme, bay leaves, and peppercorns in cheesecloth. Add the sachet, the chicken wings, and the chicken feet to the stockpot and cover with as much of the ice as possible. Bring to a simmer over medium heat and skim off all of the impurities and fats that rise to the top. As the liquid simmers, continually add the remaining ice. Simmer over low heat, uncovered, for 5 hours, skimming every 30 minutes. Strain through a chinois and reduce to 4 cups. Strain again and chill over an ice bath. Store in an airtight container in the refrigerator for up to 1 week or freeze in ice cube trays for up to 1 month.

Chicken Stock

MAKES 4 QUARTS

10 pounds chicken backs and necks
15 pounds ice cubes
1 cup diced leek, white part only
½ cup diced celery
½ cup diced celery root
½ cup sliced shallot
½ cup diced fennel
5 white peppercorns
1 bay leaf
1 sprig thyme

Rinse the chicken backs and necks well under running water for 5 minutes. Place the backs and necks in a 20-quart stockpot, top with the ice, and bring to a simmer over medium heat. Simmer for 15 to 20 minutes, skimming off all of the impurities and fats that rise to the top. After the stock is skimmed, add the leek, celery, celery root, shallot, and fennel. Make a sachet by wrapping the peppercorns, bay leaf, and thyme in cheesecloth. Add the sachet to the stock. Simmer, uncovered, for 3 hours, skimming every 30 minutes. Strain through a chinois and chill over an ice bath. Store in an airtight container in the refrigerator for up to 1 week or freeze in ice cube trays for up to 1 month.

Confit Cherry Tomatoes

MAKES 12

12 cherry tomatoes
1 tablespoon olive oil
⅛ teaspoon salt
⅛ teaspoon sugar

Preheat the oven to 200°F. Bring a large saucepan of salted water to a boil. Using a paring knife, mark a shallow X on the bottom of each tomato. Add to the boiling water for 3 to 4 seconds. Immediately transfer to an ice bath and, once cool, remove the skins with a paring knife, being careful not to cut into the flesh. Toss the peeled tomatoes in the olive oil, salt, and sugar. Place on a rimmed baking sheet lined with parchment paper and bake for 1½ hours, until the tomatoes are slightly shriveled and about one-quarter of their original size. Cool to room temperature and refrigerate in an airtight container for up to 3 days.

Corn Pudding

MAKES 2 CUPS

2 cups corn juice (from 4 quarts of corn kernels)
3 tablespoons mascarpone
¾ teaspoon salt

Heat the corn juice in a medium saucepan over medium-high heat while whisking constantly. After 1½ to 2 minutes, as the starches in the corn juice start to thicken, turn down the heat slightly to avoid scorching. Whisk until the juice reaches a puddinglike thickness, another 3 to 4 minutes. Remove the pan from the heat and whisk in the mascarpone. Season with the salt. Chill over an ice bath while whisking constantly to prevent a skin from forming. Transfer to an airtight container and refrigerate for up to 2 days.

Crème Fraîche

MAKES 6 CUPS

4 cups cream
2 cups buttermilk

In a large mixing bowl, combine the cream and the buttermilk. Whisk until smooth and transfer to a large container. Cover with cheesecloth and set in a warm place (about 75°F) for 36 hours. Strain through a chinois and refrigerate for 2 to 3 days.

Duck Stock

MAKES 4 QUARTS

10 pounds duck carcasses, cut into 2-inch pieces
4 tablespoons duck fat
4 cups sliced onion
2 cups diced carrot
2 cups diced celery
2 cups diced leek
2 cups diced celery root
5 tablespoons tomato paste
2 cups port
3 cups red wine
10 sprigs thyme
2 bay leaves
25 black peppercorns
3 pounds chicken feet
8 quarts Chicken Stock (page 499)

Preheat the oven to 375°F. Line 2 large rimmed baking sheets with parchment paper. Spread the duck carcass pieces in a single layer on the baking sheets and roast in the oven until golden brown, 1 to 1¼ hours, turning over once after 20 minutes. Melt the duck fat in a 20-quart stockpot over high heat. Sauté the onion, carrot, celery, leek, and celery root in the duck fat until they caramelize, 7 to 10 minutes. Add the tomato paste and sauté until caramelized, 5 to 7 minutes. Add the port and reduce by half. Add the red wine and reduce to a syrupy consistency. Make a sachet by tying the thyme, bay leaves, and peppercorns in cheesecloth. Add the chicken feet, duck carcass pieces, and sachet to the stockpot and cover with the stock. Bring to a simmer over medium heat and skim off all of the impurities and fats that rise to the top. Simmer, uncovered, over low heat for 3 hours, skimming every 30 minutes. Strain through a chinois and chill over an ice bath. Store in an airtight container in the refrigerator for up to 1 week or freeze in ice cube trays for up to 1 month.

Lamb Jus

MAKES 4 CUPS

10 pounds lamb bones, cut into 2-inch pieces
¼ cup canola oil
4 cups sliced onion
2 cups diced carrot
2 cups diced celery
2 cups diced leek
2 heads garlic, peeled
½ cup tomato paste
4 cups red wine
10 sprigs thyme
2 bay leaves
25 black peppercorns
4 gallons Veal Stock (page 501)

Preheat the oven to 375°F. Spread the lamb bones in a single layer on 2 large rimmed baking sheets and roast in the oven until golden brown, 1 to 1¼ hours, turning the bones every 30 minutes. Heat the oil in a 20-quart stockpot over high heat. Sauté the onion, carrot, celery, leek, and garlic until they caramelize, 10 to 15 minutes. Add the tomato paste and sauté until caramelized, 5 to 7 minutes. Add the red wine and reduce to a syrup consistency. Make a sachet by tying the thyme, bay leaves, and peppercorns in cheesecloth. Add the sachet and bones to the stockpot and cover with the veal stock. Bring to a simmer over medium heat and skim off all of the impurities and fats that rise to the top. Simmer over low heat, uncovered, for 4 hours, skimming every 30 minutes. Strain through a chinois and reduce to 4 cups. Strain again and chill over an ice bath. Store in an airtight container in the refrigerator for up to 1 week or freeze in ice cube trays for up to 1 month.

Lemon Vinaigrette

MAKES 2 CUPS

1½ cups lemon-infused olive oil
½ cup lemon juice
1 tablespoon salt

In a mixing bowl, whisk together the lemon oil and lemon juice. Season with the salt and use immediately.

Mayonnaise

MAKES 2 CUPS

2 egg yolks
1 teaspoon lemon juice
½ teaspoon Dijon mustard
1½ cups canola oil
1 teaspoon salt

Place the yolks, lemon juice, and Dijon mustard in the bowl of a food processor. With the processor running, slowly stream in the canola oil and continue blending until the mayonnaise is fully emulsified. Season with the salt. Store in an airtight container in the refrigerator for 2 to 3 days.

Pickled Mustard Seeds

MAKES 1 CUP

½ cup mustard seeds
1 cup white balsamic vinegar
2 teaspoons salt
1 teaspoon sugar

Bring a medium saucepan of water to a boil. Add the mustard seeds and cook for 30 seconds. Strain the seeds through a mesh strainer and rinse well under cold water. Transfer to a medium bowl. Bring the vinegar, salt, and sugar to a boil in a small saucepan over medium heat. Pour the liquid over the mustard seeds and cool to room temperature. Cover and let stand at room temperature overnight. Store in an airtight container in the refrigerator for up to 1 week.

Pickled Red Pearl Onions

MAKES ABOUT 40 PIECES

7 red pearl onions, peeled
2 teaspoons salt
1 teaspoon olive oil
2 tablespoons red wine vinegar

Slice each onion into 5 or 6 coins. Separate the coins into rings, keeping only the perfect pieces. You should have about 40 rings. Season with the salt. Heat the oil in a small sauté pan. Add the onions and quickly sauté over high heat for 2 to 3 seconds. Add the vinegar and toss, steaming the onions with the vinegar. Immediately transfer the onions to a small bowl and chill over ice. Drain, discarding the liquid, and store the onions, covered, at room temperature for up to 2 days.

Pickled Shallots

MAKES 1 CUP

½ teaspoon canola oil
1 cup diced (⅛ inch) shallot
½ cup red wine vinegar
Salt
Sugar

Heat the oil in a medium sauté pan over high heat. Add the shallots and sauté for 4 to 5 minutes, stirring frequently to keep the shallots from browning. Add the red wine vinegar to steam the shallots, toss, and transfer to a small bowl. Cool to room temperature, and, once cool, drain the liquid from the shallots and season with salt and sugar to taste. Store in an airtight container in the refrigerator for up to 1 day.

Potato Puree

MAKES 2 CUPS

1½ pounds fingerling potatoes
1 cup cream
¼ cup Brown Butter (page 498)
Salt

Peel the potatoes and place in a medium saucepan. Cover with cold water, bring to a simmer over medium heat, and cook for 20 to 25 minutes until tender. Drain and pass through a food mill into a large bowl. Warm the cream and brown butter in a small saucepan. Just before it begins to simmer, fold it into the potatoes until combined but still loose. Working quickly, pass the mixture through a chinois. Season with salt to taste and use immediately.

Ricotta Ice Cream

MAKES 3 CUPS

1¼ cups milk
1 cup ricotta
⅓ cup sugar
3 tablespoons Crème Fraîche (page 499)

3 tablespoons glucose syrup
2 teaspoons lemons juice
1 teaspoon salt

In a blender, puree all of the ingredients until smooth. Strain through a chinois and chill over an ice bath. Freeze in an ice cream machine. Store in the freezer for up to 1 month.

Veal Stock

MAKES 4 QUARTS

5 pounds veal bones
5 pounds veal breast, cut into 2-inch pieces
3 pounds veal feet, cut into 2-inch pieces
20 pounds ice cubes
1 cup sliced onion
½ cup diced celery
½ cup diced celery root
½ cup diced leek, white part only
2 cups white wine
10 white peppercorns
5 sprigs thyme
1 bay leaf

Rinse the bones well under running water for 5 minutes. Place the bones, veal breast, and veal feet in a 20-quart stockpot. Cover with the ice and bring to a simmer over medium heat. Skim off all of the impurities and fats that rise to the top as it simmers. After the stock is skimmed, add the onion, celery, celery root, and leeks. Make a sachet by wrapping the peppercorns, thyme, and bay leaf in cheesecloth. Add the sachet to the stock. Simmer, uncovered, for 4 hours, skimming every 30 minutes. Strain through a chinois and chill over an ice bath. Store in an airtight container in the refrigerator for up to 1 week or freeze in ice cube trays for up to 1 month.

White Balsamic Pickling Liquid

MAKES 4 CUPS

4 cups white balsamic vinegar
½ cup salt
½ cup sugar

Combine the vinegar, salt, and sugar in a medium saucepan. Bring to a boil to dissolve the sugar and salt. Cool over ice and refrigerate, covered, until ready to use.

White Balsamic Vinaigrette

MAKES 2 CUPS

1½ cups olive oil
½ cup white balsamic vinegar
1½ teaspoons salt

In a mixing bowl, whisk together the oil and vinegar. Season with the salt. Store in an airtight container in the refrigerator for up to 2 weeks.

Acknowledgments

Sandra Di Capua, our project manager, oversaw the editorial process of the book and bore the incredible responsibility of working with everyone listed below to make this idea come to life.

Bryce Shuman, our executive sous chef at Eleven Madison Park, played an integral role in the organization and execution of this book. From scheduling farm visits, to developing and writing recipes, to coordinating photo shoots, Bryce's culinary and logistical expertise is what drove this book from idea to reality.

Peter Weltman is an Eleven Madison Park alumnus and currently a sommelier at the NoMad Hotel. He has written articles for national food and travel publications and traveled across New York State to interview the fifty-eight farmers and artisans featured in this book, cultivating a true understanding of each farmer's vision.

Ben Marshall, an Eleven Madison Park line cook, tested and retested the recipes in this book, ensuring that they would be navigated as easily and as clearly as possible by the home and professional cook alike.

Christen Sturkie, head reservationist at the NoMad Hotel, worked with Peter and Bryce to edit all of the profiles and recipes in the book with a keen eye toward detail.

Leo Robitschek, our bar manager at Eleven Madison Park and the NoMad Hotel, developed the beverage recipes and shared his vast knowledge on the history of cocktails and mixology in New York.

Alexandra Stylianos assisted in the writing and editing of the book's proposal.

Michael Mabry designed this book, giving it a personality of its own with hand-drawn graphics and custom fonts. With a unique sense of whimsy, he was able to creatively interpret our vision of New York.

Amy Livingston, our longtime assistant, organizes our lives in such a way that we are able to have time to put together books like this one.

David Black, our incredible book agent and friend, brought this book to Ten Speed Press, giving us the motivation we needed to turn this book into a reality.

Aaron Wehner and Julie Bennett of Ten Speed Press guided us through the process of making this book and believed in it from the very beginning. Their professionalism, creativity, and inherent spirit of collaboration made them the ideal partners for this project.

Our managers and sous chefs, at both Eleven Madison Park and the NoMad—Abram Bissell, Adam Smith, Amanda Maxwell, Angela Pinkerton, Ashley Abodeely, Austin Johnson, Billy Peelle, Bradley Ray, Brandon Laterveer, Brian Lockwood, Camilla Warner, Chris Flint, Chris Ono, Connie Chung, Daniel DiStefano, Dmitri Magi, Dustin Wilson, Jackie DeGiorgio, James Kent, Jeff Tascarella, Josh Harnden, Josh Morgan, Julian Proujansky, Julian Sherman, Kelly Jeun, Kirk Kelewae, Kristen Millar, Kristen Schleiden, Laura Wagstaff, Leo Robitschek, Mandy Laterveer, Marcia Regen, Mark Bartley, Mark Welker, Mary Helen Crafton, Max Snyder, Megan Vaughan, Stephen Kelly, Taylor Thorne, Thomas Pastuszak, and Zachary Schultz—are the backbone of our restaurants. We are forever appreciative to them for their dedication to our company.

Our families (Frank and Juliette Guidara; Brigitte and Roland Humm; Geneen, Colette, Vivienne, and Justine Humm) have always been by our sides to provide us with the support, advice, and love we need to make even our wildest dreams come true.

Index

Westfield Memorial Library
Westfield, New Jersey

Westfield Memorial Library
Westfield, New Jersey

Copyright © 2013 by Made Nice, LLC

Photographs copyright © 2013 by Francesco Tonelli

Illustrations copyright © 2013 by Michael Mabry

All rights reserved.

Published in the United States by Ten Speed Press, an imprint of the
Crown Publishing Group, a division of Random House, Inc., New York.

www.crownpublishing.com
www.tenspeed.com

Ten Speed Press and the Ten Speed Press colophon
are registered trademarks of Random House, Inc.

I♥NY. is a registered trademark of the NYS Dept. of Economic Development,
used with permission. Plan a New York State Getaway! Visit iloveny.com

Library of Congress Cataloging-in-Publication Data
Humm, Daniel.

 I love New York : ingredients and recipes / Daniel Humm and
Will Guidara.—First edition.
    pages cm
 Includes index.

1. Cooking, American. 2. Cooking—New York (State)—New York.
3. Local foods—New York (State)—New York. I. Guidara, Will. II. Title.
 TX715.H89445 2013
 641.59747—dc23
 2012026491

ISBN 978-1-60774-440-5
eISBN 978-1-60774-441-2

Printed in China

Design by Michael Mabry
Production by Sarah Pulver

10 9 8 7 6 5 4 3 2 1

First Edition